Some Serious, Popular

FALSE DOCTRINES

Some Serious, Popular

FALSE DOCTRINES

Answered From the Scriptures

By

John R. Rice

SWORD of the LORD PUBLISHERS

P.O.BOX 1099, MURFREESBORO, TN 37133

Library of Congress
Catalog Card Number:
73-126630

ISBN 0-87398-282-7

NOTE: Dr. John R. Rice published this book in 1970. Some of the books he listed as references may now be out of print. You may find them in a store that sells used books.

Printed in U. S. A.

Table of Contents

Introduction

In this book we discuss *some* false doctrines, not all. We have dealt with the doctrines that seem hurtful to more people.

We have used here the material that God has given in answer to different needs. For example, we deal with the errors of Romanism here as those errors have come up and not in a well-organized, complete theological discussion of all the errors of Rome. We feel this way, perhaps, is more practical and helpful, not so much for the theologian as for the common Christian who would most likely be misled by these false doctrines.

Some may protest perhaps that we should never "talk about other Christian faiths." That viewpoint is short-sighted, and, of course, contrary to the plain teaching of the Scriptures and to the practice of Jesus and the apostles.

Jesus openly exposed the bad teaching of the Pharisees about Corban, and about oaths, and about duty to government. He answered the false doctrines of the Sadducees about the resurrection. In I Corinthians 14, Paul rebuked the Corinthians for their tongues heresy, much like the tongues teaching and practice today. He rebuked the legalizer for trying to enforce the Sabbath and other Old Testament ceremonies (Col. 2:11-17), and he would do exactly the same today with Seventh-Day Adventists, no doubt, concerning the same heresies.

The whole book of Galatians is a vigorous refutation of the heresy of salvation by the law, and by ceremonies. And when Paul said, "But though we, or an angel from heaven, preach any other gospel unto you than that which we have preached unto you, let him be accursed. As we said before, so say I now again, If any man preach any other gospel unto you than that ye have received, let him be accursed," he was sharper than anything said in this book. He plainly said in Galatians 5:12, "I would they were even cut off which trouble you."

Yes, we are not left to our own opinions as to whether we should oppose false doctrine. In Titus 1:9-13 the Apostle Paul was inspired to write about the duties of a pastor, "holding fast the faithful word as he hath been taught, that he may be able by sound doctrine both to exhort and to convince the gainsayers. For there are many unruly and vain talkers and deceivers, specially they of the circumcision: Whose mouths must be stopped, who subvert whole houses, teaching things which they ought not, for filthy lucre's sake. One of themselves, even a prophet of their own, said, The Cretians are always liars, evil beasts, slow bellies. This witness is true. Wherefore rebuke them sharply, that they may be sound in the faith."

So those who "subvert whole houses" with false doctrine must be answered and their mouths stopped by God's scriptural answers. Those who fall into false doctrine are to be rebuked sharply "that they may be sound in the faith."

We should be glad if in this book the same kind of answers I have given to Christians for years in letters and in the pulpit and in THE SWORD OF THE LORD, turn many Christians from deceitful doctrines and make them "sound in the faith."

Jesus said, "Beware of false prophets" (Matt. 7:15). In Jude 3 we are plainly told it is necessary to "earnestly contend for the faith." One is not a better Christian for ignoring God's commands. If you would be true to Christ you must earnestly defend the faith and must beware and teach others to beware of false doctrine, false teachers.

Oh, since false teaching damns many souls and causes strife and division and unrest among God's people, then we should love the Word of God and seek most earnestly to teach it with love and kindness and fidelity to the Bible.

Some of these false doctrines are false teachings held

by unconverted people, doctrines that affect the plan of salvation. For example, one who depends partly upon the Mass or on baptism to save is not likely to be converted. Certainly there is no other sacrifice for sin except the atoning death of Christ and equally certain it is that baptism does not bring salvation, is not a step toward salvation.

However, a Catholic may have seen beyond the ceremony, beyond the priesthood, and the church and may have come to Christ in the heart, with saving faith. The Catholic forms and ceremonies and priesthood did not save him, and will not save anybody else. But one who comes to trust in Christ is saved, even if he comes in ignorance but honestly turns to Christ in penitent faith.

Also, some may have been led astray in doctrine after having been truly converted. So, no doubt, there are some in Christian Science who know Christ as The Way and not "the Way-Shower" as Mary Baker Eddy taught. Some converted Christians are misled by Christian Science as they seek healing. But some surely have trusted in the blood of Christ, not in so-called "divine science," for forgiveness of sins.

Doubtless there are Catholics who are saved, Church of Christ people who are saved, Christian Scientists who are saved, possibly even some Jehovah's Witnesses who are saved. But Catholic Mass and Confession, Baptismal Regeneration teaching, that of Rutherford or Mary Baker Eddy or of Herbert Armstrong, do not lead men to saving faith and salvation. Some are better off in heart than in their poor mistaught heads. All who penitently turned from sin and trusted in Christ enough to call upon Him for forgiveness and salvation, have, we believe, received it. "Whosoever shall call upon the name of the Lord shall be saved" is the plain promise of Romans 10:13.

A sick man may be healed without knowing all about the medicine needed, if he goes to the right doctor. But we must warn that those who teach of salvation to be earned by good works or church rites, surely lead to eternal ruin all who follow their teaching who never learn to turn to Christ in saving faith. Because millions die in sin, lost forever, as a result of false teaching, we must warn of these false doctrines.

But there are doctrines which are taught by some saved people who teach a saving Gospel, errors in doctrine which do great harm. We do extended teaching here on the false doctrines of Seventh-Day Adventists. We believe many a Seventh-Day Adventist has trusted in Christ and is saved. But to teach that Sabbath keeping is part of the Gospel is a snare that dishonors the Bible truth of salvation by grace. To give honor to Mrs. White as a seeress or authoritative prophetess dishonors the Bible as the exclusive, eternal Word of God. To stress salvation partly by law is surely a snare and detracts from the Gospel of salvation by trusting in Christ's atoning death when they preach it.

Then, Pentecostal people who teach the false doctrine that all should speak in tongues; that speaking in tongues is the "initial evidence of the baptism of the Holy Spirit," are usually fervent, godly people who preach the Gospel and who hold to the essentials of the Christian faith. We count them our brothers in Christ. But the emphasis on tongues makes them usually a divisive force, critical of all other Christians, even of the most devout and most useful. It leads them to unethical proselyting to get people who are interested in soul winning to leave soul-winning churches to talk in tongues. It leads to pious boasting and leads people away from the Bible doctrine of the fullness of the Spirit as an enduement of power for soul winning. So, this teaching which does so much harm and causes so much division and strife and perverts the Bible doctrine of the Holy Spirit, should be answered here, we think.

Hyper-Calvinists, although generally Christian people, do great harm in turning God's people from soul winning to intellectual fancies.

So we speak in this book, not only of heretical cults and antichristian forces, but we talk about some false doctrine promoted by good Christian people which does great harm.

And now may God's people learn to love the Word of God and follow it with devotion and love for all of God's people. And may God teach us charity and compassion for those who love the Lord Jesus, believe the Bible, but who go wrong on minor matters. And let us be bold and plain in opposing those doctrines which are antichristian and which damn souls.

March, 1970

John R. Rice

1

Errors of Romanism

1. Knights of Columbus Publish Seven Falsehoods

No! The Bible Is Not a Catholic Book!

In THE SWORD OF THE LORD we reproduced a photostatic copy of an advertisement published widely in secular magazines by the Knights of Columbus.

A Sunday school teacher wrote that a sixteen-year-old girl was greatly troubled by this advertisement and asked me to answer. Many others have inquired, so I want to take time to show that this advertisement holds at least seven errors, misstatements, untruths which ought to be exposed.

It is true that these statements would deceive only the ignorant, but of course there are many ignorant of the facts in the case. Many honest, well-meaning people would be misled by such an advertisement if it were not answered. But in the cause of Bible Christianity and to save people from being misled, we call your attention to the most palpable errors in the ad on this page. The ad says, "The Bible is a Catholic book." That is simply not true in the sense claimed here, and that is easy to prove.

It is true that the Bible is a catholic book if you mean that it is universal, that it is written for all mankind. But if you mean Roman Catholic church or the Catholic church in any sense as a denomination, then the Catholic church did not originate the Bible, does not guarantee the Bible, and has generally been against the spread of the Bible.

Seven Outstanding Errors Listed

Please read this list of striking errors:

1. It says there are 73 books in the Bible. That is wrong. There are only 66.

2. The ad says that the "list of the 73 inspired books" of the Bible "was given to the world by the Catholic Church almost three full centuries after the crucifixion of Jesus Christ."

Scholars simply know that that is not true. In the first place, there was no Catholic church like the present Roman Catholic church "almost three full centuries after the crucifixion of Jesus Christ." But the organization that was even then heading toward the heretical monstrosity which is now the Roman Catholic church did not settle on the list of the canon of Scriptures at that time.

3. This advertisement says, "Established by Jesus Christ Himself and rapidly spread among the nations of the world, the Catholic Church was carrying on Christ's work for the salvation of men some 60 years before the Apostle John wrote his books of the New Testament."

Jesus did not establish the Catholic church. It is a growing accumulation of error through the years and new doctrines and principles are added continually like the doctrine that the body of Mary was taken to Heaven, adopted November 1, 1950.

4. The Knights of Columbus ad says, "They were members of the Catholic Church who, under God's inspiration, wrote the New Testament in its entirety." But Matthew, Mark, Luke, John, Paul, Peter, James and Jude never heard of the Catholic Church. It did not exist then!

5. This ad says, "It is the infallible authority of the Catholic church that always has been the only sure guarantee of its inspiration." False!

6. Knights of Columbus here declare that "the complete revealed truth of God" was delivered to the Catholic church "from the beginning." That is not true. There was no Catholic church then and the Bible was not given to the Catholic church.

7. Knights of Columbus here declare that "the Catholic church has faithfully unfolded the meaning of the written Word of God to past generations of mankind—and does so today." That, we shall see, is false.

Now consider these points one by one. Check up from the Bible, from the *Encyclopedia Britannica,* from the *International Standard Bible Encyclopedia,* from the *Catholic Encyclopedia,* from any other reliable source, and find out for yourself. Here are seven terrible misstatements, errors, falsehoods, written by blind leaders of the blind, and intended by Satan to mislead the ignorant and the unwary.

1. Knights of Columbus Wrong on How Many Books in the Bible

The Catholic Bible has 73 books. They get that many by adding some books of the Apocrypha, that is, books which were not inspired of God and ought not to be part of the Bible. Many years after the New Testament was completed, some of these books began to be published with the Bible. But they do not show internal evidences of inspiration, they were not accepted by Christians in Bible times as inspired, and we do wrong to count these apocryphal books inspired now. They add no new revelation at all. They are interesting historically, but they are not helpful spiritually. They do have some definitely false doctrine. From some of these apocryphal books Catholics try to prove that we should pray for the dead.

There are two simple facts which prove the Knights of Columbus and other Catholics are wrong about the number of books in the Bible. First, the Jews in the time of Christ in Palestine had already decided on the canon of the Old Testament. That list of books was not made up by Catholics at all. Some Jews in Alexandria, Egypt, had some of the apocryphal books, but Jews in Palestine never believed that the apocryphal books were divinely inspired.

Even Catholics never agreed fully on this until modern times and the Jews in Palestine never did accept any of the apocryphal books as part of the Old Testament. They had exactly the same Old Testament books as we have today in the King James Version of the Bible and in other Protestant translations.

The other fact is that the Catholics themselves have the same 27 books in the New Testament that we have. So when Catholics set out to force on others these books which are not inspired, they do it without any authority and without even the backing of the best scholars.

2. The Catholic Church Did Not Give the Present Catholic List of 73 Books They Think Is Inspired "Almost Three Full Centuries After the Crucifixion of Jesus Christ"

The Knights of Columbus would have the unsuspecting reader of their paid ads to believe that the Catholic church decided on the 73 books which they think are part of the inspired Bible, the Catholic canon of Scriptures, and that they gave this list to the world "almost three full centuries after the crucifixion of Jesus Christ." Several things are wrong with that statement.

First of all, they did not make up the list of the books of the Old Testament. The Jews had already done that before Christ came. Remember that there is a gap of almost five hundred years between the Old Testament and the New Testament, and the Old Testament canon was well established and decided upon before any Catholic ever saw the light of day!

And even the apocryphal books which some Jews in Alexandria, Egypt, decided should be published along with the regular Old Testament canon of Scriptures were selected by these Jews, and were not selected originally by the Catholic church. Then there were hundreds of years of controversy in the Roman Catholic church as it grew into its present enormous man-made proportions, before the canon of Scriptures was "officially" decided by the church councils.

Saint Jerome himself, the Catholic scholar who translated the Latin Vulgate Bible from the original Greek and Hebrew, did not believe that the apocryphal books were part of Scripture and said so! Saint Augustine, the great Catholic bishop of Hippo, did not believe that the apocryphal books were inspired, though he favored publishing them. (See the *International Standard Bible Encyclopedia,* Volume I, page 562.) Pope Gelasius, an early Catholic pope from the years 492 to 496 A.D., "issued a decretal or list in which he included the Old Testament Apocrypha. Yet even after this official act of the papacy, the sentiment in the Western church was divided. Some followed the strict canon of Jerome, while others favored the larger canon of Augustine, without noting his cautions and the distinctions he made between inspired and uninspired writing."

"At the Council of Florence (1442 A.D.), 'Eugenius IV, with the approval of the Fathers of that assembly, declared all the books found in the Latin Bibles then in use to be inspired by the same Holy Spirit, without distinguishing them into two classes or categories' (cf. Gigot, *General Intro,* 71.) Though this bull of Eugenius IV did not deal with the canonicity of the apocryphal books, it did proclaim their *inspiration.* Nevertheless, down to the Council of Trent (1546 A.D.), the apocryphal books possessed only inferior authority; and when men spoke of canonical Scripture in the strict sense, these were not included."

But the Reformation came on. Luther and other reformers denounced the Apocrypha as not inspired. So the Catholic Council of Trent, April 8, 1546, declared that the apocryphal books were equal in authority and canonical value to the other books of sacred Scripture and pronounced an anathema on all who would not receive them.

So it is foolish for anyone to pretend that the Catholic church gave to the world "almost three centuries after the crucifixion of Christ" the present Catholic list of books which they claim to be canonical, a part of the Bible. It is simply not true. The Catholics never had any authority to decide what books were truly part of the Bible and Catholics had never agreed fully on it until an official bull from the pope came in modern times!

3. The Catholic Church Definitely Was Not Established by Jesus Christ

One of the easiest things in the world to prove is that there was no Catholic church in New Testament times. There was no pope in Bible times. There were no priests in the New Testament church. There was no sacrifice of the Mass. There were no nuns. There were no monks. There was no confessional. There were no prayers to Mary. There was no teaching of purgatory. Neither the Roman Catholic organization nor anything even remotely like it existed. The present doctrinal stand of the Catholic church did not exist nor was there anything remotely like it in the New Testament churches.

On the contrary, there were simple local congregations

of Christians. Everybody who was saved was baptized and received as a member in a local congregation. The word "bishop" in the New Testament refers to a pastor of a local congregation. There were no denominational bishops, secretaries, popes, or cardinals. All of these have been invented later by worldly-minded men.

Peter never went to Rome. He was not accepted as superior by Paul, but was openly rebuked when he was wrong (Gal. 2:11-14). He was never regarded as infallible. He did not even preside in the Council at Jerusalem (see Acts 15). He never went to Rome. When Paul wrote to Rome, among many, many people he greeted, Peter was not ever mentioned. When the book of Acts tells how Paul came to Rome, it makes quite clear that Peter was not in Rome. In all the letters Paul wrote from Rome he never mentioned Peter. On the contrary, Peter was at Babylon, as he plainly tells in his epistle, which was far in the other direction (I Pet. 5:13).

(See chapter 3 in this section.)

The whole idea of priesthood, nuns, monks, popes, bishops, of purgatory, Masses, prayers for the dead, prayers to the Virgin Mary and all the statues and images, feast days and programs of the Catholic church —all were wholly unknown in Bible times. Anyone who is aquainted with the Roman Catholic organization, doctrine, and practice would not have found anything even remotely like them in New Testament churches.

Jesus organized no denomination. The word "church" in the Bible never means denomination. It always means a local assemby or that general assembly including every person ever saved in all the ages who will be caught up to meet Christ in the air at the rapture. That group of all ages who are born again will be the body and bride of Christ in Heaven, and in that sense, those who are saved are in the true church. The worldly idea of a human super-church organization like the Roman Catholic system is not taught in the Bible. Jesus would have had nothing to do with it when He was on earth. He did not start it. And the Catholic religion is not at all New Testament Christianity, either in doctrine, in organization, or in historical sequence.

The monstrosity of heresy and worldliness which is the Roman Catholic church today is a growth through the centuries. It was not until 1870 that the Catholic church officially decided on the doctrine that the pope is infallible when he speaks officially. At the same time, it was decided as a law of the church that the church tradition is as authoritative as the Bible.

It was not until 1950 that it became official Catholic doctrine that the body of Mary was taken to Heaven. In doctrine and in organization and practice, the Roman Catholic church has far departed from Bible Christianity. Jesus built no denomination and of all the denominations, He would most certainly have repudiated Catholicism as being untrue to the Bible, untrue to what He Himself taught and trained His apostles to teach. No, Jesus did not establish the Catholic church and only the most biased or ignorant could so declare.

4. The Knights of Columbus Ad Says, "Yes, the Bible Is Truly a Catholic Book. They Were Members of the Catholic Church Who, Under God's Inspiration, Wrote the New Testament in Its Entirety"

That advertisement simply says that Matthew, Mark, Luke, John, Paul, Peter, Jude, the inspired writers of the New Testament, "were members of the Catholic Church." There is not a shred of truth in the statement.

Again, let me say that Jesus did not found the Catholic church. In New Testament times they never heard of a pope. They had no priests in the New Testament, no monks, no nuns. They had no confessional. They had no Mass. They never heard of the foolish, unscriptural doctrine of purgatory. They had no statues, they never prayed to the saints. They never prayed to Mary. They did not have any of the Catholic feast days and programs.

If you had asked Paul if he were a member of the Catholic church, he would have looked perplexed, since there was no Catholic church then and he would have answered that the local church at Antioch, after prayer and fasting, had sent him and Barnabas out on their missionary journeys, and that he counted that as his local home church (see Acts 13:1-4).

Of the about 110 or 112 times that the word "church" is used in the New Testament, it is used approximately one hundred times about local congregations of Christians. It is used one time about Israel as an assembly at Mount Sinai and the rest of the times about the heavenly assemblage when all the saints are caught up to meet Christ in the air. The word is never used about the Catholic church or about any other human denomination. And every historian in the world knows that the Catholic church as such did not exist in New Testament times and that the men who wrote the New Testament were not members of the Catholic church.

5. The Catholic Church Is Not "The Infallible Authority . . . That Always Has Been the Only Sure Guarantee" of the Bible's Inspiration

It is a blasphemous claim that the Catholic church makes: "It is the infallible authority of the Catholic Church that always has been the only sure guarantee of its [the Bible's] inspiration." The Catholic church has no authority from God. The Catholic church cannot guarantee the inspiration of the Bible or speak for God in any other matter. They misinterpret some Scripture to teach so, as I will show you.

When Jesus rose from the dead, He breathed on the disciples and gave them this blessed promise: "Whose soever sins ye remit, they are remitted unto them; and whose soever sins ye retain, they are retained" (John 20:23).

Again in Matthew 18:17-19 is a similar Scripture. There Jesus said: "And if he shall neglect to hear them, tell it unto the church: but if he neglect to hear the church, let him be unto thee as an heathen man and a publican. Verily I say unto you, Whatsoever ye shall bind on earth shall be bound in heaven: and whatsoever ye shall loose on earth shall be loosed in heaven. Again I say unto you, That if two of you shall agree on earth as touching any thing that they shall ask, it shall be done for them of my Father which is in heaven."

From these Scriptures the Catholic popes claim that they have received power to bind on earth and to loose on earth and to act for God on earth.

However, any open-minded reading of the Scriptures will show that they say no such thing. In the first place, these Scriptures do not even mention the pope. They were not given to Peter only, nor even primarily, but to all the apostles. And Matthew 18:17 indicates that they were given to the local congregation, the church.

If Jesus gave special authority to the twelve apostles, it was not intended to be handed down to anyone else. There have been no apostles since Bible times. Jesus never hinted that any other apostles should take the place after these apostles died and after the New Testament was written. He trained His own disciples and gave them the work He wanted them to do. There have been no apostles since those Jesus appointed, including Paul.

However, it may well be that when Jesus said, "Whatsoever ye shall bind on earth shall be bound in heaven," He really meant, "Whatsoever ye shall bind on earth *shall have been bound* already in heaven." The future and future perfect are the same form in the Greek here. That is, Jesus may have meant that the Holy Spirit would simply reveal to the Spirit-filled apostles what God had already settled in Heaven. In the Greek, the future perfect and the simple future are the same. The late Dr. Mantey, a Greek scholar of the Northern Baptist Seminary in Chicago, is the authority for this statement. Hence that right is given to every Christian in the world.

If God's Spirit is on me, I might declare to some what God had revealed from Heaven. Or more clearly, I might, on the authority of the Bible, declare to men what God had already settled in Heaven. For example, when a lost sinner trusts in Christ, I may tell him boldly that he is then a born-again child of God, that his sins are forgiven the moment he trusts in Christ. Thus I can declare on earth what has been settled in Heaven.

At any rate, the Bible never hints that Simon Peter, or any successor of his, would have more authority and more power than others of the apostles. And the Bible never hinted that a pope or a priest or a human organization would have the power to forgive sins on earth, as the Catholic church claims to do. The Bible certainly does not teach and Jesus never taught that a Catholic pope would be able to speak for God on earth. The infallible authority claimed for the Catholic church simply does not exist. The pope is a poor, frail man like any other man. He is a sinner who needed to be saved by the blood of Christ, just the same as I needed to be saved and as any drunkard or infidel would need to be saved.

The Bible is clear that no person on earth can speak for God except when he speaks in the power of the Holy Spirit and on the authority of the Word of God. No one has a right to make any new doctrines, no one has a right to change any of the Bible commands.

The Catholic church sinned against God when it taught people to pray to Mary, when it taught people to pray for the dead. The Catholic church sinned against God when it invented the wicked doctrine of purgatory. The Catholic church sinned against God when it pronounced the law that priests could not marry. It is a blasphemous usurpation of the authority of Jesus Christ which the Catholic church claims. The church cannot guarantee the inspiration of the Bible. The Bible guarantees its own inspiration. God's Spirit inspired men to write the Bible. God has providentially protected the manuscripts.

6. Catholics Falsely Claim "the Complete Revealed Truth of God" Was Delivered to the Catholic Church "From the Beginning"

The Bible was never delivered to the Catholic church by God. Paul did not write his epistles to the Catholic church. Peter did not write his first and second epistles to the Catholic church. Read the book of James and you will see that it was not written to the Catholic church. The Catholic church did not even exist when the New Testament was completed.

There was no pope at Rome. There were no bishops in the Roman Catholic sense. God had parts of the Bible written to specific people who are named. The books of Luke and Acts are written by Luke and addressed to Theophilus. The book of Revelation was written to the seven local congregations in Asia Minor which are named. The book of James was written to Jews scattered abroad. The book of Hebrews was written to Jews at Jerusalem before the city was destroyed. The epistles of First and Second Timothy were written by Paul the apostle to the young preacher Timothy. So with Titus and Philemon. They were written to the men named by the Apostle Paul.

It is wholly contrary to the fact, and the falsehood can be easily discovered by anybody who reads the New Testament, when Catholics claim that God delivered "the complete revealed truth" to the Catholic church.

7. The Catholic Church Has Not "Faithfully Unfolded the Meaning of the Written Word of God to Past Generations of Mankind" and It Is Not True That She "Does So Today"

The simple truth is that the Roman Catholic church has developed further and further away from the New Testament pattern and from the truth of God. The very idea of a great superchurch with a princely pope claiming to be in the place of God on earth is itself a departure from Bible principles and from the truth of God. The idea that one needs priests to whom he can confess his sins, priests to offer sacrifices, is itself a departure from God's truth. The idea that the traditions of the church are as authoritative as the Bible, is a most serious and fundamental departure from the truth of God. The authority claimed by the pope and by priests who act for him is a blasphemous assumption of authority.

If you want to see whether the Catholic church has "faithfully unfolded the meaning of the written Word of God to past generations of mankind," and if it "does so today," I suggest that you go to South America or Central America, or to Spain, or anywhere else that Catholicism has had free rein without the help of Protestantism. Everywhere Catholicism has had full authority, the people have been led into ignorance and superstition and sin. There is one sure way for any nation to be a benighted nation of ignorance, superstition and proverty. That is to give the Roman Catholic church absolute power and authority there and shut out all other religions. That has been proved around the world for many centuries.

And does the Catholic church really promote the reading of the Bible? Only in Protestant countries! Only in places where Catholics hear Protestant preachers on the radio and read Protestant magazines, and where they constantly mingle with Protestants, only in such cases does the Catholic church advise Catholics to read the Bible.

If you go to South America, you will find that Catholic priests burn Bibles almost as fast as Protestant missionaries can give them out! It was so in the days of Wycliffe. It was so in the days of the Reformation. The Catholic church thinks much of the church but little of the Word of God. Priests themselves are generally ignorant of the Word of God and the most fervent and sincere Catholic people are notoriously ignorant of the Bible. The Catholic church has failed more in this one thing than in almost anything else. It has not "faithfully unfolded the meaning of the written Word of God."

Teaching people to offer Masses for the dead and try to pray them out of purgatory! Teaching people that they are to confess their sins to a man, an unmarried priest, and expect him to forgive them! Teaching people to pray to Mary, hoping that she will intercede with Christ for them! Teaching people that salvation is in the church instead of in Jesus Christ! Teaching people it is a sin to eat meat on Friday or during Lent! That is how far the Roman Catholic church has been from "faithfully unfolding the meaning of the written Word of God."

No, my friend, the Bible is not a Catholic book.

Thank God, the Bible is God's Book. No church, no human denomination has a right to claim it as peculiarly their own. It belongs to me, and to every other Christian who has received it, but it is not given to me by any denomination and its authority does not rest on the say-so of any denomination or pope. The Bible is not a Catholic book.

We read in Ephesians 3:1, "For this cause I Paul, the prisoner of Jesus Christ for you Gentiles. . . ." This is significant. Paul was in jail for being true to the trust God had committed to him. He was a prisoner because he was an apostle to the Gentiles. Paul and Peter had a dispute, as we read in Galatians 2:11-14. Peter was sincere, and Paul was, too. The trouble was that Peter was talking out of turn. He was not an apostle to the Gentiles; so Paul rebuked him. If Peter had brought circumcision into the body of Christ, he would have hampered the early church and they would have lost a good many members. Paul and Peter were not in disagreement about the doctrines of the virgin birth, the incarnation, the vicarious blood atonement, or the bodily resurrection of our Lord. The trouble was that one of them was called for one definite purpose, and the other one was called for another definite purpose.

2. Was Peter the First Pope?

Did Christ Give Peter the Power to Forgive Sins? Did the Catholic Church Get This Right From Peter? Was the True Church Founded on Peter or on Christ?

"*And I say also unto thee, That thou art Peter, and upon this rock I will build my church; and the gates of hell shall not prevail against it. And I will give unto thee the keys of the kingdom of heaven: and whatsoever thou shalt bind on earth shall be bound in heaven, and whatsoever thou shalt loose on earth shall be loosed in heaven.*"—Matt. 16:18,19.

Catholics say that Christ founded His church upon Peter. They say that Peter was the first pope, or head of the church, and that this primacy of Peter descends to other Catholic popes. Therefore, they claim that the Catholic church is the true church, that only the Catholic church can forgive sins, etc.

Now that can be easily answered from the Bible, and I hope you will give it careful consideration and check up for yourself and see if this answer is not thoroughly satisfactory.

1. Jesus Did Not Say He Would Found His Church Upon Peter

The church is not founded upon Peter but upon Jesus Himself. A note upon these verses in the Scofield Reference Bible says:

> There is in the Greek a play upon the words "thou art Peter [*petros*--literally, "a little rock"], and upon this rock *[Petra]* I will build my church." He does not promise to build His church upon Peter, but upon Himself, as Peter himself is careful to tell us (I Pet. 2.4-9).

First Peter 2:4-9 says:

"*To whom coming, as unto a living stone, disallowed indeed of men, but chosen of God, and precious, Ye also, as lively stones, are built up a spiritual house, an holy priesthood, to offer up spiritual sacrifices, acceptable to God by Jesus Christ. Wherefore also it is contained in the scripture, Behold, I lay in Sion a chief corner stone, elect, precious: and he that believeth on him shall not be confounded. Unto you therefore which believe he is precious: but unto them which be disobedient, the stone which the builders disallowed, the same is made the head of the corner, And a stone of stumbling, and a rock of offence, even to them which stumble at the word, being disobedient: whereunto also they were appointed. But ye are a chosen generation, a royal priesthood, an holy nation, a peculiar people; that ye should shew forth the praises of him who hath called you out of darkness into his marvelous light.*"

From the above Scripture you can tell that all Christians are living stones, built up into a spiritual house. But the chief corner stone is Jesus Christ. Always in Scripture Jesus is the Rock, the Chief Stone. So He is the Foundation Stone.

That is exactly what I Corinthians 3:10,11 says: "*According to the grace of God which is given unto me, as a wise masterbuilder, I have laid the foundation, and another buildeth thereon. But let every man take heed how he buildeth thereupon. For other foundation can no man lay than that is laid, which is Jesus Christ.*"

No foundation can be laid but Jesus Christ.

Isaiah 28:16 has a prophecy about Jesus Christ which says, "Therefore thus saith the Lord God, Behold, I lay in Zion for a foundation a stone, a tried stone, a precious corner stone, a sure foundation: he that believeth shall not make haste."

This Scripture speaks of Christ as a foundation stone, a precious corner stone. Jesus is both. Many times in the Old Testament the Lord Himself is called a Rock. Psalm 18:2 says, "The Lord is my rock, and my fortress, and my deliverer; my God, my strength, in whom I will trust; my buckler, and the horn of my salvation, and my high tower."

You see, the Rock or Stone, upon which the church is built, is Jesus Christ Himself, and not Peter. Jesus said to Peter, "Thou art Peter [a boulder, or a little rock, the word means], and upon this rock [Christ, the foundation bedrock, a different Greek word] I will build my church."

Peter had just said to Jesus, "Thou art the Christ, the Son of the living God" (Matt. 16:16). So Jesus is telling Peter that upon Himself the church would be founded. Christ is the Chief Cornerstone, the Foundation Stone, the Head of the church and the Foundation. A great old song teaches this same thing,

"The church's one foundation
Is Jesus Christ her Lord."

2. Jesus Did Not Give Peter the Keys to Heaven or the Keys to the Church

In Matthew 16:19 Jesus said, "And I will give unto thee the keys of the kingdom of heaven: and whatsoever thou shalt bind on earth shall be bound in heaven: and whatsoever thou shalt loose on earth shall be loosed in heaven."

Catholics think that Jesus gave Peter the keys to Heaven and the keys to the church, and that whatever Peter or his successor (for so they call the pope) requires, must be done if we want to get to Heaven. In other words, they say that the Catholic church, with its pope and priesthood, has the authority given to Peter, and that therefore only through the Catholic church can one be saved. But they misunderstand and misinterpret the Scripture altogether. Again, let me give you the most widely accepted interpretation of this passage. The Scofield Reference Bible, in a note on this verse, says,

> Not the keys to the church, but of the kingdom of heaven in the sense of Mt. 13., i.e. the sphere of Christian profession. A key is a badge of power or authority (cf. Isa. 22.22; Rev. 3.7). The apostolic history explains and limits this trust, for it was Peter who opened the door of Christian opportunity to Israel on the day of Pentecost (Acts 2.38-42,) and to Gentiles in the house of Cornelius (Acts 10.34-46).
>
> There was no assumption by Peter of any other authority (Acts 15.7-11). In the council James, not Peter, seems to have presided (Acts 15.19; cf. Gal. 2.11-15). Peter claimed no more for himself than to be an apostle by gift (1 Pet. 1.1), and an elder by office (1 Pet. 5.1).
>
> The power of binding and loosing was shared (Mt. 18.18; John 20.23) by the other disciples. That it did not involve the determination of the eternal destiny of souls is clear from Rev. 1.18. The keys of death and the place of departed spirits are held by Christ alone.

It is important to note that Peter himself never

claimed the power to save people or damn them. Peter never pretended that he was the head of the church. Peter never pretended to forgive sins on his own authority. He never said, as Roman Catholic priests say, "*Te absolvo,*" or "*I forgive you.*" Rather Peter preached about Jesus that "To him give all the prophets witness, that through his name whosoever believeth in him shall receive remission of sins" (Acts 10:43).

There Peter preached to Cornelius and his household that whoever would believe in Christ or trust in Him should have remission of sins. It was not on the basis of the Mass, or the basis of a priesthood, or doing penance, or saying prayers, or baptism. Those who put their trust in Christ would have all their sins remitted, forgiven, Peter said.

You see, Peter never pretended that he was given the power to forgive sins. So Peter understood what Jesus meant better than do the Catholics.

3. In Bible Times Neither the Other Apostles Nor Peter Thought That Peter Was the Head of the Church

In Ephesians 2:19 and 20 we are told:

"*Now therefore ye are no more strangers and foreigners, but fellowcitizens with the saints, and of the household of God; And are built upon the foundation of the apostles and prophets, Jesus Christ himself being the chief corner stone.*"

You see, Jesus Christ is the Chief Cornerstone as well as the Foundation, and the apostles and prophets were built upon Christ, all of them alike, and then we who are left follow them.

In building a building you have first the foundation, then you put on other stones, in this case the apostles and prophets. Then in succession, others who were saved were added to this church or building, which is "fitly framed together," as "an holy temple of the Lord." You see that here the apostles and prophets are all alike a foundation upon the one main Foundation. Nothing is said more for Peter here than for the other apostles and the prophets.

In Acts, chapter 15, there was a big council at Jerusalem to decide whether or not Gentiles needed to be circumcised. Before that council Peter made a speech, as you see in Acts 15:7-11. Then Paul and Barnabas made speeches, as you see in verse 12. Then when everybody else was through, James made a speech and settled the matter; he said in verse 19, "Wherefore my sentence is, that we trouble not them, which from among the Gentiles have turned to God: But that we write unto them, that they abstain from pollutions of idols, and from fornication, and from things strangled, and from blood."

You see, James had the final say. Then all the apostles and elders agreed, and they wrote letters carrying out the sentence, or the decision, of James. Certainly, at Jerusalem, James was as important as Peter when it came to authority in the church. Peter was no more a pope than was James. He was no more a pope than Paul and Barnabas were. He was a preacher and an apostle, but that was all.

Later Paul was preaching at Antioch. Gentiles were saved. Peter was glad they were saved and he laid aside his old Jewish prejudices and ate with them. But when some Jews came from Jerusalem, Peter was afraid of them. So he withdrew himself from Gentiles. He led other Jews likewise to do wrong, even Barnabas. So what did Paul do? He boldly rebuked Peter, before everybody! Galatians 2:11-14 tells the story by divine inspiration:

"*But when Peter was come to Antioch, I withstood*

him to the face, because he was to be blamed. For before that certain came from James, he did eat with the Gentiles: but when they were come, he withdrew and separated himself, fearing them which were of the circumcision. And the other Jews dissembled likewise with him; insomuch that Barnabas also was carried away with their dissimulation. But when I saw that they walked not uprightly according to the truth of the gospel, I said unto Peter before them all, If thou, being a Jew, livest after the manner of Gentiles, and not as do the Jews, why compellest thou the Gentiles to live as do the Jews?"

Does that look like Peter was the head of the church, a pope? Does that look like he pretended to have the keys to Heaven, and save people or damn them? Absolutely not! Peter was only a man, a good preacher, one of the first of the twelve apostles, but he had no more authority than Paul or the other apostles, and when he did wrong they felt perfectly free to rebuke him.

Peter never claimed to be the head of the church nor to have the power to forgive sins. If anyone says so, then they simply do not know the Bible. And Peter certainly knew whether he was a pope or not and whether Christ had put him at the head of the church, and whether only he and others appointed by him could give salvation, could forgive sins. No such thing is taught in the Bible, and Peter did not think anything like that.

4. There Are Several Good Reasons Why Peter Could Not Have Been the First Pope

First, Peter would not make a good pope because he was married. Matthew 8:14,15, and two other passages, tell how Jesus healed Peter's wife's mother, who was sick of a fever. Long later, Peter still had his wife, for Paul spoke of him (Cephas, another name here) in I Corinthians 9:5, "Have we not power to lead about a sister, a wife, as well as other apostles, and as the brethren of the Lord, and Cephas?"

You see, Peter still had his wife. There is nothing wrong with a preacher having a wife. First Timothy 3:2 says, "A bishop then must be blameless, the husband of one wife." But, contrary to the Scriptures, popes do not marry, so Peter would not have made a good pope.

Second, there is not a single scrap of evidence that Peter ever went to Rome. The Bible never mentions his going to Rome; when Paul went to Rome, Peter was evidently not there, as Paul does not mention him at all in letters written from Rome, and there is not any secular history which reliably mentions Peter's going to Rome. That is only a myth, a tradition, unconfirmed by any reliable history and unconfirmed by the Bible.

3. Peter Was Never at Rome

The whole Catholic church is formed and founded on the claim that Peter was a pope, the first pope at Rome, that he was the vicar of Christ, that is, that he was the voice of Christ, had all of Christ's authority and power, kingly powers and authority over all the earth, and that all succeeding popes at Rome inherit that authority.

Note carefully, there could not be a particle of argument for the pope as Christ's ruler on earth if Peter himself was not a pope. Elsewhere we discuss the fact that Peter was never a pope, never claimed to be. There is no hint in the Bible that he carried any of the authority claimed for the popes. But here our subject is the simple fact that Peter was never even at Rome! If we prove that Peter was never at Rome, then we prove he was never a pope, and prove that the whole Catholic organization is not a Christian organization, that its claims are false, that Catholicism is a false religion—not the Christian religion, and the Catholic church is not "the church of Christ" on earth as it claims to be.

I say again, the Catholic church has not a particle of foundation if Peter was never in Rome. And that we can prove, and we invite every honest Bible believer to check the evidence which we give.

I. Overwhelming Lack of Bible Evidence That Peter Went to Rome

Peter is the third most often mentioned man in the New

Testament. Of course, there is far more about Jesus Christ, and there is more about the Apostle Paul, but besides these, Peter is the most often-mentioned person in the whole New Testament. He is discussed in Matthew, Mark, Luke, John, the book of Acts, and I Corinthians. He wrote the two epistles, I and II Peter. And yet there is never a hint that he was to be a pope, that he was to have authority over the other apostles, and there is not even an inference that he went to Rome or that he ever would go to Rome! The Catholic tradition that Peter went to Rome, that he was the first pope there, that he was crucified there head downward, as a martyr—all that is purely fraudulent tradition without a particle of historical evidence, without even a hint in the Bible that Peter was ever at Rome.

He is called Peter, or Simon Peter, I think, 162 times in the New Testament, Simon 30 times and Cephas six times. We read about his being a fisherman and being called to be a disciple. We read about his walking on the water and sinking, and about his going with Jesus on the Mount of Transfiguration and in the Garden of Gethsemane. We read that it was revealed to Peter that Jesus was the Christ of God. We read that he cursed and swore and denied Jesus, and quit the ministry, and that Jesus called him back again to serve Him. When the Great Commission was given to the disciples, we do not find a hint that any special emphasis was given to Peter, or any authority given to Peter more than to the others.

We read in the book of Acts how Peter preached at Pentecost, how he was used of God to work miracles, how he preached to Gentiles at the household of Cornelius, how he was imprisoned by Herod. This latter incident was recorded in the twelfth chapter of the book of Acts, not halfway through. The Holy Spirit then dismisses the story of Peter, and Paul takes the center of the stage. It is Paul who goes to Rome; it is Paul who teaches the New Testament churches; it is Paul who is the apostle to the Gentiles.

Peter is mentioned as being at Bethsaida, at Capernaum, at Cana, at Nain, at the country of the Gadarenes, at Jericho, at Jerusalem, at Bethany. The Bible reports that he was at Samaria, at Joppa, at Lydda, at Caesarea, at Antioch, at Sychar. Now if Peter was at Rome for years, was the chief of all the Christians there, the most important person at Rome, and God wanted him to be so received, would not the Bible have said so? It did not. The whole idea of Peter being at Rome is a false, idolatrous man-made tradition of people who want to exalt their denomination above Jesus Christ.

Now any sensible person must see that if Jesus Christ had intended Peter to be a pope, He would have said so. And in all the mentions of Peter—if he was to go to Rome to establish the Roman church—the Scripture surely would have hinted it or referred to it somewhere! It never did, because Peter was not a pope, and Peter never went to Rome.

In this case, since the Catholic claim is that the one single, most important thing about Peter is that he went to Rome and became pope, then when that is not mentioned in the Bible, it becomes an obvious fabrication. If Peter was to become the spiritual ruler of the world and that his successors, popes of Rome down through the ages, were to be rulers of the world for Christ, the Bible somewhere surely would have hinted it, referred to it, or stated it. The silence of the Bible in this matter is absolute and overwhelming evidence: Peter never went to Rome.

II. The Scriptures Clearly Designate Peter as an Apostle to Jews, Not to Gentiles

Paul was an apostle to Gentiles. The Bible expressly says so more than once. When Paul was converted, the

Lord said to Ananias about Paul, "...he is a chosen vessel unto me, to bear my name before the Gentiles, and kings..." (Acts 9:15). Paul was arrested in Jerusalem, where he had gone contrary to the plain instructions of the Holy Spirit, because he wanted to preach primarily to Jews, when God wanted him to go to the Gentiles. There Paul himself reported that God had said to him, "Depart: for I will send thee far hence unto the Gentiles" (Acts 22:21). And Paul was inspired to say in Romans 11:13, "For I speak to you Gentiles, inasmuch as I am the apostle of the Gentiles, I magnify mine office." In II Timothy 1:11, Paul was inspired to write, "Whereunto I am appointed a preacher, and an apostle, and a teacher of the Gentiles."

Since Paul was to go to the Gentiles, the matter is very explicitly taught in the Scriptures in the account of his going to the Gentiles and his ministry among them. But with Peter it is not so. He preached to Cornelius and his household against his will, and there is no record of his going to other Gentiles. In fact, Peter even refused to eat with the Gentile converts, as we see from Galatians 2:12, and Paul found it necessary to rebuke him openly.

But when Paul went up to Jerusalem to get acquainted with the apostles and compare the Gospel which he preached with theirs, they could add nothing to the revelation God had given Paul.

"*But contrariwise, when they saw that the gospel of the uncircumcision was committed unto me, as the gospel of the circumcision was unto Peter; (For he that wrought effectually in Peter to the apostleship of the circumcision, the same was mighty in me toward the Gentiles:) And when James, Cephas, and John, who seemed to be pillars, perceived the grace that was given unto me, they gave to me and Barnabas the right hands of fellowship; that we should go unto the heathen, and they unto the circumcision.*"—Gal. 2:7-9.

Note carefully, the Bible is abundantly clear: Paul was to be the apostle to the Gentiles; Peter was to lead in giving the Gospel to the Jews. The "gospel of the circumcision was [committed] unto Peter" (Gal. 2:7). So they gave Paul and Barnabas "the right hands of fellowship;" that Barnabas and Paul should go unto the Gentiles and "they unto the circumcision." It could not be clearer than the Bible makes it. Peter was to preach to Jews, not to the Gentiles. So Peter did not go to Philippi, Thessalonica, Berea, Athens, and then to Rome; he went to the Jews in Jerusalem and at Joppa and at Caesarea, and then eastward to Babylon, to the Jews of the Dispersion, Jews who had been scattered out to all that country. If Peter had gone to Rome, it would have been against the clear command of God, that he was to go to "the circumcision." And the Bible tells us very plainly that Paul was assigned to that role, to go into Europe and to Rome; but Peter was not.

Paul was in Jerusalem sometime after the crucifixion of Christ and His resurrection and ascension. After Paul was converted (Acts, chapter 9), then, we think, probably after some time at Damascus, then three years of preaching in Arabia and then again at Damascus (Gal. 1:17; Acts 9:22,23), he came to Jerusalem. And Peter was there, and the other apostles, and Barnabas recommended him (Acts 9:26,27; Gal. 1:18). That was probably about the year 38 or 40 A. D. or possibly later. Then, fourteen years later Paul came up to Jerusalem again and saw Peter there again. Ussher and Unger have the Jerusalem council about 50 A. D. (see Gal. 2:1-9). Note that Peter was still in Jerusalem.

Again (we do not know the date), "when Peter was come to Antioch," and compromised and needed to be rebuked by Paul (Gal. 2:11-14), then Peter went to Babylon. And I and II Peter, his epistles, are from Babylon, and he sent greetings from the church there (I Pet. 5:13). And notice that in his first epistle he announces himself as "Peter, an apostle of Jesus Christ, to the strangers scattered throughout Pontus, Galatia, Cappadocia, Asia, and Bithynia, Elect according to the foreknowledge of God the Father. . . ," that is, to the Jews. More literally translated, it was to "sojourners of the dispersion." He was an apostle to the circumcision, not to the Gentiles.

Notice carefully that some thirty-five years later, when the book of Revelation was written, it may symbolically refer to Rome as Babylon; but nobody had called Rome "Babylon" before that time. And The Revelation is a prophecy of the future destruction of that monstrous "whore," the Roman church. So when Peter previously sent word from the church at Babylon, he was not at Rome. Peter never went to Rome.

Notice that the epistle of II Peter was written shortly before Peter died in Babylon: II Peter 1:14 says, "Knowing that shortly I must put off this my tabernacle, even as our Lord Jesus Christ hath shewed me." And that second epistle was probably written in 66 A. D., according to the best scholarship. Peter at that time was in Babylon, and that was about the time Paul was beheaded in Rome!

III. When Paul Wrote the Letter to Romans, Peter Was Not There

Paul's epistle to the Romans "was written from Corinth during the apostle's third visit to that city (2 Cor. 13.1), in A. D. 60," says the Scofield Reference Bible. It is quite clear that, knowing the claims of the false Roman religion, God set out to give abundant evidence that Peter was not at Rome when this letter was written. In Romans 16, Paul named some twenty-eight persons and their families, and sent them greetings. Yet he does not even mention Peter. These others were at Rome; Peter was not.

It is unthinkable that God would have a pope at Rome, set up to be the spiritual ruler of the world and have God's own authority over everybody else, and that the Apostle Paul would write to the Christians at Rome and not even mention Peter! Peter was not even there, and of course he was not a pope.

IV. The Apostle Peter Was Not at Rome During Paul's Stay There

Acts, chapter 28, tells of the arrival of Paul in Rome, we suppose about the year 63 A. D. When he arrived in Rome, "it came to pass, that after three days Paul called the chief of the Jews together. . ." (Acts 28:17). And when they came together, he told them of the charges against him and why he was sent to Rome. This is their answer: "We neither received letters out of Judaea concerning thee, neither any of the brethren that came shewed or spake any harm of thee. But we desire to hear of thee what thou thinkest: for as concerning this sect, we know that every where it is spoken against" (vss. 21,22).

Will you note carefully, most of the Jews at Rome had not even heard the Gospel. Peter was not there. He did not meet Paul there. He is not mentioned in the whole account. "And Paul dwelt two whole years in his own hired house, and received all that came in unto him" (vs. 30), but Peter is not mentioned. He was not there.

Paul wrote a number of letters from Rome, called "the prison epistles." The first of these epistles was Ephesians, and they were sent by Tychicus, as named. Peter is not mentioned.

The letter to the Philippians was written from Rome, and he mentions some Christians who are to be greeted by name! "The brethren which are with me greet you. All the saints salute you, chiefly they that are of Caesar's household" (Phil. 4:21,22). No mention is made of Peter; he is not there.

In his letter from Rome to the Colossians, Paul sends greetings from Epaphras, from Luke, the beloved physician, and from Demas (Col. 4:12,14).

And when he writes from Rome the second epistle to Timothy, Paul says, "Demas hath forsaken me, having loved this present world, and is departed unto Thessalonica; Crescens to Galatia, Titus unto Dalmatia. Only Luke is with me" (II Tim. 4:10,11). Just before Paul's martyrdom at Rome Peter was not at Rome. Nobody with Paul but Luke! Peter was not there.

The letter to Philemon was also written from Rome. In it Paul sends greetings from Epaphras, Marcus, Aristarchus, Demas, Lucas (vss. 23,24). Paul does not mention Peter. Peter is not there.

If one goes by the Bible, there can be only one honest conclusion; Peter was never at Rome when Paul was there. He was not there when Paul wrote to Rome, and he was not there when Paul arrived. He was not there when Paul wrote these letters, nor when Paul died.

4. Pope Pushes Fraud

Claims "Convincing Proof" That Bones of St. Peter Were Actually Found Buried Under St. Peter's Basilica in Rome

The June 27, 1968 daily papers published the following from the United Press:

Pope Says Proof Shows Bones Those of St. Peter

Vatican City (UPI)—An "exultant" Pope Paul VI announced yesterday that years-long investigations have produced 'convincing' evidence that bones found beneath St. Peter's basilica were those of the Apostle Peter.

The pontiff made the announcement at his weekly general audience in the basilica to a crowd of several thousand persons who greeted it with applause.

The Pope did not specify what "convincing" proof had been found.

But Prof. Margherita Guarducci of Rome University, one of the leading scholars in the inquiry, said later the announcement merely "recognized that which I already concluded in 1965."

Professor Guarducci published a book then in which she said she had determined the bones were definitely those of St. Peter, who was crucified about 1,900 years ago, according to tradition, and is recognized by the Roman Catholic Church as the first pope.

"I knew that the Holy Father was completely convinced of what I had written," Prof. Guarducci said. "But it was a surprise to me that he announced it today."

> Scholars as well as Catholics and Protestants have disputed for years over the question. Some Protestants have even questioned whether Peter ever came to Rome.
>
> Proof that he did would be of more than historical or archaeological importance. The claim of the popes to be vicars of Christ rests on their contention that they are the successors to Peter, to whom Jesus Christ said: "Thou art Peter and upon this rock I shall build my church. . . ."

Yes, I said that it is fraudulent for anybody to claim any proof that Peter was ever in Rome or that Peter was the first pope or that Peter's bones have been found in Rome. The pope said there was "convincing proof" but "the pope did not specify what 'convincing' proof had been found." It would not stand the light of day. There is no convincing proof of that which never happened.

In this matter the pope starts out with fraud in claiming to be the vicegerent of God on earth, claiming that he got his authority directly from Peter, claiming that the Roman Catholic monstrosity is the true church of Christ on earth and that he, the pope, is the highest official of Christ on earth. Nothing in the Bible substantiates any such claim. All that is a heathen tradition developed falsely through the years and for personal, selfish reasons by men who set out to rule kings and countries and enslave the minds of men and to claim the power of Heaven and Hell over people.

But when I say that the pope's claim is fraudulent, I am not simply calling names but speaking as a scholar in saying that which I can clearly prove to intelligent and informed people.

What a History of Fraud in the Traditions of the Roman Church!

Sensible people who know history have a right to

believe that the Roman church has not changed, but still manufactures traditions and relics and doctrines which are contrary to the Bible and to known facts.

Note the false inventions about Mary. They show in Jerusalem a cave over which the Church of St. Anne was built, saying that Mary's mother was named Anne, that they lived in Jerusalem. There is no hint, either in history or in the Bible, that Mary's mother was named Anne or that they ever lived in Jerusalem. Mary, we suppose, stayed in Jerusalem after Christ's ascension. She was in the prayer meeting of Acts 1:14.

They have now formed the doctrine and made it a matter of faith which the church claims one must believe in order to be saved, and that is that Mary went bodily to Heaven. And they will show you the place in Jerusalem where Catholic tradition says this occurred.

They say that Mary was a perpetual virgin, that she never had other children, though the Bible plainly names the children of Joseph and Mary, conceived and born after Jesus was born: they included James, who wrote the book of James; Jude, who wrote the book of Jude; one named Simeon and some sisters who are not named (Matt. 13:55,56). And Psalm 69:8 is a prophecy about Jesus: "I am become a stranger unto my brethren, and an alien unto my mother's children." The New Testament quotes the next verse: "For the zeal of thine house hath eaten me up; and the reproaches of them that reproached thee are fallen upon me," as referring to Jesus (Ps. 69:9; John 2:17).

Catholic tradition says that prayers to Mary will get through to God better than any other way and that Mary, not Jesus, is the mediator between God and men.

The Catholic tradition is that in the Mass the bread actually becomes the body of the Lord Jesus and the wine actually becomes the blood of Jesus, and that thus a new sacrifice of Christ is made every time the Mass is observed and that despite the express statement of the

Scriptures in Hebrews 10:14, "For by one offering he hath perfected for ever them that are sanctified." And that after one is converted to Christ, "their sins and iniquities will I remember no more. Now where remission of these is, there is no more offering for sin" (Heb. 10:17,18).

In a thousand places where Romanism has gone, extravagant and unbelievable traditions have been manufactured to obtain the devotion and the money of the ignorant. There are many little bits of wood, "pieces of the true cross," there are "nails from the true cross." There is the handkerchief or scarf with which St. Veronica is said to have wiped the face of Jesus and left the imprint of His face there! There are the bones of this saint and the other saint. And these traditions and inventions are being propagated continually.

I was in the Mamertine Dungeon in Rome and now we found what had not been there these years before—there was an indentation in the stone where it is said that the Apostle Peter, when he was in Rome, was imprisoned and bumped his head there! And it is so labeled.

The Church of the Holy Stairs in Rome is based on the tradition that these twenty-eight steps were brought to Rome from Palestine, that they were the steps to Pilate's Judgment Hall in the Fortress of Antonia in Jerusalem and Queen Helena, mother of Emperor Constantine, is said to have found them and brought them to Rome. Actually she was not in Palestine until 275 years after the crucifixion and after Jerusalem had been utterly destroyed again and again. And she picked out also the cave in which she says the Saviour was born in Bethlehem, although the Bible says nothing about a cave. She picked out the site where now the Church of the Holy Sepulchre is built in Jerusalem, which is supposed to cover the place of the crucifixion and burial of Christ and she is supposed to have found that site by some wondrous magic!

In Nazareth the Catholic church is built over a cave which Queen Helena and others said was the home of Mary and Joseph and the boy Jesus, although there is no Bible indication that they lived in a cave and, of course, there are no houses remaining these two thousand years that could be called the home of Mary and Joseph.

And now the pope claims that the bones of St. Peter have been found under the basilica of St. Peter's. However, a few years ago the Catholic priests sold me a booklet in Rome claiming that the Church of St. John the Lateran had had, since the twelfth century, I believe, the bones of Peter and the bones of Paul! That was sold to me in the Church of the Holy Stairs by priests. They do not sell it any more, now that they have another set of bones of Peter, at St. Peter's Church!

No, Rome cannot be trusted with its fictitious traditions to mislead the people and collect their money and get honor which no pope should have.

5. Catholic Tradition, or the Bible?

Letter to a Catholic Friend Showing the Sin of Following Human Tradition and the Shifting, Unreliable Nature of Catholic Traditions

Dear Mrs. B————:

Thank you for sending me the clipped article from your Catholic magazine, *Our Sunday Visitor.* The Rev. G. Stuart Hogan, Catholic priest, is right in labeling his article, "Tradition Called a Key to Catholicism." That is the sad truth. It is based upon human tradition and not upon the Word of God.

You may remember that I told you in a former letter that I took *Our Sunday Visitor* for years, that I studied carefully *Faith of Our Fathers* by Cardinal Gibbons, and referred again and again to the *Catholic Encyclopedia.* I feel I may claim to be really better informed on the history and doctrines of Catholicism than most Catholics.

In answer to your kindly letter and the article I must call your attention to several very serious mistakes in reference to facts, in this article, "Tradition Called a Key to Catholicism," in *Our Sunday Visitor.* I will call your attention to several of these errors of fact.

1. The idea that the Catholic church has never changed from the doctrine and practice of the apostles

is a fallacy, known, first, by all historical scholars and known, second, by all students of the Bible.

All well-informed students of church history know that the Catholic church has steadily changed and grown further and further from the Bible. We can go back in history and find when the church changed from baptism by immersion to baptism by sprinkling; when it changed from baptism of believing converts to the sprinkling of infants, and teaching the doctrine of baptismal regeneration. Practically all scholars agree, including Catholic scholars, that baptism in the days of the apostles was by immersion.

In ancient Catholic churches built up to the twelfth and thirteenth centuries, the baptistry itself was a large pool for immersion, and some such buildings remain today. The Catholic church simply changed from immersion to sprinkling. The *Catholic Encyclopedia,* under the subject *baptism,* frankly admits that the church here changed from and left the apostolic doctrine and practice.

In the *Catholic Encyclopedia,* sponsored by the Knights of Columbus, with the imprimatur of Cardinal Farley, Volume II, page 259, under the heading: "BAPTISM, II, Etymology," is the following:

> The word baptism is derived from the Greek word *bapto* or *baptizo,* to wash or to immerse.

On page 261, Volume II, second column, we read:

> The most ancient form usually employed was unquestionably immersion. This is not only evident from the writings of the Fathers and the early rituals of both the Latin and Oriental churches, but it can also be gathered from the Epistles of St. Paul, who speaks of baptism as a bath (Eph. V, 26; Rom. VI, 4; Titus III, 5). In the Latin Church, immersion seems to have prevailed until the twelfth century.... Infusion and aspersion, however, were growing common in the thirteenth century and gradually prevailed in the Western Church."

2. Church history students know when the Catholic

church left the apostolic way of administering the Lord's Supper the way Christ Himself gave it, in both kinds, that is, with both bread and the fruit of the vine.

The Catholic church had no compunction in throwing away what Jesus Christ said and creating a new tradition of the church. They followed human tradition here instead of the Bible, just as they did about baptism.

John A. O'Brien, Catholic authority, in the book, *The Faith of Millions,* page 223, says:

> It was the common custom for the first twelve centuries to give communion under both kinds.

He says:

> The present law of giving communion to the laity only under the form of bread dates from the Council of Constance in 1415.

3. The Catholic traditional requirement of celibacy of the priesthood, that is, that priests should not be allowed to marry, is wholly based on human reasoning and is especially contrary to the command of Christ and the apostles.

Peter himself was married. See Mark 1:30 where his wife's mother is mentioned and Jesus healed her fever. The Apostle Paul, by divine inspiration, wrote: "A bishop then, must be blameless, married but once. . ." (I Tim. 3:2); as translated in the Catholic Confraternity edition of the New Testament. And this Catholic New Testament adds a note: "3,2: **Married but once:** priestly celibacy as a law is of later ecclesiastical institution." Any new "ecclesiastical institution" like requiring priests not to marry, is an innovation manufactured by men, in direct opposition to the command of the apostles and the teaching of Jesus Christ Himself. To say that the Catholic church does not make any new doctrines, does not change from the apostolic way or the teaching of Christ, is simply not true, as all scholars everywhere know.

The celibacy of the priesthood (that is, that priests could not marry) was decreed by Pope Gregory VII in 1079. Is not this a fulfillment of the Scripture in I Timothy 4:1-3:

"*Now the Spirit speaketh expressly, that in the latter times some shall depart from the faith, giving heed to seducing spirits, and doctrines of devils; Speaking lies in hypocrisy; having their conscience seared with a hot iron; Forbidding to marry, and commanding to abstain from meats, which God hath created to be received with thanksgiving of them which believe and know the truth.*"

4. The papacy itself is an invention unheard of in the days of Christ and the apostles and during the first century of the Christian era.

Catholic tradition says that Peter was the first pope. Who, then, was the second one? Who were the popes of the first three centuries? All good students of history know there were no popes. There were no pastors who even claimed the authority and position that the Roman pontiff now claims. In fact, this tradition of the papacy has developed and changed bit by bit.

Dr. Loraine Boettner tells us that the title of pope or universal bishop was given to Boniface III, by Emperor Phocas, in 607, after Gregory I had refused it. It was not until 1870 that the doctrine of papal infallibility was accepted officially by the Catholic church itself through its cardinals and bishops in council.

5. Mariolatry or the idolatrous worship of Mary and praying to Mary has been a slow growth in the Catholic religion, an ever-increasing tradition of men contrary to the teaching of Christ and the apostles.

In the first Christian centuries there was no worship of Mary, no doctrine of Mary's Immaculate Conception and sinlessness, no prayers to Mary, no Ave Maria. As the church went further and further into the darkness of the

Middle Ages and further and further away from Christ and the apostles, this doctrine of legendary human tradition increased more and more.

If you will look at St. Mark, chapter 3, verses 31-35 in your Confraternity translation of the New Testament by Catholic scholars, you will see that Jesus plainly taught that His mother was no better than other godly people who did His commands. His mother sent for Him and Jesus did not come. Instead, verses 33 to 35 say: "Who are my mother and my brethren? And looking round on those who were sitting about him, he said, 'Behold my mother and my brethren. For whoever does the will of God, he is my brother and sister and mother.'"

In St. Luke 1:47 Mary calls Christ "God my Saviour." If Jesus was the Saviour for Mary, then she had been a sinner. That is not what the Catholic church now teaches. But it is exactly what the Catholic church taught for centuries. In fact, St. Augustine, the great Catholic father, is on record on this. "St. Augustine says that Mary was more blessed in that she believed in Christ than in that she had given Him birth" (*De virginibus*, III). Check for yourself or have your priest check and see. Catholic theologians know that within the last hundred years there has been a very definite increase in the Catholic tradition about Mary.

Pope Pius IX, on December 8, 1854, gave a decree that Mary was immaculately conceived, that is, with no sin, which could be said of nobody else in the world. Augustine, Chrysostom, Eusebius, Thomas Aquinas, and others differed, and plainly insisted that Mary did have the taint of sin, as everybody else does, except Christ. Then there naturally followed the Catholic teaching that Mary was impeccable, that is, that she never did sin and, like Jesus Christ, she was conceived without sin and lived without sin, according to this Catholic tradition from 1854.

On November 1, 1950, Pope Pius XII pronounced with papal authority that "Mary's body was raised from the grave shortly after she died, that her soul and body were reunited, and that she was taken up and enthroned as Queen of Heaven," as Boettner states it. And now it is a mortal sin not to believe what all Catholics are now commanded to believe, as the pope, called "infallible in the realm of faith and morals," has stated. So Catholic tradition grows!

6. There were many other changes in Catholic tradition, doctrine and practice.

I could name a hundred details in which Catholic theology and Catholic practice and worship have changed. Where were the Masses in the days of the apostles? Good students of church history know that the Mass did not develop until long after the time of the apostles, nor the Catholic doctrine (tradition) of the Mass. All Bible students know there was no practice of the Mass in the days of the apostles and of Christ. There was a simple memorial supper, with no trappings, no priests. We know that the doctrine and practice of the Mass was slowly developed. It was not derived from Christ and the apostles.

We know that the confessional does not come down from New Testament times. It is a later invention of men, a perversion of the teaching of Christ and the apostles. Catholics now try to quote Scripture for the confessional and that the church can forgive sins, but they should honestly admit that in the first centuries after Christ the confessional as now used was unknown. *And there is no reference to the practice in the New Testament.*

The Catholic church in recent centuries has changed in many other matters besides the doctrine of papal infallibility. Once the church sold indulgences. Remember, that was an official and universal practice supported by the tradition of the church. Now the church does not sell indulgences officially. Some corrupt priests in Latin American countries have a very similar practice, not perhaps endorsed by the church.

Once the Catholic church burned people at the stake for reading their Bibles, even Catholic translations. Now, under the pressure of public opinion and the example of the Protestants, the church often encourages the reading of the Bible. I suggest that you check up on this matter and you will see that until modern times, no pope encouraged the reading of the Bible by the laity.

How Wicked to Go by the Changing, Legendary, Mythical, Human Tradition Instead of the Word of God

Yes, the Catholic priest, Father Hogan, in the Catholic magazine, *Our Sunday Visitor,* was right when he wrote his article entitled, "Tradition Called a Key to Catholocism." And that means it is a false religion, not a Bible religion and not the Christian religion.

Surely you can see that Catholic tradition is a frail and changeable thing. If you do not see that, then you have not quite honestly read the preceding statements and checked up for yourself on their truth. One who is willing to accept Catholic tradition accepts the authority of a changing mass of superstitions, and men's opinions wholly different from the Christianity taught by Christ and the apostles.

Wherever these superstitions rule and reign, there is spiritual and intellectual darkness. For example, in Latin American countries Catholics have had their best chance to show what Catholic tradition could do, with the fullest help of the state and without competition from Protestants. The result has been heathenism, the vilest immorality and intellectual apathy. On the other hand, wherever people accept the Bible as authoritative and where the Bible itself, God's holy Word, comes to be loved and read and taught and preached and followed, there comes great enlightenment and morality, education and righteousness.

I am not now primarily making a distinction between Catholics and Protestants. I am making a distinction between Catholic tradition and the Word of God. All that is the best in our American civilization and English civilization came from the emphasis upon the Bible. The great wave of immorality in America today, the anti-religion sentiment lamented by both Catholics and Protestants, results from turning away from the Bible.

But one does not need to go by one's own judgment in this matter of human tradition. Jesus Himself has warned us of the sin of following tradition. If you will read St. Mark, chapter 7, verses 5-13, you will see that it is a sin to follow tradition in matters of religion. In verse 8 He said, "For, letting go the commandment of God, you hold fast the tradition of men." In verse 13 Jesus said, "You make void the commandment of God by your tradition, which you have handed down; and many suchlike things you do." I am quoting from your own Catholic version, the New Confraternity translation of the New Testament.

In the last book of the Bible, (Revelation, we call it), the Apocalypse, chapter 22, verses 18 and 19, Jesus Christ gave the following command:

"I testify to everyone who hears the words of the prophecy of this book. If anyone shall add to them, God will add unto him the plagues that are written in this book. If anyone shall take away from the words of the book of this prophecy, God will take away his portion from the tree of life, and from the holy city, and from the things that are written in this book."

It is a terrible sin to add any word of men as authority alongside the Bible. It is a terrible sin to take from any part of the Bible or to change its teachings, as the Catholic church, by its shifting, varying tradition, has done. And all who take the traditions of men instead of the Word of God will have to give an account to an angry God.

Dear friend, I write with love and tenderness, and I write as a man of God giving you an honest and loving warning. Oh, in Jesus' name, turn away from human traditions and myths and opinions, to the infallible Word of God.

6. Answer to a Catholic Priest

Dear Rev. D———:

I am glad you read the article on "Catholic Tradition, or the Bible." I am sorry that, in the face of many, many plain Scriptures from the Word of God, you still prefer tradition to the Bible.

I should like to answer briefly some of the questions raised by your letter, and I do it, I trust, in the spirit of Christ. Our viewpoint is not the same, of course, and you do not see things just as I do; yet it is only fair to give you an honest, intelligent and kindly answer.

Persecution by Catholics

1. You say, "Hence, you never see the Catholic Church or hear her, for that matter, attack the sincerity of any man, be he Jew, Protestant or pagan."

Forgive me, brother, but as a well read man, a college teacher, an editor for many years, I well know all the bloody persecution of Rome, the Spanish Inquisition and worse. And I know this persecution in many countries has not ceased. It goes on even now in Spain, in Brazil, and other Latin American countries. You are either misinformed, or you pass off bloody atrocities and murders very lightly. I assure you on this matter that I have the information from abundant, reliable and unquestioned sources, that in many countries the church of Rome still carries on her murders and persecutions of sincere, Bible-believing, holy-living Christians. Before you speak on such matters, you should have both information and sincerity. I trust you have the sincerity and not the information. If you have the information, then how could you be sincere in professing such kindly attitude toward true worshipers of Christ?

Christ's True Church Not a Huge, Worldly Denominational Machine

2. You speak plaintively of the fact that there are various divisions of Protestantism. However, several things need to be said to clarify that point. The most important is that you have wholly misunderstood the prayer of Jesus that His disciples might be one. You think He was talking about one great earthly organization, but you get your idea from your Catholic background and not from the Bible. If you were really anxious to know the will of God and would go with an unbiased mind to the New Testament, there you would find no hint of the great ecclesiastical and worldly machinery which is Romanism.

Then there were independent local congregations of churches. Each one was called a church. Of about one hundred and twelve times the word *ecclesia* is used in the Greek New Testament, fully ninety-eight or ninety-nine times it means a local congregation. The other times it refers to that mystical body of Christ, not a human organization at all, not a visible organization at all, into which every one who is truly converted, truly born again, is entered by the work of the Holy Spirit.

Not one time is the word "church" in the Bible used to represent any human organization larger than one local congregation.

When a group of local congregations are mentioned, they are called "churches" (plural, not singular), as in Galatians 1:2, "the churches of Galatia," Galatians

1:22, "the churches of Judaea," and in Revelation 1:11, "the seven churches which are in Asia."

So you see that while men seek to have an organic union, a big supercolossal, worldly empire with human wealth and human prestige, Jesus Christ simply prayed that Christians should be of one mind, of brotherly love and of unity of doctrine.

The truth is that great, human organizations always tend away from the Bible and toward worldliness and sin, just as Romanism took up the holidays and worship forms of heathenism at the beginning of the Catholic church under Constantine (see any good encyclopedia), and just as the Federal Council of Churches in America among Protestants has done. What Jesus prayed for is that people would follow the Bible, take it at face value and agree together in brotherly love.

In this matter I practice what I preach. You speak of the divisions of Protestantism. The simple truth is that in spirit the great bulk of Protestants are in happy fellowship. My work, for example, is interdenominational and everywhere I go my doctrinal preaching on the great fundamentals of the Christian faith is accepted alike by all principal denominations. Baptists, Methodists, Presbyterians, United Brethren, Christian and Missionary Alliance, Assemblies of God and many other groups unite heartily under my preaching year in and year out. Different organizations do not imply strife and lack of unity of spirit.

Worship of Mary Antichristian

3. You say, "How anyone can claim to have read *The Sunday Visitor* for years and Cardinal Gibbon's *Faith of Our Fathers,* and still come up with the notion that Catholics worship Mary is a complete mystery to me."

But you quibble when you say it. You know as well as I do that the adoration of Mary, the prayers to

Mary, the exaltation of Mary amount to worship. You may remember that President Abraham Lincoln once asked, "If you count a dog's tail a leg, then how many legs does a dog have?" A friend answered, "Five." But Lincoln said, "No, even if you count a dog's tail a leg, it is still not a leg, and the dog only has four legs."

In 1854, Pope Pius IX proclaimed the immaculate conception of the virgin Mary, that is, that she was conceived without the taint of original sin. Then there naturally followed the tradition that Mary lived without personal sin. In 1950 Pope Pius XII proclaimed the assumption of the virgin Mary, that is, that she was bodily carried to Heaven shortly after her death. And everywhere Catholic authorities teach that Mary is a mediatrix, intervening between a Christian and Jesus. The honor is given to her which ought to be given to Jesus.

In actual practice I well know, and you do, too, that multitudes of Catholics give far more attention to Mary than to Jesus Christ. They bow before shrines of Mary, but you say it is not worship. They adore Mary as the "Mother of God and Queen of Heaven," but you say it is not worship. They make their prayers to Mary, yet you say it is not worship. They ascribe to her the sinless perfection which the Bible gives only to Christ, and yet you say it is not worship. Common people know better and certainly intelligent, unbiased scholars know better.

You implied that I lied in saying I had read *The Sunday Visitor* and Cardinal Gibbon's *Faith of Our Fathers* and other Catholic authorities. I pass that by. That is a device of a debater who has a case too hard to prove and so must attack the character of his opponent. And to say that if I would read these things I would not understand them, is childish.

No Popes in Bible Times or Till Long After

4. You sent me a list of the popes according to Cath-

olic tradition, in the little booklet, *The Truth About Catholics.* I have had a copy in my possession for years, studied it very carefully. However, a very embarrassing fact has occurred. Within the last ninety days Catholic authorities have changed this list you sent me and a Vatican authority has published a new list, leaving out one or two of these, and I believe adding another. You will get it through official sources eventually. It merely illustrates the vagaries and unreliability of changing human tradition.

Actually, it is quite clear from history that there was no Catholic pope for the first three centuries. Peter is called "chief of the apostles," but not prince of the apostles, in the Bible. We are plainly told in Galatians 2:11-14 that Paul rebuked Peter to his face for being wrong. Paul did not accept the authority of Peter. In the first church council, which is recorded in Acts, chapter 15, we find that it was James who seems to have presided and who certainly gave the final sentence that circumcision and the ceremonial law were not to be required of Gentile converts. Peter was on a level with the other disciples.

No reputable secular historian can give any evidence that Peter was ever at Rome. The Bible itself has all the evidence against it.

To Follow Roman Tradition Is to Renounce the Bible

5. You admit that "certainly the celibacy of the priesthood is an outgrowth of tradition...as all tradition must be based on sacred Scripture, so must this be and, as a matter of fact, is."

No, that is not based on Scripture but in fact exactly contradicts the Scripture, for the Scripture plainly commands, "A bishop then must be blameless, the husband of one wife...having his children in subjection with all gravity" (I Tim. 3:2,4). Read your note in the new Catholic version, the Confraternity Translation of the New Testament. There your note says that this refers to priests and bishops. It is true that Paul urges those who can do so to "remain even as I," but clearly explains that this is not given to some, that it must be a matter of personal choice and that it is better to marry than to burn. The Bible exactly contradicts the tradition of the Roman church on this matter, as on many other matters.

6. You say, "You wonder where there is the 'Ave Maria' in the Scripture," and you quote from Luke 1:28. Of course all Bible readers know the words of the angel to Mary, but it was not a prayer. It was a simple address announcing she had been chosen to be the mother of Christ. It is farfetched indeed to have prayers addressed to Mary with any such title, and certainly nothing like that occurred in New Testament times.

You started your letter with a tribute to my sincerity. Then you accused me of lying about reading *The Sunday Visitor,* Cardinal Gibbon's *Faith of Our Fathers,* then said, "You can't fool all the people all the time." Then you say, "Misquote me here sometime, if you please to." It appears to me you must be hard run for argument.

You are enthusiastic about your church, but have you ever really been converted to Christ? You are enthusiastic in dogma, but do you know that your sins are forgiven, that your soul is saved, and that you have everlasting life? That, dear friend, is far more important than this quibbling over human traditions and human organizations.

Under separate cover I am sending you my pamphlet, *Sermon From a Catholic Bible,* which is so kindly in tone and has been so widely received that I think you would be interested in it.

In Jesus' dear name, yours,

John R. Rice

7. Why Catholic "Church" Not the Church of the Bible

The Catholic Church Could Not Be "The True Church," as Catholics Claim

This is true for several reasons.

1. Because a Worldwide, Man-Made Organization Is Not Mentioned in the Bible

First, Catholics misunderstand the meaning of the word "church." In the Bible, the word "church" sometimes means a local congregation, like "the church of God at Corinth" (I Cor. 1:2), or "the churches of Galatia," or "the church of the Laodiceans" (Rev. 3:14). A local congregation is a church, in the Bible sense. It is a called-out assembly.

The Bible also uses the word "church" to refer to the whole body of Christ, including all the saved whose names are written in Heaven. Christ is the Head of this church. Everyone who is converted, born again, thus becomes a part of that heavenly body that will be called out and assembled in Heaven when Jesus comes. All the saved of all ages will be in that church.

But the Catholic church is not a local organization. And it is not a spiritual body including all the believers of the ages. Instead of that, it is simply a human organization on earth, headed by the pope and cardinals, and under them the archbishops, bishops and priests and monks and people. It is as much a human organization as any earthly government, as any business corporation. It owns property, it carries on its business on a worldly basis.

No Catholic who is intelligent even pretends that all Catholics are converted, born-again Christians. No Catholic priest in the world will tell you that all Catholics go to Heaven. Every Catholic priest in the world is taught to say Masses for the dead, trying to pray them out of purgatory, and hoping that it can be done, but not sure of it. So the true church, as pictured in the Bible, could not be the Catholic church, this human, carnal, worldly organization, a denomination. When Jesus said, "On this rock I will build my church," He could not have meant the Catholic denomination, for that is not the Bible kind of church.

2. The Catholic Church Is Fatally Wrong on God's Plan of Salvation

Next, the Catholic church could not be the true church because it is unscriptural on the most vital doctrines of all. It does not even teach the true plan of salvation. That plan of salvation as given by Jesus, was this, "For God so loved the world, that he gave his only begotten Son, that whosoever believeth in him should not perish, but have everlasting life." In John 3:18, John 3:36, John 5:24, John 6:40, John 6:47, Jesus plainly said that all who would personally believe in Him or trust in Him would have everlasting life. Salvation was made wholly on the basis of a personal dependence, a personal trust in Christ as a personal Saviour.

Certainly that is not the doctrine taught by Catholics. They try to save people through the church and not by direct personal faith in Christ. They try to save people by Mass, by confession, by doing penance, by saying over and over certain prayers, etc. Catholics are utterly different from Jesus Christ on the plan of salvation, so they could not be the right church.

Incidentally, Paul and Barnabas preached exactly the same plan of salvation. In Acts 13:38,39, at Antioch they preached, "Be it known unto you therefore, men and brethren, that through this man is preached unto you the forgiveness of sins: And by him all that believe are justified from all things, from which ye could not be justified by the law of Moses." To the jailer in Acts 16:31 Paul and Barnabas preached, "Believe on the Lord Jesus Christ and thou shalt be saved." All New Testament preachers and apostles preached the same plan of salvation, which is utterly foreign to the doctrines of the Catholic church. The Catholic church, therefore, could not be the true church.

3. Based Largely on Tradition, the Catholic Church Could Not Be the Bible Church

The Catholic church could not be "the true church" because it is based so largely on tradition instead of the Bible. The decrees of popes, who are declared to be infallible in questions of faith and morals, and the decrees of church councils are received as the principal basis for the doctrines and practices of the Roman church. Catholic scholars would all agree that baptism in Bible times was by immersion (see the *Catholic Encyclopedia*). Tradition changed that. Catholic scholars agree that the celibacy of the ministers is not taught in the Bible. The Catholics forbid priests and nuns to marry. And for centuries they commanded the people to abstain from meats on Fridays and in Lent. This clearly shows that the Catholic church fulfills the "doctrines of devils" plainly prophesied in

I Timothy 4:1-3. In the Bible times pastors and preachers were supposed to marry. Catholics changed that. Tradition made that rule. The Bible says nothing about Rome being the center of the Christian religion. That is a matter of tradition. The Bible does not teach that Mary was conceived immaculately, without original sin, that she lived a sinless life, that she was taken bodily to Heaven after her death. That is all a matter of tradition.

The doctrine of purgatory is not mentioned in the Bible. It is the product of Catholic tradition. That a priest could forgive sins, or that the Mass could be a sacrifice—these are not taught in the Bible; they are a man-made tradition.

So the authority of popes and councils and the traditions of men are made a basis for faith, and thus they bring the curse of the Lord Jesus in Revelation 22:18 on the Roman church. Jesus said, "For I testify unto every man that heareth the words of the prophecy of this book, If any man shall add unto these things, God shall add unto him the plagues that are written in this book." God there announces the close of the canon of inspiration. To put any other authority equal with the Bible, or as an added revelation to the Bible, brings a curse of the plagues of the book of Revelation.

One of the certain marks of a false cult is if it has some other authority besides the Bible. So Christian Science puts the writings of Mary Baker Eddy along with the Bible and really above the Bible. So Jehovah's Witnesses put the writings of Pastor Russell and Judge Rutherford. So Seventh-Day Adventists regard the writings of their prophetess, Mrs. White. So the Anglo-Israel people place the Great Pyramid as the divine revelation. The fact that the Roman church forms its doctrine and methods from human tradition means it could not be "the true church" representing Jesus Christ.

That was the complaint that Jesus had against the Pharisees and scribes in New Testament times. In Mark 7:6-9 He said:

"*Well hath Esaias prophesied of you hypocrites, as it is written, This people honoureth me with their lips, but their heart is far from me. Howbeit in vain do they worship me, teaching for doctrines the commandments of men. For laying aside the commandment of God, ye hold the tradition of men, as the washing of pots and cups: and many other such like things ye do. . . . Full well ye reject the commandment of God, that ye may keep your own tradition.*"

Again, in Mark 7:13 He said: "Making the word of God of none effect through your tradition, which ye have delivered: and many such like things do ye."

Any religion accepting human tradition as authoritative is a false cult.

In Bible times, the Lord Jesus gave the communion or the Last Supper and taught people to take this supper, both the bread and wine, in remembrance of Him. Catholics changed it and claim the bread and wine actually to be the body and blood of Jesus, instead of representing it, and then they take the wine away from the people and the priests take all the wine. And instead of having it in memory of Jesus, to remind people that they are saved only by faith in His shed blood and broken body, Catholics put saving power in the ordinance itself, which is wrong. Hence the Catholic church could not be the true church. It is unscriptural in so many vital doctrines.

4. Rome Could Not Be the True Church Because the Bible Pictures Her as a "Great Whore" to Be Destroyed

In fact, in Revelation, chapter 17, we have a picture

of the Roman Catholic church as "the great whore that sitteth upon many waters, With whom the kings of the earth have committed fornication." Rome is also called "MYSTERY, BABYLON THE GREAT, THE MOTHER OF HARLOTS AND ABOMINATIONS OF THE EARTH." Read that chapter and you will see in it the Spanish Inquisition, and the murder of martyrs by the Catholic church. Notice the scarlet colors in verse 3. Then in verse 18 we are told, "And the woman which thou sawest is the great city, which reigneth over the kings of the earth." That surely is the city of Rome. Verse 9 says, "The seven heads are seven mountains, on which the woman sitteth." Those are the seven hills of Rome, of course.

You see that the Catholic church, called "the great whore," "THE MOTHER OF HARLOTS AND ABOMINATIONS OF THE EARTH," the false church at the city of Rome, ruling over the kings of the earth, is an abomination to God and could not be the true church.

It is true that the picture given in Revelation, chapters 17 and 18, of the great state church that will cooperate with the Antichrist and will be destroyed as a false religion, is a picture of Rome as it will be then. One cannot misunderstand the "seven mountains, on which the woman sitteth" (Rev. 17:9), but it is fair to say that we expect other false religions, religious liberals, "wolves in sheep's clothing," to join with Rome in a great, one-world, superchurch after Christ returns to take away born-again saints. Unconverted Protestants, those who have taken the name of Christian but not believing or following the Bible, not trusting Christ as Saviour, will be left behind; and we believe they will join with the monstrous organization of Rome in this "great whore"—the harlot church.

And it is fair to say that those among Catholic friends who have trusted in Christ and know Him as Saviour will not be in that great city and organization when it is destroyed under the curse of God. Those who came to trust in Christ and love Him and depend on Him for salvation are saved whether they are in the Roman church or in the Protestant church or in no church. And all such will be caught up to meet the Lord Jesus when He comes. There are saved Catholics and there are lost Protestants. But the organization pictured in Revelation 17, that religious harlot, is surely the culmination of the church of Rome. That means, of course, that it could not be the true church of Christ.

I have gone into this matter pretty carefully, and I hope you will read the Scriptures and check up on these things for yourself.

It is true that the Catholic Bible has some books that the Protestant Bible does not have. The reason for this is that the Catholics simply picked out some writings and decided that they wanted to have them in the Bible. They were never recognized by Jews in Old Testament times as part of the Word of God, even the part which was written then.

The books of the Maccabees, for example, were of great interest, and the Jews kept them but did not regard them as inspired. They never were counted part of the Word of God. They do not seem to be, nor prove themselves to be, like other books of the Bible. They do not add any divine revelation. They do not make plain any other doctrine. So why should we add to the Bible these other books?

These other books called "the Apocrypha" are in print and available all over the country if people want to buy them. They do not buy them—neither Catholics nor Protestants— in important amounts. Really, the books are not especially interesting and not especially helpful, and clearly they are not inspired as the Bible itself is. Just as the Catholic church felt free to change God's plans and go against the Bible in many other matters, commanding priests not to marry, forbidding common people to take the Lord's Supper "in both kinds," that is, with bread and wine both, and perverting the Bible plan of salvation, so Catholics presumptuously added these other books to the Bible. Before the famous Council of Trent they were never regarded as part of the Bible by very many people.

I do not say that no Catholics are real Christians. Any who have personally repented of their sins and have trusted Jesus Christ to forgive their sins and save their souls are saved. In spite of the trappings and forms of Romanism, some, no doubt, have in their hearts found the Saviour. But Romanism is a terrible curse. Any true children of God who are in this unscriptural organization which pretends to forgive sins and pretends to have the sole authority of Christ on earth should come out and follow the Bible, the Word of God itself, instead of following the teachings and traditions of the unscriptural Roman Catholic church.

8. Priest Says Kept by Grace Encourages Sin

A Catholic Priest, Who Thinks People Must Rely on the Church and Good Works, Berates the Editor for Preaching Salvation by Grace

The priest of St. Mary's Church, Toledo, Ohio, wrote under date of November 26, 1952, berating the editor. Here are some statements from his letter:

> Your doctrine is very encouraging to sinners. They can live in adultery, promiscuity, they may be guilty of all the crimes enumerated by St. Paul and yet have no fear of eternal punishment. You encourage iniquity, malice, avarice, murder, detraction, pride, disobedience, infidelity.
>
> You are adept, Dr. Rice, at distortion and corruption of Holy Scripture. You are a master of perversion and deception. St. Paul says, I Corinthians 4:4: "I am not conscious to myself of anything. Yet am I not hereby justified; but he that judgeth me is the Lord." You can twist this text, of course, to deceive those who wish to believe your corrupt doctrine of faith without virtue, religion without creed, Heaven without merit, Christianity without baptism.
>
> You refuse to hear the Original Christian Religion. You despise the Apostles and their successors. Therefore, you despise Christ and the God who sent Him. Luke 10, 16. You should have read up the Apostolic Fathers

on these texts, which you mutilate, truncate, pervert and corrupt. How guilty you are of all the crimes and sins and wickedness which follow from your dogmas, which discourage virtue and foster and encourage vice, only God knows. After reading the "Report to Protestants" by Marcus Back on the fanatic, the lunatic fringe, Holy Roller, Pentecostal Jumper, Jehovah's Witnesses, the Mormons, there is no way of conjecturing the responsibility of psychopaths, Catamonts, crackpots, etc.

Dr. Rice, you are a promoter of vice and wickedness, perversion and corruption, irreligion and barbarism.

The Editor Answers

December 5, 1952

Mr. ————
St. Mary's Church
Toledo, Ohio

Dear Mr. ————:

One should always be glad to hear from an honest man. And it is only proper Christian charity to suppose that you are honest in your letter of November 26. It is true that you said many foolish things, you made irresponsible charges without evidence, which is against all Christian principles. But I will try to assume that your words were hasty, that you did not consider how these Christian principles should apply in this case, and so I welcome your letter, and answer it as sincerely as I know how.

On sober second thought, I hope you will consider the slanderous and wicked charges that you made so carelessly, without evidence. You say:

> Your doctrine is very encouraging to sinners. . . . You encourage iniquity, malice, avarice, murder, detraction, pride, disobedience, infidelity. . . . Dr. Rice, you are a promoter of vice and wickedness, perversion and corruption, irreligion and barbarism.

Thousands Turned From Sin to Holy Living Prove the Priest False in His Charges

But you do not give any evidence of your slanderous charges. All over America in great revival campaigns my preaching has resulted, by God's mercy, in the turning of drunkards to Christ and sobriety, the turning of harlots to purity and godliness, the turning of profane, adulterous worldlings into consecrated, dedicated Christian people.

When I was pastor in Dallas, Texas, so many drunkards were converted and turned to sobriety and holy living that it was well-known all over the city. And my people were so strict in their conception of godliness that some people mocked us, but all the churches were specially anxious to have some of our members as teachers and workers because of their knowledge of the Bible and godly lives.

I could tell you of thousands turned from drink, of many, many thousands who left the profane oaths of the lodges, of multiplied thousands who turned from filthy habits, from the lewdness of the commercialized movie theater, under the influence of my preaching from the pulpit and through literature. You will never be able to find even one person who says that he decided to live a wicked and sinful life because of my teaching. Therefore, I charge that your slanders are absolutely false, inexcusably, wickedly, devilishly false.

More than that, I protest that had you really been concerned to know the truth, you could have found out. The traces of my ministry have been spread widely enough that one could well check for himself what kind of people they are who listen to my preaching and believe the doctrine I present from God's Word. Therefore, again in charity, granting that you are probably an honest man who made hasty charges, I ask you to either give evidence of your slanders or retract them. I believe that any honest man will try to do the one or the other, and I trust you are an honest man.

But did you think that such doctrine as that people are saved by faith, through the grace of God, not by human merit, not by human works, not by the rites of the church—did you think that that kind of doctrine has in the past turned people to sinfulness and license and sin and crime? Was that the result in Presbyterian Scotland where they believed, fully as strictly as I do that one is saved by faith without works, through the merits of the atoning blood of Christ, and thus kept by the power of God to salvation—do you believe that Scotland, under this doctrine in the old days, was a cesspool of iniquity? On the contrary, you will know that it was once, under the flaming preaching of John Knox and his successors, more nearly a model of virtue to the nations than almost any other.

This doctrine was held very strictly by the Dutch Reformed people in the Netherlands, we will say under that great Christian premier Kuyper.

In the greatest revivals of religion in America under D. L. Moody, R. A. Torrey, J. Wilbur Chapman, and Billy Sunday, we see the kind of results wrought by this doctrine which you hate and slander. All these men believed as I do and as I have stated the case in the booklet, *Can a Saved Person Ever Be Lost?* which you despise. They believed that men must be saved by the grace of God, without human merit, by simple faith in the atoning work of Jesus Christ. They believed that people are kept through faith by the power of God unto salvation. They believed that God must do the saving and keeping, and that those who are saved do not merit the saving and do not merit the keeping.

Catholic Doctrine of Trusting the Church and Good Works Has Kept Mexico, Latin America and Spain in Sin and Ignorance

And do you really believe that the doctrine of your church, the Catholic church, that people are saved by the church, saved by good deeds—do you really believe that that makes men more godly than the Bible doctrine of salvation by grace? Everywhere I go I am shocked to see announcements of bingo parties and other gambling events sponsored by Catholic churches! I am shocked to see Catholics who have no conscience on drink and that in communities where Christian people who believe as I do live clean and godly lives without gambling, without alcoholic drink, and without worldliness.

Of course, no Protestant group is perfect, and no Catholic group would be expected to be perfect. But by comparison, one is bound to see that the doctrine to which you adhere and which you preach does not make the same kind of Christian as the doctrine I preach. People who follow my preaching quit their profanity, quit their gambling, quit their beer drinking. I do not believe you will claim that even the average Catholic quits all those things. And where Catholics have had complete control for long, long years and where Protestants have been in a very small minority, as in Latin America, for example, the general standards of morality are much lower than where the Gospel which I preach of salvation by faith in the shed blood of Jesus Christ, salvation by grace, not on the basis of human merit, is preached.

So on the basis of the history of the kind of doctrine I preach, compared with the doctrine you preach, your charges were false and foolish and wicked. You ought to retract them with a sincere apology.

False Cults and Arminian Groups All Agree With the Priest on Keeping Saved by Good Works

I note what you say about certain cults and sects, "Holy Roller, Pentecostal Jumper, Jehovah's Witnesses, the Mormons," etc. But unfortunately for your position, none of these people believe in the eternal security of a born-again child of God. On the contrary, they believe, with you, that one must keep his salvation by his good works. So your argument there is a little silly.

And now very seriously, I call your attention to a great truth of the Christian religion. There are only two doctrines, really, about salvation. One doctrine is that men can be saved by something they do themselves, whether it is good works or prayers or submission to rites of the church, etc. To that group you belong, along with the Mormons and Jehovah's Witnesses and others which you mention.

On the other hand, there is the doctrine which the Apostle Paul, by divine inspiration, so clearly expressed: "For by grace are ye saved through faith; and that not of yourselves: it is the gift of God: Not of works, lest any man should boast" (Eph. 2:8,9). We believe that Christ does all the saving, and saves people who do not deserve it, when they commit themselves to Him and trust Him to do what He promised. You join with those who believe in salvation by human merit. I stay with those who believe in salvation by the blood of Christ.

God Keeps No One Saved but Born-Again Believers, With New Hearts

For another matter, you utterly ignore the principal part of my teaching and that of evangelical Christianity. You speak as if I taught, or other evangelical Christians taught, that God keeps wicked, unconverted, unregenerate sinners and saves them. I never taught any such thing. There was not a hint of that in anything I ever wrote. That was either the naive and ignorant misunderstanding of my teaching or a deliberate perversion on your part.

I teach what all Bible preachers who believe the great fundamentals of the Christian faith teach, that one needs to be born again, needs a new heart, needs to be regenerated by the miraculous power of God, and given a new nature, a new heart, a new outlook. I have never taught anywhere that God would keep anybody who did not repent of his sins.

Once a preacher who held to your position told me, "If I believed as you do, I would trust Christ and then I would go out and have my fill of sin." I told him, as I tell you, if you have not already had your fill of sin, then you have never been converted, never been born again, and you are not a child of God.

God keeps those who are born into His family, those who have a new heart, those who have in their hearts turned from sin and so want to do right. God plainly says about such people that He will write His laws in their hearts "and on their minds will I write them." God keeps Christian people, not heathen worldlings. God keeps His own born-again children, not children of the Devil.

I wonder if you really do not know anything about the Bible doctrine of the new birth? I wonder if you have ever yourself been genuinely born again, that is, in sincere repentance and faith received Christ into your heart to make you a new creature? If you have not been born again, have not been given a heart to love righteousness and to hate sin, a heart to want to please God, then I beg you, in Jesus' name, get that matter settled first and then you will understand what I preach and what I am talking about now.

I call your attention earnestly to the words of Paul in Romans 10:1-3:

"*Brethren, my heart's desire and prayer to God for*

Israel is, that they might be saved. For I bear them record that they have a zeal of God, but not according to knowledge. For they being ignorant of God's righteousness, and going about to establish their own righteousness, have not submitted themselves unto the righteousness of God."

So many people are going about to establish their own righteousness and have never submitted themselves to the righteousness of God. Christ Himself is the end of the law for righteousness to everyone who believes, the Scripture tells us.

Now let me thank you for writing me freely. And thank you for reading my answer. I hope that you will, like a kindly, good man must do when he finds he has been in error, retract your slanderous charges which are untrue, and which no good man ought ever to have made without having the proof at hand.

In the Saviour's name, yours,

John R. Rice

I mailed to the priest the booklet, *Eight Gospel Absurdities if a Born-Again Soul Ever Loses Salvation.* If you wish to study what the Bible clearly says on this question of the security of a believer, we hope you will write for it. You may also want to order *Can a Saved Person Ever Be Lost?* You may order from the Sword of the Lord Publishers, Box 1099, Murfreesboro, Tennessee 37130.

We recommend *Roman Catholicism* by Loraine Boettner, Presbyterian Reformed Publishing Company and *The Other Side of Rome* by John D. Wilder, Zondervan Publishing Company, (out of print). Also, *Roman Catholicism in the Light of Scripture* by F. C. H. Dreyer and E. Weller, paperback, Moody Press. (out of print).

2

Baptismal Regeneration

1. An Unscriptural Heresy
2. Answer to a Church of Christ Preacher
3. Mistakes of a Church of Christ Preacher

1. An Unscriptural Heresy

Dear Friend:

Thank you for your letter, and I will try to answer in detail and honestly, the best I can, the questions you raise. And I hope that the dear Lord will open your eyes and mind to the truth and give you the humility of heart to receive the Scriptures as openly as a Christian should.

I can understand your rearing and your training. It is of a very distinctive kind, and easily recognized in Church of Christ and Christian Church preachers and debaters. But I dare say that the Scriptures themselves can be understood. They never contradict themselves, they should be taken at face value by honest hearts. That I trust I will do and I hope you will do also.

I. "SAVED BY FAITH" IS A BIBLE DOCTRINE REFERRING TO WHAT A SINNER MUST DO TO BE SAVED

1. The Bible Does Teach That One Who Trusts in Christ Is Saved

Unless one starts with the plain, honest intention to take the Bible at face value and not argue against any clear statements in the Bible, of course he cannot expect to come out right. And many Scriptures plainly say that one who trusts in Christ then has everlasting life, or is not condemned, or shall not come into condemnation, or is saved.

"*That whosoever believeth in him should not perish, but have eternal life. For God so loved the world, that he gave his only begotten Son, that whosoever believeth in him should not perish, but have everlasting life.*"—John 3:15,16.

"*He that believeth on him is not condemned: but he that believeth not is condemned already, because he hath not believed in the name of the only begotten Son of God.*"—John 3:18.

"*He that believeth on the Son hath everlasting life: and he that believeth not the Son shall not see life; but the wrath of God abideth on him.*"—John 3:36.

"*Verily, verily, I say unto you, He that heareth my word, and believeth on him that sent me, hath everlasting life, and shall not come into condemnation; but is passed from death unto life.*"—John 5:24.

"*And this is the will of him that sent me, that every one which seeth the Son, and believeth on him, may have everlasting life: and I will raise him up at the last day.*"—John 6:40.

"*Verily, verily, I say unto you, He that believeth on me hath everlasting life.*"—John 6:47.

"*To him give all the prophets witness, that through his name whosoever believeth in him shall receive remission of sins.*"—Acts 10:43.

"*And they said, Believe on the Lord Jesus Christ, and thou shalt be saved, and thy house.*"—Acts 16:31.

"*For by grace are ye saved through faith; and that not of yourselves: it is the gift of God: Not of works, lest any man should boast.*"—Eph. 2:8,9.

Here is a Bible doctrine repeated again and again. To quibble about it or to try to make it mean something else besides what it plainly says would not be an honest dealing with the Scriptures. Now, if we approach the Bible with an honest, open heart to the truth, we will find that all the other teaching about salvation fits in with these clear, plain statements that one who trusts in Jesus Christ is saved, is born again and has everlasting life.

To an honest, unsophisticated reader, these verses assure the one who trusts in Christ that he is then and there "saved," has "everlasting life," "is not condemned," "shall not perish." Now did God mean to say what these verses say, or is God like a shyster lawyer, making it appear on the surface as it really is not? Does God have some hidden parts of His contract not stated here? Does God hide some conditions in His contract in smaller print elsewhere? In other words, is God not quite open and aboveboard in dealing with poor, ignorant sinners on the matter of salvation? To ask such a question ought to answer it for honest people. Away with all this foolish way of complicating the plan of salvation, trying to find other Scriptures that contradict or limit what God so clearly promises here. So, one who believes in Christ, trusting Him to forgive, has salvation then and there, according to many, many plain statements in the Bible.

2. "Saved by the Blood," "Saved by Grace," Does Not Contradict at All the Clear Teaching That a Sinner May Simply Trust in Jesus Christ for Salvation and Be Instantly Born Again

You quote Alexander Campbell as is the custom among his followers. He said, "That faith by itself neither justifies, sanctifies, nor purifies, is admitted by those who oppose immersion for the forgiveness of sins.

They all include the idea of the blood of Christ." But Alexander Campbell was not logical, and I fear not even sincere in making that kind of a statement.

When I talk about what a sinner must do to be saved or when the Bible talks about what a sinner must do to be saved, it often says something like: "Believe on the Lord Jesus Christ, and thou shalt be saved," or "He that believeth on the Son hath everlasting life." It is obvious that "saved by grace" refers to God's grace, not the sinner's grace. When we say "saved by the blood," it is obvious that we are talking about the blood of Christ, not the blood of the sinner. No sensible person ever claims that the sinner must provide the grace or that the sinner must provide the blood for salvation. One who brings that up either is simply following a pattern he has been taught, or he wishes to confuse the issue.

Of course we believe in the atoning blood of Christ. But that is God's part. Of course we believe in the loving grace of God unmerited that provides salvation for all who will believe. But that is God's part. When we speak of what a sinner must do to be saved, it is still the plain teaching of the Bible that "He that believeth on the Son hath everlasting life" (John 3:36), and "Believe on the Lord Jesus Christ, and thou shalt be saved" (Acts 16:31).

3. Being "Born Again" Is What the Sinner Gets in Salvation, Not What He Does

You say, "In John 3:3,5, Christ said that if we wanted to enter the kingdom of God we must be born again." Again, surely every honest Bible student knows that God speaks here of what He does. When one is born of God, it is God who does it. When one is "born of the Spirit," it is God, the Holy Spirit, of course, who makes that change. That does not change nor does not limit the clear statement of many Scriptures that one who puts his trust in Christ is born again. God works the miracle of the new birth according to II Peter 1:4: He is made a partaker "of the divine nature." That miraculous change in nature, making one a child of God, is what God does, not what the sinner does.

4. Repentance as a Condition of Salvation Does Not Deny the Teaching of "Saved by Faith," Is Not a Separate Act of the Sinner but Part of the Same Decision

It is true that God does teach repentance as the plan of salvation. (Notice I did not say as *one* plan of salvation, but it is *the* plan of salvation, the same plan as faith.) People are commanded to repent and repentance is indicated as the way to be saved in Matthew 3:2, in John the Baptist's preaching; Matthew 4:17 where Jesus said the same thing, "Repent: for the kingdom of heaven is at hand." It is clearly taught in Luke 13:3,5, "Except ye repent, ye shall all likewise perish." In Luke 16:30, the rich man in Hell is quoted as knowing that his brothers must repent or go to Hell. In Acts 2:38, Peter commanded those at Pentecost to repent. Acts 17:30 says that God hath "commanded all men every where to repent." In II Peter 3:9 we are told that God is "not willing that any should perish, but that all should come to repentance." So repentance is the way of salvation, and repentance is what a sinner must do to be saved.

But as many, many Scriptures tell us, believing or trusting in Christ is the way to be saved. Then, God must mean that repentance and faith are together, that they are inseparable, that one who repents has believed, and one who believes has repented, understanding always that we mean what the Bible means by heart repentance and heart trust in Christ. Since "He that believeth on the Son hath everlasting life," then, evidently he has repented.

You see, repentance and faith simply describe two views of the heart attitude a sinner has when he turns to Christ for salvation. He turns *from his sins,* and so we call that repentance. He turns from his rebellion against God and his sins against God, so we call that repentance. But no one can genuinely turn from his sins, in the Bible sense of repentance, without turning to Christ. So, one who turns to Christ, depending on Him for salvation, has believed in Him, but he also turned from his sins. The one great heart-turning, the one great decision that took place, involved repentance if you mean one's attitude of mind toward his sin and God; it was faith if you mean his reliance on Christ for forgiveness. So, faith and repentance are called "inseparable graces" and so they ought to be called. And what God hath joined together let not man put asunder. To try to make these plain statements of Scripture contradict each other is not only twisting the Word of God but it is wickedly wrong and no one ought to do it.

When the prodigal son *left* the hogpen and his sinful course, he was repenting, he was turning, but he was headed *toward* his father and reliance on his father's mercy and forgiveness, and so that was faith, too. And that is a proper illustration of saving faith and honest repentance. They are a part of the same thing or they are simply different ways of looking at the same matter. The prodigal son was going *from* the hogpen. He was going *toward* his father. But it was one decision in his heart and one trip that he made. So it is with repentance and faith. When one turns *from* his sin in his heart to *trust in Jesus* for forgiveness and salvation, he has both repented and believed (or trusted).

So the Bible says and means it when it says, "He that believeth on the Son hath everlasting life." So the Bible says and means it, that God "is not willing that any should perish, but that all should come to repentance." It is never right to use one Scripture against another or to interpret one Scripture to contradict another.

II. WHAT DOES "BAPTIZED INTO CHRIST" MEAN IF NOT THAT BAPTISM SAVES?

You say, "Won't you agree with me that to be 'in Christ' is to be 'saved' and to be 'not in Christ' is to be 'unsaved'? If you agree with me on that and believe that baptism does not save, what does Romans 6:3 and Galatians 3:27 mean?"

Romans 6:3 says, "Know ye not, that so many of us as were baptized into Jesus Christ were baptized into his death?" Galatians 3:27 says, "For as many of you as have been baptized into Christ have put on Christ."

Now, what do these verses mean?

I think that Romans 6:3-5 tell very clearly the intent of baptism, its form and meaning. It is a burial, a planting (not a birth): "Therefore we are buried with him by baptism into death: that like as Christ was raised up from the dead by the glory of the Father, even so we also should walk in newness of life. For if we have been planted together in the likeness of his death, we shall be also in the likeness of his resurrection." So baptism pictures the burial and resurrection of Christ and of our participation in His death and burial. We count the old man dead and buried. We are raised up to live a new life because we have a new heart. Baptism thus is a picture, a ceremony with a definite meaning.

Notice also that twice in verse 5 it is called "the likeness of his death," and "the likeness of his resurrection."

Now does "baptized into Jesus Christ" mean that baptism puts us in Christ? Again your trouble is in the little preposition *into*. It is the translation of the Greek word *eis*, used some eighteen hundred times in the New Testament. It is an indefinite preposition of reference.

It is variously translated *in, at, unto, toward,* etc. The simplest meaning is "referring to," or "with reference to." So, Romans 6:3, ". . . that so many of us as were baptized into Jesus Christ were baptized into his death," simply means "that so many of us as were baptized referring to Jesus Christ were baptized referring to his death."

And in Galatians 3:27 the meaning simply is, "For as many of you as have been baptized referring to Christ [or pointing to Christ] have put on Christ," that is, have publicly and symbolically acknowledged Christ.

You see, we have an exact copy of that use of the word in I Corinthians 10:1,2, "Moreover, brethren, I would not that ye should be ignorant, how that all our fathers were under the cloud, and all passed through the sea; And were all baptized unto Moses in the cloud and in the sea." And that "baptized unto Moses" again uses the little preposition *eis,* so the Bible says, "baptized *eis* Jesus Christ," "baptized *eis* his death," and "baptized *eis* Moses." So if baptism puts the penitent sinner into Christ, then all the nation Israel were put into Moses. If the one is literally put into, then the other is literally put into. In this inspired Scripture, God uses exactly the same language.

But if you take the way the word is used throughout the New Testament and as an indefinite preposition of reference, then the Israelites were baptized in that crossing of the Red Sea, surrounded by the cloud and the sea, were baptized with reference to Moses and his leadership just as a Christian is baptized with reference to Jesus Christ, pointing to His death and resurrection. We ought to use the terms like the Bible uses them and we ought to mean what the Bible means. And to take it that these Scriptures contradict the other plain statement, that one who believes in Christ is already saved and has no condemnation, is misusing the Word of God. No Scripture ever contradicts another Scripture, if it be rightly interpreted.

III. ACTS 2:38 DOES NOT GIVE BAPTISM AS ESSENTIAL TO SALVATION

Acts 2:38, which you mention in your former letter, with verse 39 following, says:

"*Then Peter said unto them, Repent, and be baptized every one of you in the name of Jesus Christ for the remission of sins, and ye shall receive the gift of the Holy Ghost. For the promise is unto you, and to your children, and to all that are afar off, even as many as the Lord our God shall call.*"

Some things I call to your attention is clear to the humble Bible-believer who has an open mind.

1. It Is Clear Here That These People Wanted Two Things

They said, "Men, and brethren, what shall we do?" They did not say simply, "What must I do to be saved?" the question that is so plainly asked and answered in Acts 16:30, 31. Peter has been talking to them about this great outpouring of the Holy Spirit upon the Christians, how it was foretold by the Prophet Joel and how Christ whom they crucified has now shed forth this power of the Holy Spirit. So they want to be saved and they want what Peter and the other Christians have. They wanted to be saved and they wanted to be filled with the Holy Spirit.

And the answer takes that in mind. First, they were to repent and thus be saved. Then they were to be baptized, referring to the remission of their sins which they would have gotten when they repented and then they would receive the gift of the Holy Ghost. So repentance is here the way to salvation; and baptism, if it be with the heart that understands its meaning and really means to be raised up to live a new life and do the soul-winning work of Christ, is here mentioned as the way to "the gift of the Holy Ghost."

2. And Here Is the Problem, Too, Which You Mentioned, That in Acts 2:38 Jesus Said, "Repent, and Be Baptized Every One of You in the Name of Jesus Christ FOR the Remission of Sins . . ."

And you have thought and some others have thought that "for the remission of sins" meant "in order to get remission of sins," or "so that they would get remission of sins." However, that is not the meaning. The preposition here translated *for* is again the little Greek preposition *eis,* an indefinite preposition of reference used so many times in the Bible. Just as I Corinthians 10:2 speaks of the children of Israel baptized with reference to Moses, so here Peter spoke of being baptized with reference to their remission of sins which they would receive when they repented.

The Holy Spirit very carefully and exactly selected the words that He used. There is a Greek preposition *hina* which means "in order to," or "so that." That is not the preposition used here. That Greek preposition *hina* is used in the New Testament according to *Young's Analytical Concordance* and translated one time *albeit,* one time *because,* one time *so as,* twice as *so that,* and 542 times as simply *that* and *to the intent* one time and *to the intent that* one time. So, if Peter had meant "baptized that ye may receive the remission of sins," he would have used that Greek preposition. The Greek terms are very exact.

The Greek preposition *eis* is never used to mean "in order to," or "to the end that."

It is true that the word *eis* is here translated "for," but even with that translation it would not necessarily mean that one should be baptized in order to get remission of sins. A man is paid *for* his work already done, not in order to get him to work. A woman is praised *for* her beauty, not in order to make her beautiful. A child is punished *for* his disobedience, not in order to get him to be disobedient. To make a meaning here which would contradict the use of the preposition all through the Bible and which would contradict the clear Bible teaching on the plan of salvation as given in many other verses, is the wrong use of the Scriptures, is the wrong interpretation.

IV. "BORN OF WATER" IN JOHN 3:5 DOES NOT MEAN BAPTISM

In John 3:5 Jesus said to Nicodemus: "Verily, verily, I say unto thee, Except a man be born of water and of the Spirit, he cannot enter into the kingdom of God." This has been widely quoted as teaching that baptism is essential to salvation. However, people did not get the doctrine from the Scripture; they got the interpretation of the Scripture from a doctrine they already established. Our Catholic friends taught salvation by rites of the church, and those who follow after this human reasoning twist Scriptures to make them fit the doctrine they have already accepted. Note the following evidence:

1. Baptism Is a Picture

Romans 6:5 says, "For if we have been planted together in the *likeness* of his death, we shall be also in the *likeness* of his resurrection."

First Peter 3:20 and 21 says that just as Noah and his eight souls were "saved by water... *The like figure* whereunto even baptism doth also now save us." In only some figurative sense was Noah saved by water, and baptism is here called a "figure."

But baptism is a figure of death and resurrection and not a figure of birth! People are baptized picturing the burial and resurrection of the Saviour and picturing the fact that we count the old sinner dead and now raised up to live a new life in Christ. If Jesus had wanted to use baptism as a picture of a birth He could have done so, but He did not, nor did any other Bible writer.

2. Water Is Used as a Symbol of the Word of God, and the Part It Plays in Salvation

Ephesians 5:25 and 26 says, "... Christ also loved the church, and gave himself for it; That he might sanctify and cleanse it with the washing of water by the word." Here the Bible is saying that Christ loved those He would save, gave Himself on the cross for them, and this body, including all the Christians, He sanctifies or sets apart and cleanses with *the washing of water by the Word.* So the Word of God has a part in salvation.

That is what Psalm 19:7 says: "The law of the Lord is perfect, converting the soul."

So I Peter 1:23 says, "Being born again, not of corruptible seed, but of incorruptible, by the word of God, which liveth and abideth for ever."

And Romans 1:16 says, "I am not ashamed of the gospel of Christ: for it is the power of God unto salvation to every one that believeth." So evidently God uses two elements in His part in regeneration. He uses the Word of God, the Gospel. He uses the Holy Spirit to convict and regenerate. No one is ever saved without this twofold work which God does when one believes in Christ. One hears the Gospel and as he turns repentantly to trust in Christ, he is born of the Spirit. So in John 5:24, "Verily, verily, I say unto you, He that heareth my word, and believeth on him that sent me, hath everlasting life, and shall not come into condemnation; but is passed from death unto life." The Bible so clearly and repeatedly teaches that the Word of God is used in saving a sinner, that one must hear the Gospel in order to be saved. We can be sure the same meaning is intended here.

Titus 3:5 bears witness to John 3:5, "Not by works of righteousness which we have done, but according to his mercy he saved us, by the washing of regeneration, and renewing of the Holy Ghost." There is the twofold element again of cleansing through the Gospel, the washing of regeneration, and the renewing of the Holy Ghost.

No, Jesus did not say that salvation meant born again in baptism. And no Christian ought add that meaning to the Scripture and thus set out to contradict many, many other Scriptures all through the Bible on the plan of salvation.

It is evidently intentional that the second "of" in John 3:5 is not in the original, so in the King James Version it is put in italics. What the Scripture says in the Greek is "born of water and Spirit." That is one act of God, that is, of the Gospel preached and the Holy Spirit who regenerates the believing person.

V. EXPLAIN "HE THAT BELIEVETH AND IS BAPTIZED SHALL BE SAVED" FROM MARK 16:16

Let us read the whole verse: "He that believeth and is baptized shall be saved; but he that believeth not shall be damned." What is it that damns a person? It is that he does not believe or trust in Christ.

Again we must remember that all Scriptures fit together and no Scripture contradicts another Scripture. And again the Bible can be taken at literal face value, so it does not take an extra amount of logic or argument to settle any principal matter. Certainly God did not leave the plan of salvation without a clear teaching. And, as we mentioned before, many, many times the Lord has plainly said, "He that believeth on the Son hath everlasting life," and "Believe on the Lord Jesus Christ, and thou shalt be saved."

So the one who believes in Christ here is saved when he believes. When he is baptized, he is still saved. So both Scriptures are true and they both fit together.

But note carefully that believing and being baptized are not the same thing. Some people would explain away the Bible teaching that one who trusts Christ is immediately saved by saying that baptism is a part of faith, and that one never has completed faith until he is baptized. No, for the Bible here clearly says, "He that believeth *and* is baptized." So believing does not include baptism.

However, in Bible times it was customary and proper and right for people to be baptized immediately when they were saved as in the case of the Philippian jailer who was baptized at night, in Acts 16, and as in the case of the Ethiopian eunuch who was baptized immediately when he was saved on the highway. One cannot see faith in the heart, but one can see the public profession of faith in baptism. So it is proper and customary to put the two together, for they go together. People who believe in Christ and get saved should be baptized immediately as a public profession of their faith. And one who believes in Christ has everlasting life; he is not condemned, he is passed from death to life, as many Scriptures say. But if you want to say, "He that believeth and is baptized shall be saved," it is still true. He was saved when he believed. He is still saved when he is baptized. And why make it mean something else that would twist the Scriptures and pervert other plain statements? And it is clear in the same verse that "he that believeth not shall be damned."

VI. FIRST PETER 3:21 SAYS, "BAPTISM DOTH ALSO NOW SAVE US"

But that is not all this Scripture says, and its meaning

is clear if you note the context. There, speaking of the Word of God which Christ preached through the Spirit in Noah before the flood, I Peter 3:20,21 says, "Which sometime were disobedient, when once the longsuffering of God waited in the days of Noah, while the ark was a preparing, wherein few, that is, eight souls were saved by water. The like figure whereunto even baptism doth also now save us (not the putting away of the filth of the flesh, but the answer of a good conscience toward God,) by the resurrection of Jesus Christ."

It is obviously only a figure of speech to say that Noah and eight souls were saved by water. And then we should not be surprised in verse 21 that the Scripture says "*the like figure* whereunto even baptism doth also now save us." Here baptism is simply mentioned as a figure, a symbol, of salvation. It pictures the sinner, the old man dead and now buried, and the new person risen to live in Christ. Why avoid the clear statement that just as you might say figuratively, Noah and his family were saved by water, so, "the like figure whereunto even baptism doth also now save us"? Baptism is a figure, a symbol, a picture of salvation. It does not save. It declares salvation.

And the next verse is evidently intended to safeguard us on that matter so we would not misunderstand the Scripture, for the same verse goes on to say, "(not the putting away of the filth of the flesh, but the answer of a good conscience toward God,) by the resurrection of Jesus Christ." So baptism does not put away the filth of this old carnal nature. It is simply "the answer of a good conscience toward God." And the saving that we get is "by the resurrection of Jesus Christ," after His death on the cross, which is pictured in baptism. And this is "the answer of a good conscience," a conscience already purged, before one is baptized.

Our Catholic friends say that when Jesus gave the Lord's Supper and He said, "This is my body," He meant that the bread actually becomes the body of Christ and the cup actually contains the blood of Christ literally, and that these are a new sacrifice. That is unscriptural. But to make baptism a saving ordinance by misinterpreting I Peter 3:21 is the same sin, the same perversion of Scripture.

VII. DID PAUL WASH AWAY HIS SINS IN BAPTISM?

You claim that baptism saves or that one cannot be saved without baptism and sometimes quote Acts 22:16 as evidence that baptism saves. There we are told that Paul, speaking in the Hebrew tongue to the great crowd who would mob him in Jerusalem, said that Ananias came to him, told him of God's wonderful call to him and Paul quotes Ananias as saying, "And now why tarriest thou? arise, and be baptized, and wash away thy sins, calling on the name of the Lord." Here the Bible tells us what Paul said that Ananias said. Of course, we do not suppose that Paul was claiming to give exact quotation, and he probably did not. The Bible does not guarantee that all the things that men say, which are reported in the Bible, were true. Sometimes the Devil is quoted and good and bad men are quoted. We know that the record of Paul's quotation is right and that Paul actually reported that Ananias said, "Arise, and be baptized, and wash away thy sins. . . ." But what the Spirit of God tells us actually happened, in inspired language, in Acts 9:17 was: "And Ananias went his way, and entered into the house; and putting his hands on him said, Brother Saul, the Lord, even Jesus, that appeared unto thee in the way as thou camest, hath sent me, that thou mightest receive thy sight, and be filled with the Holy Ghost."

Ananias, in words not given here in the inspired account in Acts 9, may have said the very words that Paul quoted him as saying. But they are not put in the divine account of the conversion in Acts 9, and evidently for a good reason. But Paul, speaking to the Jews who were familiar with the ceremonies of the law and knew all the object lessons and types of the passover, the sacrifices, the priesthood, and the Temple service, would be accustomed to figures of speech in religious matters. And so Paul here used the figurative language which he quotes from Ananias, "Arise, and be baptized, and wash away thy sins, calling on the name of the Lord."

Are we to suppose then that here God has another plan of salvation different from John 3:15,16; John 3:18, John 3:36, John 5:24, John 6:40, John 6:47, Acts 10:43, Acts 16:31, Ephesians 2:8,9? Is Paul here contradicting his own plain statement to the jailer in Acts 16:31, "Believe on the Lord Jesus Christ, and thou shalt be saved"? Does Paul here mean to contradict his own plain statement to the people of Antioch in Acts 13:39, "And by him all that believe are justified from all things," that is, that they were already saved before baptism? Of course, no contradiction is intended and Paul did not mean to teach here what he otherwise plainly did not teach, that baptism is essential to salvation. It is not.

In fact, Paul goes into great detail in I Corinthians 1, verses 13-19, that he came not to baptize, that he baptized very few himself, that he did not want to emphasize baptism "lest the cross of Christ should be made of none effect." For if you put baptism in the plan of salvation you minimize the cross and salvation by grace, and Paul many times made clear he did not want to do that.

VIII. THE BIBLE TELLS OF MANY PEOPLE SAVED WITHOUT BAPTISM

Yes, many people in the Old Testament and many people in the New Testament times were saved by faith in Christ without baptism as the Scriptures plainly tell us.

1. Old Testament Saints Were Saved by Faith Without Baptism

We have the record of many people in the Bible who were saved without baptism. I remind you that God has never had but one plan of salvation. In the Old Testament it was "not possible that the blood of bulls and of goats should take away sins" (Heb. 10:4). In fact, the eleventh chapter of Hebrews tells us of case after case of people in the Old Testament times who were saved by faith. Acts 10:43 makes clear that the only plan of salvation taught in the Old Testament was by faith in Christ, just as it was preached in the New Testament. There Peter said, "To him give all the prophets witness, that through his name whosoever believeth in him shall receive remission of sins."

Remember, there never was any plan of salvation but by faith. Every Old Testament sacrifice and ceremony was a picture and shadow and type of the Lord Jesus Christ, "the Lamb of God which taketh away the sin of the world"!

Now, all of these Old Testament saints were saved without baptism, for there is not a word in the Old Testament about baptism and no record of a single person's ever being baptized before John the Baptist began it. Baptism, then, is not a part of God's plan of salvation.

Abraham, an Old Testament saint, is used as an example of the plan of salvation both for Jews and Gentiles, in Romans, chapter 4.

This matter is so important that I take space here to quote Romans 4:1-12:

"*What shall we say then that Abraham our father, as*

pertaining to the flesh, hath found? For if Abraham were justified by works, he hath whereof to glory; but not before God. For what saith the scripture? Abraham believed God, and it was counted unto him for righteousness. Now to him that worketh is the reward not reckoned of grace, but of debt. But to him that worketh not, but believeth on him that justifieth the ungodly, his faith is counted for righteousness. Even as David also describeth the blessedness of the man, unto whom God imputeth righteousness without works, Saying, Blessed are they whose iniquities are forgiven, and whose sins are covered. Blessed is the man to whom the Lord will not impute sin. Cometh this blessedness then upon the circumcision only, or upon the uncircumcision also? for we say that faith was reckoned to Abraham for righteousness. How was it then reckoned? when he was in circumcision, or in uncircumcision? Not in circumcision, but in uncircumcision. And he received the sign of circumcision, a seal of the righteousness of the faith which he had yet being uncircumcised: that he might be the father of all them that believe, though they be not circumcised; that righteousness might be imputed unto them also: And the father of circumcision to them who are not of the circumcision only, but who also walk in the steps of that faith of our father Abraham, which he had being yet uncircumcised."

It could not be plainer. Abraham was saved by faith without baptism. That was before he was circumcised. And circumcision was simply a sign, "a seal of the righteousness of the faith which he had yet being uncircumcised: that he might be the father of all them that believe, though they be not circumcised; that righteousness might be imputed unto them also." It could not be clearer, we think, that the same plan of salvation that applies now has applied all through the centuries. It was so in David's time so that David could describe "the blessedness of the man, unto whom God imputeth righteousness without works."

And remember, it is clearly stated in Acts 10:43 that all the prophets in the Old Testament and the New Testament taught the same plan of salvation that "whosoever believeth in him shall receive remission of sins."

2. People Saved Without Baptism in the New Testament

Since the same plan of salvation was preached in the Old Testament and in the New Testament, and people were saved in the Old Testament without baptism, you would expect them to be saved in the New Testament without baptism, and they were. In Luke 7:37-50 is the story of a woman, a notorious sinner. Verses 47 to 50 in that seventh chapter of Luke tell us plainly that her sins were forgiven her and that her faith had saved her. Read carefully these Scriptures:

"*Wherefore I say unto thee, Her sins, which are many, ARE FORGIVEN; for she loved much: but to whom little is forgiven, the same loveth little. And he said unto her, THY SINS ARE FORGIVEN. . . . And he said to the woman, THY FAITH HATH SAVED THEE: go in peace.*"

Jesus plainly stated that the woman was immediately forgiven and was thus now saved by faith. She knelt at the feet of Jesus, trusted Him, and went away a saved woman. She was saved without baptism.

In Luke 18:35-43 we are told about the healing and conversion of a blind man. Verse 42 tells plainly, in the words of Jesus Himself, just how he was saved: "And Jesus said unto him, Receive thy sight: THY FAITH HATH SAVED THEE." Notice that salvation was received right there before he was baptized.

That is the same plan of salvation given throughout the book of John; in John 1:12, John 3:14-18, John 3:36, John 5:24, John 6:37, and many other places. It is the same plan taught by Peter after Pentecost (Acts 10:43). It was the same plan taught by Paul, the apostle to the Gentiles (Acts 13:38,39; Acts 16:30,31; Ephesians 2:8,9; Romans 3:28 and Romans 4:5-8). People were saved in the Old Testament by faith without baptism, were saved during the life of Jesus by faith without baptism, and were saved after Pentecost by faith without baptism.

That publican, about whom the Saviour has told us in Luke 18:13,14, was saved without baptism. Standing there in the Temple, he prayed, saying: "God be merciful to me a sinner." Jesus tells us about him then, that, "I tell you, this man went down to his house justified"! He was saved, then, without baptism.

3. The Thief on the Cross Was Saved Without Baptism

The most remarkable case of this kind is the thief converted on the cross as told in Luke 23:39-43. When that poor man turned to the Lord Jesus and asked to be in His kingdom, the Lord Jesus replied, "Verily I say unto thee, To day shalt thou be with me in paradise"! He died that day on the cross as we are told in the Scriptures and so could not have been baptized. But that day, according to the express statement of the Saviour, he went with Jesus to Paradise. And some happy day, all who trust in Christ will see him there.

No, baptism is not essential to salvation.

And again, we must remember that "to him [Jesus] give all the prophets witness, that through his name whosoever believeth in him shall receive remission of sins" (Acts 10:43). Yes, God has saved many, many people without baptism and so He saves people today without baptism.

And, dear friend, I have taken a great deal of time and work to go into this matter. I have trusted that you have an honest heart and want to know the truth. I know ahead of time, as you know, that you would prefer that it turn out that your church is right and that the teaching of Alexander Campbell and his followers is right. So you will have to overcome that bias and prejudice if you find what God really teaches on baptism.

And you can remember this: All the emphasis in the Bible is on trusting Christ, not on baptism. And those who make the most of baptism make less of the blood and make less of salvation by grace through faith.

Whether you can overcome the bias, the training, the preference, your denominational connections and training, I do not know.

IX. SAVING FAITH MEANS A PENITENT RELIANCE ON JESUS CHRIST FOR SALVATION

It is only fair to remind you what is everywhere apparent in the Bible, not all who say, "Lord, Lord," are saved, as Jesus Himself plainly tells us in Matthew 7:21-23. Not all who believe the Bible are saved, for we are plainly told that "the devils also believe, and tremble." So, acceptance of a fact mentally is not saving faith, and, of course, no one pretends that it is. If you think of faith as simply believing certain doctrinal facts, then, of course, you have missed the whole point. A fervent trust in Christ, a reliance on Christ to do what He promised to do, is faith. Mental acceptance of certain doctrines is not faith in the sense of John 3:16, and all the other blessed promises of salvation by faith.

And let me say that the more one relies on water, the less he relies on the blood. The more one relies on baptism, the less he relies on Christ. Any act of righteousness that one depends on becomes a snare.

That was the trouble with Israel. Paul said, "For I bear them record that they have a zeal of God, but not according to knowledge. For they being ignorant of God's righteousness, and going about to establish their own righteousness, have not submitted themselves unto the righteousness of God. For Christ is the end of the law for righteousness to every one that believeth" (Rom. 10:2-4). Oh, do not go about to earn Heaven by doing, doing, doing! Rely on Christ and depend on Him and give Him the credit instead of claiming it for your righteous deeds.

I have written in great detail. May God bless it to your heart.

In Jesus' name, yours,

John R. Rice

(For further reading, see the author's book of 64 pages on *Bible Baptism*.)

2. Answer to a Church of Christ Preacher

Dear Brother H———:

I am grateful that you allow that one may be converted even if not a member of the "Church of Christ" just as I freely say that I believe everyone who has personally trusted Christ for salvation is saved even though he may be wrong in doctrine. And now perhaps if I discuss briefly the points as numbered in your letters, it would help to clear up our position.

1. Wrong on Salvation, So a False Cult

Yes, I think the Church of Christ is a false cult in that, as I see it, it is wrong on the essential plan of salvation. In fact, many, many Church of Christ preachers have taught that the Church of Christ group is the true church of Christ and no one else is, and the preachers have told me that I am unconverted and I am going to Hell because I have not been baptized by a Church of Christ preacher.

I have very sadly faced the fact that often Church of Christ people despise the best Christians in their community, they mock at the best gospel preachers, they hate the Gospel, and otherwise act as one would expect false cults to act. So I believe that Church of Christ preachers, like the one whom I answered in THE SWORD OF THE LORD, lead thousands of people astray and keep them from turning to Christ for salvation.

But it is only fair to remind you, I said that I believe "many of the Church of Christ people are unconverted because they know nothing about the new birth." Notice I said "many." A man is not saved by believing a doctrine or understanding a doctrine. A man is saved because he personally trusted Christ for salvation. I believe many are saved who do not fully understand the Bible doctrine of salvation.

You see, the Lord is very merciful. He wants people saved and He has plainly said again and again in the Bible that all who come to Him for salvation receive it. For example, John 6:37, "...him that cometh to me I will in no wise cast out." Again, Romans 10:13 says, "For whosoever shall call upon the name of the Lord shall be saved." Again, James 4:8 says, "Draw nigh to God, and he will draw nigh to you."

So one who might be misled in doctrine might in his heart call on Christ for salvation and penitently, earnestly turn his heart away from sin and with some faith, however faltering, might turn to Christ for mercy. He might do that thinking that he yet needed to be baptized to be sure of salvation. Or he might do that not knowing what anybody taught about baptism, whether you or I or someone else. The simple truth is that the Lord Jesus loves sinners, wants to save them and does save everyone who penitently turns to Him for mercy.

So you do not understand what I am talking about if you think that I accuse you of being lost because you agree with the Church of Christ plan of salvation. God's salvation is so great and wonderful that none of us fully appreciate all we have. And one may have salvation between the time he believed in Christ and the time he gets baptized, although he may, I think, foolishly and unscripturally think that God will not really save him until he gets baptized.

You see, the plan of salvation, as I understand the Bible to teach it, would involve many more people than the plan of salvation as you preach it. I say that when a man honestly turns from sin and trusts in Christ, he is saved. You say that, no, after he trusts in Christ, he is not saved until he is baptized. So even a Church of Christ man like yourself who has honestly trusted in Christ, the best he knew, got saved before he knew he was saved, if you did trust Christ, as I hope you did.

However, in the nature of the case, since Church of Christ people put so much emphasis on baptism, they often obscure the plain Bible doctrine that people are saved by faith in Christ. And so many people go through the outward form thinking that is the plan of salvation and do not seek and do not have the change of heart because they are trusting on the church and the form and the ceremony and obedience and holding out faithful and many other works of men, instead of depending on Christ. One who trusts in Christ is saved whether he is clear in doctrine or not. Unfortunately, any group, such as the Church of Christ group, which adds to God's plan of salvation, often confuses the issue and keeps people from trusting in Christ, in my judgment.

2. In Mark 16:15 Jesus Says One Who Believes Is Still Saved When He Is Baptized

You say that in Mark 16:15 "Jesus gave two conditions, not one." You say there are two conditions, but God does not say so. And the next sentence does not indicate it. And to put in two conditions here where

God puts only one in John 3:16, John 3:18, John 3:36, and in many, many other Scriptures, means that you have in many cases God promising salvation with other conditions besides those stated, which would be hardly fair and hardly honest and certainly not literally honest.

I was a college teacher; I have been an editor now for thirty-five years, and I know, and informed people everywhere know, that if the Bible is to be trusted, it must be honest and straight. Whatever God says in one verse, if there were not another verse in the Bible, is still true and can be trusted. One can hang his soul's eternal welfare on any plain promise on that matter, properly understood, and to make God giving different plans of salvation and different verses is wholly foreign to the nature of God and to the integrity of the Bible.

You say, "But let us go to the Bible as the final authority on this subject." Yes, by all means, but you are trying to prove the wrong thing. I agree already that Matthew 28:19 commands us to "teach all nations, baptizing them. . . ." I suspect that I have obeyed this command better than you have. I have baptized hundreds of converts. I have a book, *Bible Baptism*, which has led thousands of others to be baptized. I am not questioning it at all that Peter commanded people to be baptized at Pentecost. So do I.

I have never questioned that "He that believeth and is baptized shall be saved. . . ." So all orthodox Christians believe. We also believe John 3:36, "He that believeth on the Son hath everlasting life," that is, is saved. And John 3:18 where Jesus said, "He that believeth on him is not condemned." One who trusts in Christ is saved. When he gets baptized he is still saved. So, of course he that believeth and is baptized is saved. But then we ought to notice that by divine inspiration that same Scripture continues, ". . . . he that believeth not is condemned." The saving or damning factor is whether or not one trusts in Christ, so say many Scriptures. You talk about taking seriously the Great Commission. My life's work is in telling people to take that more seriously and get more people saved, and I think you ought to do that, too. You surely ought not ever bring that question up to me as if I were not taking it as seriously as you do.

You think that some have been led not to be baptized because people taught what God Himself said in John 3:16, John 5:24, and other verses! My friend, you ought to be concerned far more over the thought that many are taught not to trust Christ for salvation by putting baptism in the plan where God did not put it. The plain, simple truth is that one ought to teach what the Bible says about both—about salvation and about baptism—and where that is done, then those who trust Christ for salvation also follow in baptism as an almost universal rule, as I know well from forty-eight years' ministry. Those who teach falsely about baptism do harm, whether it is a Church of Christ preacher putting baptism and human works in the plan of salvation (along with taking the Lord's Supper, taking active part in the services, holding out faithful, and doing right in every thought, word, and deed), or whether like a pedobaptist they teach sprinkling of infants and are wrong not only on the form but the meaning of baptism. Both, I think, do great harm. I think that one ought to teach simply what the Bible teaches and be sure that not a single verse contradicts another verse, if we take them at face value.

3. Acts 2:38 Teaches Baptism Referring to, or Pointing to Repentance

You make much of Acts 2:38, "baptized...for the remission of sins," but alas here you do not go to the Scriptures so much as to many so-called authorities. But you are not accurately quoting these authorities.

Somebody has victimized you and so you are quoting what other people said long ago.

For example, I knew Dr. Trantham when I was a student in Baylor University. Dr. Dana was my professor of Greek in Southwestern Seminary. Later, I knew him when he taught in Northern Baptist Seminary, and he is now dead. But neither Dr. Trantham nor Dr. Dana believed that Acts 2:38 meant that one is baptized in order to be saved.

In fact, no Greek teacher in the world thinks that, because if it meant "in order to," it would have used the Greek word *hina* instead of the little Greek preposition *eis.* So all good Greek scholars know. And if you are not a Greek scholar, then of course you could get either *Young's Analytical Concordance* or *Strong's Concordance,* which gives the original Greek or Hebrew word for every word in the Old Testament and New Testament in Hebrew and Greek, and you can see for yourself.

You see, you have been misled by going to the dictionary and going to some other books whereby you have been misled. You ought, instead, to have gone to the Bible and found out for yourself.

And it is a quibble, I think unworthy of you, to say that in Acts 2:38 it may point to the remission of sins in the future, but could not point to the remission of sins when one repented in the past. But in that you ignore the usage of the word in the Greek and the meaning of it.

For instance, in Luke 11:7, the Scripture says, "My children are with me in bed." And the word *in,* here in English, is the translation of the Greek word *eis.* The man's children were already with him in bed and it did not point to anything in the future.

And I could go through the Bible, but it is not necessary. There is no way to convince a man against his will, and if it is not against your will, then you will take it to heart and check up on it. And besides, to make Acts 2:38 contradict other plain Scriptures is foolishness and dishonors God.

4. What It Means to Believe on Christ and Be Saved by Faith

But actually, the matter is not as difficult as you have made it appear and as your friends have made it appear. It does not have to be settled by logic or by the dictionary. "He that believeth on the Son hath everlasting life." If there is any one thing stated again and again in the Bible, this is clear, that one who trusts Christ is already saved. So with John 1:12; John 3:14, 15, 18, 36; John 5:24; John 6:47; Acts 10:43, Acts 13:38, 39; Acts 16:30, 31, etc.

You can go to Romans, chapter 4, and see:

"*For what saith the scripture? Abraham believed God, and it was counted unto him for righteousness. Now to him that worketh is the reward not reckoned of grace, but of debt. But to him that worketh not, but believeth on him that justifieth the ungodly, his faith is counted for righteousness. Even as David also describeth the blessedness of the man, unto whom God imputeth righteousness without works, Saying, Blessed are they whose iniquities are forgiven, and whose sins are covered. Blessed is the man to whom the Lord will not impute sin.*"—Rom. 4:3-8.

Read it again, especially verse 5, "But to him that worketh not, but believeth on him that justifieth the ungodly, his faith is counted for righteousness." Now any time you make some other Scripture contradict that Scripture, or contradict any other one, then you are wresting Scriptures and misusing Scriptures, which no Christian ought to do. The Bible has no contradiction, and is not hard to understand. If you want to take the credit for saving yourself by good works, then you may twist Scriptures, but if you are willing for the Lord to do all the saving and get all the credit and get the praise, then you should be willing to take what He says. One who trusts in Christ is counted righteous without working, and then one who works for God does it because he is already saved.

Again, it seems to me that you dodge the issue or either you do not know what the word *believe* means in the Bible, the little Greek work *pisteuo.* You say, "Do you mean simply to believe the facts?" If that is your idea of faith, then I fear you have never been saved, because no honest reader of the Bible can come up with any such doctrine. And for you to accuse me of that is a kind of dishonesty or ignorance which makes it unworthy of you and hardly worth answering. But the simple truth is that to face what Bible faith is takes the emphasis off baptism, for Bible faith or belief as used about salvation means dependence, reliance, committal. As Paul said, "I know whom I have believed, and am persuaded that he is able to keep that which I have committed unto him against that day" (II Tim. 1:12). One who relies upon Christ and the price He has paid and the promises He has made for salvation has everlasting life. And in the nature of the case, that is incompatible with relying partly on baptism.

5. Believing on Christ Is the "Work of God," Said Jesus

You quote Matthew 7:21, "Not every one that saith unto me, Lord, Lord, shall enter into the kingdom of heaven; but he that doeth the will of my Father which is in heaven." But unfortunately, you misinterpret it and make a lie out of other Scriptures and make salvation by works instead of by faith and by grace. In fact, Jesus here is teaching the exact opposite of salvation by works. That is the trouble of those who will come and will be rejected. They have depended on works. They say, "Have we not prophesied in thy name? and in thy name have cast out devils? and in thy name done many wonderful works?" (Matt. 7:22). And that, with many, no doubt will include baptism. But that is *not* the way of salvation.

No, the one who is saved is "he that doeth the will of my Father which is in heaven," that is, the will of God *about salvation!*

To make it mean to do the will of God about baptism perverts the Scripture and loses the sense entirely of what Jesus is saying. To the same kind of people Jesus was talking to in Matthew 7:21, He gave an answer in John 6:28 and 29, "Then said they unto him, What shall we do, that we might work and works of God? Jesus answered and said unto them, This is the work of God, that ye believe on him whom he hath sent." So the will of God about salvation is to believe on Him that God has sent and this is "the work of God."

And Jesus was talking to the same kind of people as those to whom Paul referred in Romans 10:3, "For they being ignorant of God's righteousness, and going about to establish their own righteousness, have not submitted themselves unto the righteousness of God."

Alas, I wonder if you, too, have gone about to establish your own righteousness by doing good works and baptism and confession and the Lord's Supper and trying to do right "in every thought, word, and deed" as the Church of Christ Sunday school quarterly puts it, instead of depending on Christ? Unfortunately, you need to take much more seriously the plain Word of God, that salvation is not of works but of grace, not earned but given freely. And as in Romans 4:5, "But to him that worketh not, but believeth on him that justifieth the ungodly, his faith is counted for righteousness." And so you pervert Galatians 3:27 also to make salvation by works and so men get the credit instead of God.

6. Salvation by Faith Is Not a "Baptist Theory"

And again, you use the old, old Campbellite dodge that salvation by faith is "the Baptist theory." People who try to find the truth do not have to use that kind of language, that kind of sneers, and that kind of influences. You have run with bad company and taken up bad habits of language and methods of discussing scriptural truth that are unworthy of you, and they make me tremble as to whether or not you know what we mean by salvation by faith in Christ.

Again, in your discussion you follow the same old Campbellite fallacy that salvation depends on all duty. You say that anything that Paul ought to do, then not to do would mean he would be lost. So again you either ignore or you do not understand the Bible teaching on the plan of salvation by trusting Christ and what I have been saying to you and what others have.

You still insist that works are faith and that faith is works, and you nullify and wave aside all the Scriptures on that matter. But I warn you as a friend in kindness and love that you will have to meet God for that kind of use of the Scriptures.

And again, you show how you dislike the Baptists. I have no disposition to defend them. I do not teach anything as Baptist doctrine. I am more despised by many Baptists than you could be by Church of Christ people, and yet you would say about your Church of Christ friends that they are the true church, that their doctrine is correct, and you have absorbed their sneering, debating attitude about the Word of God, it seems. I do not mean to be offensive. I wish that you would listen to me enough to take it to heart and check up and see if it is not right.

7. Salvation and Fellowship Not the Same

You say if a person is saved, "he is in the body of Christ and is therefore entitled to partake of the Lord's Supper." But the Bible says nothing of the kind. On the contrary, in I Corinthians 11 the people at Corinth are plainly warned to examine themselves and judge before they take the Lord's Supper. And in I Corinthians 5 they are plainly required to withdraw fellowship, "if any man that is called a brother be a fornicator, or covetous, or an idolator, or a railer, or a drunkard, or an extortioner; with such an one no not to eat" (vs. 11). And yet in II Corinthians the person from whom they withdrew fellowship is called a brother and is restored. There is a difference which no Arminian like yourself can understand, it seems, between salvation and fellowship.

And again you talk about people "being worthy to partake of the marriage supper of the Lamb." You forget you are talking about your kind of salvation by works instead of the Bible kind of salvation without works, by faith, of people who are unworthy.

Until you learn what saving faith is and salvation by grace through faith and not of works, you are not in any condition to judge about the Lord's Supper and fellowship and other matters. And I have no disposition to defend the Baptists, although you evidently do not know anything about the two problems of salvation and fellowship as being separate problems.

Now you say that you are saved and I hope you are. Then I have some hope that you will have enough earnestness and hunger for the truth that you will take to heart and go into this thing and wait before God with the Bible to find out and get settled on the plan of salvation. If on the other hand, denominational pride and bias keep you from doing that, then I am not to blame, for as lovingly and as kindly as I know how, I have talked to you about it. And may God open your eyes.

3. Mistakes of a Church of Christ Preacher

Because a false cult disturbs many unlearned people on the plan of salvation, we publish here a letter on questions raised by a good woman concerning the teachings of the Church of Christ.

Dear Mrs. O———:

Yes, I am familiar with the Church of Christ teaching that people are saved by works and not simply by faith in **Christ,** and I am sorry that you have been disturbed by this heresy.

In the little booklet you sent me titled, *Is Salvation by Faith Only?* I note what is said about the thief on the cross.

> 4. The thief on the cross. (Luke 23:43). Many think that the penitent thief is an example of salvation without baptism, and if he could be thus saved that people today can be saved without baptism. Reply: (1) He did not ask to be saved. He merely asked Jesus to "remember" him. (2) He may have been baptized by John (Matt. 3:5). He could have been a backslider. (3) But the main point is that the thief lived and died while the law of Moses was in force, before the death of Christ, and before the terms of pardon for the New Testament dispensation were in force.

> Before one's death, his will can be changed. A will is never in force until after the death of him who made it (Heb. 9:16,17). Hence, before the death of Christ, He could forgive sins on different conditions; but since His death, and since the new will or testament is in force, there is no hope nor promise of salvation without complying with the terms of pardon as set forth for the Gospel age. It was after the death of the thief, and after the death of Christ that these conditions were revealed (Matt. 28:18-20; Mk. 16:15,16; Luke 24:46,47). Jesus made it plain that "repentance and remission of sins should be preached in his name among all nations, beginning at Jerusalem." In Jerusalem the Spirit through the mouth of the apostles said, "Repent and be baptized every one of you in the name of Jesus Christ for the remission of sins, and ye shall receive the gift of the Holy Ghost" (Acts 2:38). The thief did not become a Christian as no one was called a Christian at that time. He evidently was saved, and he may not have been baptized (no one can prove he was not), but since then the terms of pardon for all men for all ages were revealed by Christ, and the New Testament has been sealed by His blood. No one has a right to change these conditions, or to offer salvation to sinners short of them. No one today can be saved like the thief. We must come this side the cross and follow the examples of conversion as found in the book of Acts.

There are many errors in this passage by this teacher and preacher of a false cult. Note these errors.

1. The thief was saved beyond any doubt. Jesus said to him, "This day shalt thou be with me in paradise" (Luke 23:43).

2. It is not sufficient to say, "He may have been baptized by John." It is always wrong to try to teach a doctrine based on guesses. If he had been baptized by John, the dying thief would have gone to Hell just the same without coming to trust in Jesus. And when he did trust in Christ, we have no right to infer, without some Scripture statement saying so, that he was baptized by John. When the Bible speaks, we should

speak. When the Bible is silent, we should be silent on doctrine.

3. The writer shows no real understanding of the Bible plan of salvation when he says, "But the main point is that the thief lived and died while the law of Moses was in force, before the death of Christ, and before the terms of pardon for the New Testament dispensation were in force." It was just as wrong again to say, "No one today can be saved like the thief. We must come this side the cross and follow the examples of conversion as found in the book of Acts."

Here the writer probably through ignorance ignores the well-established teaching of the Bible that people have been saved in all ages exactly the same. In Acts 10:43 this is expressly stated: "To him give all the prophets witness, that through his name whosoever believeth in him shall receive remission of sins." This Scripture says that every prophet in the Old Testament and in the New Testament alike taught the same plan of salvation—that is, salvation by faith in Christ. Now it is foolish and wicked to contradict that plain statement and try to make different plans of salvation for different times.

The Bible clearly says that Abraham was justified by faith and not by works, that "Abraham believed God, and it was counted unto him for righteousness" (Rom. 4:3). The Bible says that David also believed in salvation by faith alone, that is, the righteousness of God was imputed without works to the man that believes (Rom. 4:6-8). Then in Romans 4:23,24 we are told that the example of Abraham is given that we might learn to be saved the same way: "Now it was not written for his sake alone, that it was imputed to him; But for us also, to whom it shall be imputed, if we believe on him that raised up Jesus our Lord from the dead."

It is an utterly false doctrine that one must come this side of the cross to find examples of salvation. And the man who writes this wholly misunderstands this side of the cross because he misunderstands the other side of the cross.

4. Again this false cultist perverts the Scriptures in teaching that one must be justified by works, like baptism. Again a more careful study of the Scriptures with an honest heart would have made quite clear that there is no contradiction between the teaching of Paul and the teaching of James on this question. Please note the following clear teaching. In Romans 3:20: "Therefore by the deeds of the law there shall no flesh be justified IN HIS SIGHT: for by the law is the knowledge of sin." One cannot be justified IN THE SIGHT OF GOD by works.

Again the same teaching is given in Galatians 3:11: "But that no man is justified by the law IN THE SIGHT OF GOD, it is evident: for, The just shall live by faith." We have put in capitals the important point here. Justification in the sight of God is a heart matter, and it is settled by faith. One is not justified by the law, not justified by the deeds of the law, the commandments, or by good works.

But to be justified in the sight of man, to show others our salvation, is another matter, and James discusses that, in James 2:17,18: "Even so faith, if it hath not works, is dead, being alone. Yea, a man may say, Thou hast faith, and I have works: shew me thy faith without thy works, and I will shew thee my faith by my works." Here again it is clear that James speaks of justification in the sight of man. One shows his faith by his works. One who has a new heart can show it to men only by new deeds.

Then the example of Abraham is given. James 2:21 says, "Was not Abraham out father justified by works, when he had offered Isaac his son upon the altar? Seest thou how faith wrought with his works, and by works was faith made perfect?" But notice that this time when Abraham was justified by works, in the sight of men, was many, many years after Abraham had been saved, justified in the sight of God, by faith only. And so verse 23 says, "And the scripture was fulfilled which saith, Abraham believed God, and it was imputed unto him for righteousness: and he was called the Friend of God." So we can see that a man is justified in the sight of God by faith alone.

In the sight of men he is justified by works. Men can tell our faith only by works. God can tell our faith before waiting to see any of our works.

It is true that faith that is without works is dead. But it is equally true that salvation, justification in the sight of God, comes by faith, without works.

5. This Church of Christ man teaches that salvation comes largely by baptism, and that there is no salvation without baptism. He says, "The Lord has not promised salvation before or without obedience to him." But that is a plain contradiction of many promises in the Bible. In John 3:18 Jesus says, "He that believeth on the Son is not condemned." One who has trusted in Christ is not condemned, whether he has obeyed the Lord about baptism or not.

John 3:36 says, "He that believeth on the Son hath everlasting life." One who trusts in Christ is already saved. That is the clear Word of God.

Those who are interested in what the Bible teaches on baptism would be interested, I think, to read the author's book on *Bible Baptism*.

3

Unchristian "Christian Science"

Unchristian "Christian Science"

The Mary Baker Eddy Cult a False Religion; Denies Deity of Christ, Man's Sin and Blood Atonement

Christian people ought to have great charity toward other Christians with whom they differ on minor points. A man may really be a child of God, a Christian, yet be mistaken on matters of Christian faith which are not essential to salvation, such as baptism, the Lord's Supper, when Christ will come, whether a saved person can be lost or not, whether Christians should observe Saturday, Sunday or no day as a Sabbath, etc.

Christians ought to be right on everything, but none of us are infallible. Orthodox Methodists, Presbyterians, Pentecostals and many others differ with me on some important Bible doctrines, yet we agree on the great essentials of the Christian faith, such as the inspiration of the Bible, the deity of Christ, the blood atonement, the fact of sin, and Heaven and Hell. I do not hesitate to call anyone a Christian who has trusted in Jesus Christ as his own personal Saviour and who believes that Jesus, the very Son of God, paid for his sins on the cross.

Unfortunately, Christian Science cannot be classed as any part of the Christian religion. It is not a Christian sect but must be classed with the false religions of the world, such as Mohammedanism, Confucianism, and Buddhism. This is a startling statement and we are sad that it is true, but it is true, as we can very easily show.

A traveling salesman on a Georgia train which stopped at a small town at noonday heard a colored man walking up and down the platform crying, "Hot chicken pie! Hot chicken pie! Hot chicken pie, twenty-five cents!"

The salesman bought the chicken pie, but found it unpalatable. Calling the colored man, he said, "What makes you call this hot chicken pie? In the first place it isn't chicken but beef, and it is not hot but cold. Why do you call it hot chicken pie?"

"Oh, yassah, I knows it, but that's jist the name of it!"

So Christian Science is neither Christian nor scientific. It is really not Christian Science; that is just the name of it.

Christian Science is like Grape-Nuts which are neither grapes nor nuts. It is like guinea pigs which are not guineas and not pigs. So-called Christian Science sails under false colors and is a deceptive, false, unchristian religion.

Some years ago I reviewed some of the false teachings of Christian Science as published in the official magazine, the *Christian Science Sentinel*. The doctrine taught then is the same doctrine taught now, the teachings of Mary Baker Eddy, the official teaching of the Christian Science cult. Here you will see surprising and shocking evidence that this cult which pretends to be Christian but is not, denies the essentials of the Christian faith. It denies the deity of Christ. It denies the fact of sin. It denies the blood atonement. Now read the evidence for yourself.

Some Blasphemies of Christian Science

Before me is the *Christian Science Sentinel* of December 22, 1934. On page 330 is an editorial which states part of the infidelity of Christian Science which is mentioned many times in Christian Science literature—that is, its teaching that Jesus is not God.

Here is the statement.

> Christian Science is doing much to clarify the thoughts

> of men regarding the great Way-shower. Among other things, it is correcting THE FALLACY THAT JESUS IS GOD.

The teaching that Jesus is God, Christian Science says, is a fallacy, that is, is false. Christian Science everywhere teaches that Jesus was kin to God only in the same way that every other man is. Christian Science says much about the life of Jesus, the teaching of Jesus, and so on, but denies the fact of His deity, denies that His blood atones for man's sin, denies that Jesus is very God.

Jesus expressly claims that He is God, that He is one with the Father, that He is equal with God. Notice these Scriptures.

"*In the beginning was the Word, and the Word was with God, and the Word was God. The same was in the beginning with God. All things were made by him; and without him was not any thing made that was made.*"—John 1:1-3.

"*He was in the world, and the world was made by him, and the world knew him not.*"—John 1:10.

"*And the Word was made flesh, and dwelt among us, (and we beheld his glory, the glory as of the only begotten of the Father,) full of grace and truth.*"—John 1:14.

"*I and my Father are one.*"—John 10:30.

"*If ye had known me, ye should have known my Father also: and from henceforth ye know him, and have seen him. Philip saith unto him, Lord, shew us the Father, and it sufficeth us. Jesus saith unto him, Have I been so long time with you, and yet hast thou not known me, Philip? he that hath seen me hath seen the Father; and how sayest thou then, Shew us the Father?*"—John 14:7-9.

"*Who, being in the form of God, thought it not robbery to be equal with God.*"—Phil. 2:6.

The Bible Calls Jesus "the Mighty God," Yet Christian Science Says This Is a Fallacy

Throughout the New Testament the teaching of Jesus Himself and the apostles is that Jesus is God, as eternal as the Father, and one of the Divine Trinity. The prophets of the Old Testament taught the same thing. For instance, Isaiah 9:6 says:

"*For unto us a child is born, unto us a son is given: and the government shall be upon his shoulder: and his name shall be called Wonderful, Counsellor, The mighty God, The everlasting Father, The Prince of Peace.*"

Notice the names ascribed to Jesus:

"*Wonderful*"
"*Counsellor*"
"*The mighty God*"
"*The everlasting Father*"
"*The Prince of Peace*"

Jesus is The mighty God, One with The everlasting Father! So says the Word of God. But Christian Science says, "It is correcting the fallacy that Jesus is God."

The Bible teaches that Jesus Himself is the Creator of Heaven and earth (John 1:3-10; Heb. 1:2; Col. 1:16), yet Christian Science spends its time exalting Mary Baker Eddy and trying "to correct the fallacy that Jesus is God." No religion which denies the deity of Christ can be a Christian religion. It is infidelity, pure and simple.

Christian Science has set itself to correct what it calls "the fallacy that Jesus is God." Christian Science, then, is certainly unchristian, because it denies the very heart of the Christian religion—that Jesus Christ is God. That is infidelity and blasphemy.

Christian Science is a religion, but it is a pagan religion, as different from the religion of the Bible as day is from night.

The quotation above comes from the *Christian Science Sentinel* saying, (let us read it again):

> Christian Science is doing much to clarify the thought of men regarding the great Way-shower. Among other things, it is correcting the fallacy that Jesus is God.

Notice the term applied to Jesus. He is called "the Way-shower." But Jesus says that HE HIMSELF IS THE WAY!

"*I am the way, the truth, and the life: no man cometh unto the Father, but by me.*"—John 14:6.

To the Christian Scientist, Jesus is simply a teacher, a prophet, an example, a Way-shower, a man like the rest of us. These terms are used again and again in all Christian Science literature. Christian Science teaches—its literature teaches, its lecturers teach, its official textbook by the founder, Mary Baker Eddy, teaches—that Jesus was just a man, ever so good and wise, but just a man.

Another Blasphemy — That Man Is Perfect, That There Is No Real Sin

In this copy of the *Christian Science Sentinel* for December 22, 1934, on page 327, is an article with the heading, "Man Is, Not Shall Be, Perfect and Immortal." The first sentence in that article shows that this is a primary teaching of Christian Science:

> In an illuminating statement in "Science and Health With Key to the Scriptures," Mrs. Eddy states (p. 428):

> "The great spiritual fact must be brought out that man is, not shall be, perfect and immortal."

A little later in the article is the following statement:

> Man is without beginning or end–changeless–THE SAME YESTERDAY AND TODAY AND FOREVER. All that constitutes man "is, not shall be," perfect and complete. All his qualities, faculties, and attributes are spiritual, and immortal, now.

This false, antichristian religion, calling itself Christian Science, denies all that the Bible says about sin. Instead of admitting that man is a sinner, as the Bible explicitly says, Christian Science denies it and places all men on an equal with Jesus Christ. In fact, you will notice in the above quotation that Christian Science uses about all men the term which the Bible uses about Jesus only. The Bible says, "Jesus Christ the same yesterday, and to day, and for ever" (Heb. 13:8). Christian Science says that it is true about all men! It takes the deity away from Christ and denies the sinfulness of man, saying, "Man is without beginning or end—changeless—the same yesterday, today and forever."

Compare this blasphemy with what the Bible says about man's sin and imperfection.

"*All we like sheep have gone astray; we have turned every one to his own way; and the Lord hath laid on him the iniquity of us all.*"—Isa. 53:6.

"*The heart is deceitful above all things, and desperately wicked: who can know it?*"—Jer. 17:9.

"*Behold, I was shapen in iniquity; and in sin did my mother conceive me.*"—Ps. 51:5.

"*What then? are we better than they? No, in no wise: for we have before proved both Jews and Gentiles, that they are all under sin; As it is written, There is none righteous, no, not one: There is none that understandeth, there is none that seeketh after God. They are all gone out of the way, they are together become unprofitable; there is none that doeth good, no, not one.*"—Rom. 3:9-12.

"*. . . for there is no difference: For all have sinned, and come short of the glory of God.*"—Rom. 3:22,23.

"*This is a faithful saying, and worthy of all acceptation, that Christ Jesus came into the world to save sinners; of whom I am chief.*"—I Tim. 1:15.

Nothing in the Bible is clearer than that men are sinners, that men are not perfect.

The clear teaching of Christian Science is that men are already perfect, that there is really no such thing as sin, that Christ did not need to atone for our sins, that men do not need to be born again, that there is no eternal punishment for the wicked. Christian Science actually and definitely denies nearly all the great fundamentals taught in the Bible.

"Man Is the Unfallen, Spiritual Child of God, Perfect as His Heavenly Father"—Says Christian Science

In the same issue of the *Christian Science Sentinel* mentioned above is another statement of this blasphemous teaching. On page 323 (the first page of that number) is the following statement:

> The lowly stable where Jesus was born, the manger where the Virgin-mother cradled her babe, were typical of the majestic humility which characterized the earthly career of the great Nazarene, who brought to the world the revelation that MAN IS THE UNFALLEN, SPIRITUAL CHILD OF GOD, PERFECT AS HIS HEAVENLY FATHER.

This is the kind of teaching put out by Christian

Science. The Bible teaches that man fell in the Garden of Eden and that since then all are sinners. Christian Science teaches "that man is the unfallen, spiritual child of God, perfect as his heavenly Father"!

Mary Baker Eddy Fulfilled the Promise of Jesus of the Comforter — Says Christian Science

Why is Christian Science so fundamentally opposed to the Scripture? How could it deny so many fundamentals of Bible teaching and yet claim to be Christian? Simply because Christian Science has another textbook besides the Bible. The book by Mary Baker Eddy, *Science and Health With Key to the Scriptures,* is regarded as inspired, a revelation from God. Actually it is part of the Bible of Christian Science. Christian Science could not have gone so far wrong by honestly trying to find what the Bible teaches. It goes wrong by accepting another book as a revelation from God and by following that instead of the Bible.

This is the official teaching of Christian Science, repeated many, many times, that the writings of Mary Baker Eddy were inspired revelations from God.

For instance, in this *Christian Science Sentinel* for December 22, 1934, in an article on "Happy Christmas," page 323, is the following paragraph:

> As patriarch and prophet foretold the coming of the Messiah, so did Jesus himself promise a future and further unfoldment of the truth which he taught and demonstrated. When speaking of this, he used the beautiful word "Comforter:" "And I will pray the Father, and he shall give you another Comforter, that he may abide with you for ever, even the spirit of truth." THIS PROPHECY WAS FULFILLED OVER SIXTY YEARS AGO, WHEN, AT A TIME OF GREAT MENTAL AND RELIGIOUS UNREST AND DISSATISFACTION, MARY BAKER EDDY CAME BEFORE THE WORLD WITH HER DISCOVERY OF CHRISTIAN SCIENCE,

> THE COMFORTER which has brought and is bringing health, joy, good success, freedom and peace with God to thousands of weary, suffering mortals all over the globe."

Jesus promised in the fourteenth chapter of John that after He went away He would send the Holy Spirit, the Comforter. That certainly was fulfilled when after the ascension of Christ, at Pentecost the Holy Spirit was poured out in great power. We are plainly told in the Bible that every Christian has the Holy Spirit dwelling in him (I Cor. 3:16,17; I Cor. 6:19,20; II Cor. 6:16; Rom. 8:9). But Mary Baker Eddy claims that she and her writings fulfill the promise of the coming of the Holy Spirit. This is blasphemy, infidelity, and the curse of God is upon it.

Christian Science Honors Mary Baker Eddy Equal to the Holy Spirit and Christ

Notice again the above quotation from the *Christian Science Sentinel*. The first sentence puts Mary Baker Eddy on a plane with Jesus and her writings on a plane with the New Testament:

> As patriarch and prophet foretold the coming of the Messiah, so did Jesus himself promise a future and further unfoldment of the truth which he taught and demonstrated.

Christian Science teaches that just like Jesus was the fulfillment of the prophecies, so Mary Baker Eddy fulfilled the prophecy of Jesus concerning the coming of the Holy Spirit, the Comforter! Notice that Christian Science is called a "further unfoldment" of the teachings of Jesus. The teachings of Jesus surpass the teachings of the prophets. So, according to Christian Science, the teachings of Mary Baker Eddy surpass the teachings of Jesus!

The fact is that in claiming to fulfill the prophecy of

the coming of the Comforter, the Holy Ghost, Mary Baker Eddy practically claims deity for herself. The Comforter promised, to manifest and further reveal Jesus, was really the Holy Spirit of God, one of the Divine Trinity. If she is that Comforter and her writings are His work, then you can see that she claims deity.

In fact, many times in her writings she is put on an equal with Christ. You can see why they hate the idea that Jesus is God and claim that man is perfect.

The fact that Christian Science deifies Mary Baker Eddy is manifest throughout Christian Science literature. Her writings are called a revelation from God and are counted inspired like the Bible. Christian Science publications, when referring to her as leader or founder, print it, "our Leader" or "the Founder," capitalizing any title referring to her just as they capitalize titles referring to Jesus Christ! Strange as it may seem, carved on Christian Science churches one can find side by side two quotations, one from Jesus and the Bible, and the other from Mary Baker Eddy, both given equal prominence! They call her book, *Science and Health With Key to the Scriptures,* "The Text Book of Christian Science." The Bible is not the textbook of Christian Science, but Mary Baker Eddy's writings are! This they openly announce.

Any religion that puts the writings of a woman equal with the sayings of Jesus Christ and calls her the fulfillment of the coming of the Holy Spirit is blasphemy, is infidelity and antichristian.

Christian Science Lecturer Says Jesus Not Unique, His Works Not Miraculous

"Christian Science" lecturers regularly deny the fact of sin, the deity of Christ, the blood atonement, the need for personal, supernatural regeneration, and the eternal punishment of the wicked. To a Christian Scientist, the Bible is no more inspired than the works of Mary Baker Eddy, and Christ is no more divine than she was. A great many good people are deceived by so-called Christian Science, thinking it to be Christianity, but in fact it is not.

The following paragraphs were clipped from an Oklahoma City paper.

> The want of an ever-increasing number of persons is a religion that will help them here, on earth, now, Robert Stanley Ross, C. S. B., New York City, declared Friday night in a lecture on Christian Science at the Shrine auditorium.
>
> "An ever-increasing number of persons are searching for a practical religion," Ross said. "They are no longer satisfied with promises regarding a future-world salvation....
>
> "Unwilling to accept the common belief that the marvelous works of Jesus were supernatural occurrences peculiar to him alone, instead of natural effects of a Divine law available to all, Mary Baker Eddy, through the process of reason, revelation and proof, won her way to the point where she discovered the Divine principle of Christian healing."

Mary Baker Eddy and Christian Science were "unwilling to accept the common belief that the marvelous works of Jesus were supernatural occurrences peculiar to him alone," said this official Christian Science lecturer, in the copy which he turned in to the Oklahoma City newspaper. Christian Science plainly teaches that Jesus was not supernatural but natural, that He was no more divine than other men, that His works were no more supernatural miracles than Christian Science practitioners can work. They deny the deity of Christ. "Christian Science" itself, like modernists, infidels, atheists, and pagans, denies the Bible teaching that Jesus is "Wonderful, Counsellor, The mighty God, The everlasting Father, The Prince of Peace" (Isa. 9:6).

Are Christian Scientists Ever Christians?

Christian Science itself is thoroughly unchristian and antichristian and directly opposed to the teachings of the Bible on the great fundamentals.

Christian Science does not teach that the Bible is God's revealed Word, different from all other writings in the sense that it claims to be, because they accept Mary Baker Eddy's writings as inspired along with it.

Christian Science does not believe in Christ as God, but only as a good man, not different in kind from other men.

Christian Science does not believe that man is a sinner, that man needs to repent and be born again, but believes that man is already perfect, unfallen and like God.

Christian Science therefore does not believe in the atonement made by Christ on the cross for us, as taught in the Bible.

Christian Science does not teach the personality of the Holy Spirit, but that Mary Baker Eddy and her writings fulfilled the promise of the Comforter.

Christian Science does not believe in the personality of the Devil, nor the reality of sin nor Hell.

Christian Science, so-called, is as unchristian as the teachings of Bob Ingersoll, Tom Paine and Voltaire! In fact, Christian Science has much in common with these infidels.

But while the teachings of Christian Science are thoroughly unchristian, some individual Christian Scientists are Christian people, I sincerely believe. They were saved people before they were deluded by the wicked falsehoods of Christian Science. People who have already trusted in the blood of Christ may sometimes be led into foolish cults and isms like Christian Science.

But be it understood that Christian Science never makes Christians. Christian Science does not teach people to repent, to seek forgiveness and a change of heart, to trust Christ as a personal Substitute and a Saviour from sin. Christian Science teaches people to follow the example of Jesus in His life, calling Jesus the "Way-shower" but denying that He is literally what He called Himself, "the way."

Christian Science has no doctrine to teach a sinner he needs saving, no doctrine to show how a sinner may be saved. It beclouds the Bible by adding to it the writings of Mary Baker Eddy so that the sinner will not be convicted by the Word. Christian Science does not present a Saviour whose blood can save, nor a sinner who needs saving.

Christian Science does not make Christians. It misleads ignorant Christians, proselytes troubled Christians, and steals the sheep from other flocks.

Real Christians must love Christian Scientists, so-called, but must love them as they love lost, unconverted sinners. Every Christian ought to pray for those of his friends deluded by this wicked, unchristian, false religion. Pray for them as you pray for other infidels who deny that Jesus is God. Pray for them as you pray for other unconverted moral men who say that man is good and does not need to be born again. Pray for them as you would for other idolaters, for their worship and reverence for Mary Baker Eddy is wicked idolatry, putting her before God. Pray for them as you would Mohammedans who follow the Koran instead of the Bible. Pray for them as you would Hindu people who rely upon the Vedas instead of the Bible as the Word of God. Pray for them as you would Mormons who take the Book of Mormon instead of the Bible. In other words, pray for poor, deluded Christian Scientists as you would for other unconverted sinners who must be forever lost in Hell because of their sins which they deny and for their rejection of Christ as their personal Saviour and very God.

There are many good people who are deceived by the foolish vagaries and unscriptural teaching of Christian

Science. They were not thoroughly grounded in the plain teaching of the Bible and were led astray.

I do not doubt their sincerity, and I do not mean to cast any reflection on them. However, I know beyond a doubt that the Christian Science system of teaching is unchristian, deceitful, wicked blasphemy and that its official statements are in direct opposition to Bible Christianity.

Christian Science Healings

Are people ever really healed through Christian Science? I think that very likely they are. We are told that the Devil will come as an angel of light (II Cor. 11:13-15), and to do that he must appear good and beautiful.

Read that passage and you will see how false apostles and deceitful workers apparently do good, because the Devil uses them to deceive.

"*For such are false apostles, deceitful workers, transforming themselves into the apostles of Christ. And no marvel; for Satan himself is transformed into an angel of light. Therefore it is no great thing if his ministers also be transformed as the ministers of righteousness; whose end shall be according to their works.*"—II Cor. 11:13-15.

Certainly Satan would be willing to heal people occasionally if he could thereby keep people from believing in the deity of Christ and trusting in His blood for salvation.

Do not doctors who are infidels and atheists treat sickness successfully? Do not unbelieving surgeons perform successful operations? Then why should it be thought strange that Christian Scientists often report cases of healing? Yes, I have no doubt that people are often healed through "Christian Science" just as they are through infidel doctors. But that does not prove Christian Science is of God.

Jesus tells in Matthew 12:43-45 about how an unclean spirit sometimes goes out of a man without being cast out by the Lord, but He says that the last state of that man is worse than the first. Sometimes men reform without being reborn. The system of religion the Pharisees held in the time of Christ presented outwardly a beautiful moral character but it covered a rotten heart. The Devil often does things that appear good in order to lead people away from the Bible and from God. So the Devil has some attractive and good features in every false religion. I remind you that the magicians of Pharaoh's court worked miracles when Moses came before him (Exod. 7:10-12).

What will happen when thousands of so-called "Christian Science" practitioners come before Christ to tell of their good deeds and to claim a part of Heaven? Doubtless Jesus had them in mind as well as others when He said,

"*Many will say to me in that day, Lord, Lord, have we not prophesied in thy name? and in thy name have cast out devils? and in thy name done many wonderful works?*"—Matt. 7:22.

But to every one who came denying that Jesus is God, denying that man is a sinner, denying any need for atoning blood, it is already settled what the Lord Jesus will tell them.

"*And then will I profess unto them, I never knew you: depart from me, ye that work iniquity.*"—Matt. 7:23.

That is what the Lord Jesus said will happen to people who prophesy in His name, in His name cast out devils, and in His name do many wonderful works or cures. Jesus will send them away into outer darkness because He never knew them in personal regeneration and salvation.

If Christian Science healers actually get people healed from sickness, then that is no more than Judas did who is now in Hell, and no more than many other false teachers have done who are unconverted and must face Christ in the judgment with other lost sinners. Healings do not prove that Christian Scientists are Christians. In fact, Jesus plainly said that there would be wonder-workers who were unconverted and not Christians though they would pretend to be.

Mental Healings, or Answers to Prayers?

For that matter, I remind you that the healing methods of Christian Science are more or less a system of mind cure which has been practiced often by many other people not pretending to be Christian Scientists. Coue taught people to say, "Every day in every way, I am getting better and better." Actually, a cheerful frame of mind does help to heal the body, as every physician knows. In fact, physicians know that a very large part of most healing is psychological. Many doctors have given bread pills and all doctors try to impart a cheerful, hopeful attitude. In that way, doubtless, the Christian Science system of healing has often promoted healing.

Denying a Fact Does Not Always Change It

Mental suggestion often does good. It sometimes banishes fear and removes worry and so helps to restore normal heart action, proper digestion, gland secretion, etc. But Christian Science often fails because mental suggestion does not always remove the fact.

You have heard of the boy who started to cross a field with his grandmother but was scared by a billy goat. The grandmother was a Christian Scientist and she said, "Now, now, Jimmie, remember your Science. You know the goat couldn't hurt you, so don't be afraid."

"Yes," said the boy, "I know the goat can't hurt me and you know the goat can't hurt me, but Grandmother, the goat doesn't know it!"

Denying the fact might not keep the goat from butting.

Another case might have involved the same boy and his grandmother. "Grandmother," said the boy, "Grandfather is sick."

"No, no," said this good devotee of Christian Science, "remember your Science. We know there is no such thing as sickness and pain and evil. You should have said, 'Grandfather THINKS he is sick.'"

The boy went about his business but later returned to say to his grandmother, "Grandmother, Grandfather thinks he is dead!" The doctors and the undertaker thought so, too, and they buried him!

So it is with the folly of Christian Science. Mental suggestion cannot change the fact of the terrible wickedness of the human heart. To deny that there is sin when the Bible again and again states that all have sinned and that there is none righteous, is folly. To deny sin when day by day the millions of earth are dying under its curse, is wickedness. To deny that there is sin when Jesus died a terrible death to save us from the penalty of it, is unchristian, unscriptural and devilish.

Satan can well afford to help heal the sick if he can get men to deny the fact of sin, the need to be born again, the deity of Christ, and the power of His blood.

God Sometimes Answers Prayer for Real Christians Among Christian Scientists

Doubtless, also, many sincere Christians who call themselves Christian Scientists honestly pray to God for healing and get it. I believe in prayer for the sick. Christian Science certainly did not invent that doctrine, for it is plainly taught in the Bible, and there are thousands of Christians, not Christian Scientists, who know from happy experience that God does heal the sick in answer to prayer.

The mercy of God is so great that He gives us far more than we deserve. Has He not answered your prayers when you were ignorant of His Word and unworthy of His blessings? Do you not believe that He sometimes answers the prayers for healing of the body of Pentecostal people and others who hold to the "tongues" doctrine, or who teach sinless perfection? God has answered many of my prayers when I did not deserve it and when I did not have full light on the Scriptures.

So we may know that when a real Christian, a born-again child of God, has ignorantly accepted some of the tenets of Christian Science but nevertheless prays in faith to God for healing, that prayer is answered. The Scripture says, "The prayer of faith shall save the sick" (Jas. 5:15). But such healings are not triumphs of Christian Science. Thousands pray such prayers and are answered who know that Christian Science is unscriptural. All of us ought to believe what the Bible teaches about prayer and we ought to practice it, concerning every need, whether physical, mental or spiritual. We have done wrong to let Christian Science take the credit for healing in answer to prayer. We should testify more often of the power of God to heal.

But whether the sick are healed by the power of the Devil that he may delude Christian Scientists into thinking Jesus is not God and that sin is not real, etc., or whether the Christian Scientists induce a hopeful attitude of mind which helps nature to heal, or whether sincere Christians among them really pray to God for healing, in the Bible sense of prayer, and get it—these things do not change at all the fact that Christian Science is an unchristian religion, opposed to the Bible and leading astray many thousands of souls.

And if there reads this one who has not confessed himself a sinner and fled to a crucified Saviour for mercy and personal salvation, then I beg you, do so today. Jesus *IS* the Son of God. He is "The mighty God." He is "the way"—the only way. He is real, a real Person. Sin is real. You are a guilty sinner—may I say it kindly, a condemned sinner—if you have not received Jesus by faith as your Saviour.

Do not be led away by this modern, false, unchristian religion, less than one hundred years old. Do not let its textbook take the place of the Bible your mother believed! Heaven, Hell, eternity, and judgment are REAL! So today, repent and be saved.

Bible Promises a Curse on Christian Science

Christian Science adds to the Bible the writings of Mary Baker Eddy and so brings upon it the curse of God mentioned in Revelation 22:18,19.

Christian Science brings, not the old Gospel of Christ who is God dying to save sinners but a new gospel; therefore, let it be accursed, for we are told in Galatians 1:8,9:

"*But though we, or an angel from heaven, preach any other gospel unto you than that which we have preached unto you, let him be accursed. As we said before, so say I now again, If any man preach any other gospel unto you than that ye have received, let him be accursed.*"

The attitude of real Christians toward this pagan, unchristian, false religion should be that which is commanded in the second epistle of John, verses 9 to 11:

"*Whosoever transgresseth, and abideth not in the doctrine of Christ, hath not God. He that abideth in the doctrine of Christ, he hath both the Father and the Son. If there come any unto you, and bring not this doctrine, receive him not into your house, neither bid him God speed: For he that biddeth him God speed is partaker of his evil deeds.*"

We are to love individual Christian Scientists, but we are not to receive into our houses teachers of this doctrine, nor bid them Godspeed, lest we be partakers of their evil deeds.

If you have a Christian Scientist neighbor, friend, or relative, then pray earnestly that he may be delivered from the deception of Satan and believe the Bible instead of this false doctrine. People who are deceived in this matter need your love, sympathy and careful teaching from the Bible itself. And Christians everywhere ought to believe and be able to prove and testify that God does answer prayer about health, and jobs, and peace of mind, and daily bread, and above all, He forgives the sins of those who put their faith in Jesus Christ as the God-Man, "our Lord Jesus Christ." Real Bible Christians have far more to boast of than this falsely so-called Christian Science. Therefore, Christians, let your light shine!

(We recommend *Christian Science in the Light of Holy Scriptures* by I. M. Haldeman, Revell Publishers.)

4

Errors of Seventh-Day Adventism

1. Saturday, the Jewish Sabbath, Was Ceremonial Law, Never Commanded for N.T. Christians
2. Help for a Seventh-Day Adventist
3. Hidden Heresies of Seventh-Day Adventists
4. Seventh-Day Adventist's Protests Answered

1. Saturday, the Jewish Sabbath, Was Ceremonial Law, Never Commanded for New Testament Christians

The fourth of the Ten Commandments in Exodus 20:8-11 is as follows:

"*Remember the sabbath day, to keep it holy. Six days shalt thou labour, and do all thy work: But the seventh day is the sabbath of the Lord thy God: in it thou shalt not do any work, thou, nor thy son, nor thy daughter, thy manservant, nor thy maidservant, nor thy cattle, nor thy stranger that is within thy gates.*"

Generally it has been held that this commandment applies to the New Testament Christians. Without any discussion, Christian people for centuries have preached and believed that Sabbath-keeping was enjoined upon us.

However, we have applied the commandment to Sunday, the first day of the week, instead of Saturday, the seventh day. The Scripture plainly says, "Six days shalt thou labour and do all thy work: But the seventh day is the sabbath of the Lord thy God." It is clear that the Sabbath of the Ten Commandments is Saturday, the seventh day of the week. Yet for generations people have been speaking of Sunday, the first day of the week, as "the Christian Sabbath." Sunday school has been called "the Sabbath school."

If asked to explain why they observe Sunday as a Sabbath instead of Saturday as commanded in the Ten Commandments, most preachers and Bible teachers simply say that when Jesus rose from the dead the Sabbath was changed from Saturday to Sunday. Since Christ rose upon the first day of the week, they say, therefore the apostles and other New Testament Christians changed the Sabbath day from Saturday to Sunday.

However, there is no record in the New Testament of the Sabbath being changed from Saturday to Sunday. Acts 20:7 tells how the Christians at Troas met upon the first day of the week to break bread. In First Corinthians 16:2 Paul commanded Christians to lay by them in store money for the collection for the poor saints at Jerusalem. But neither of those Scriptures nor any other command that New Testament Christians were to observe Sunday as a Sabbath. There is no Bible evidence for the saying that the Sabbath was changed from Saturday to Sunday by the apostles or by Jesus after His resurrection. In saying so, we have followed the example of Roman Catholics.

The Roman Catholic church calls Sunday the Sabbath. That church claims the right to speak with authority, without basing their teachings on Scripture. As they attempt to transfer the priesthood of the Old Testament Jewish worship into New Testament churches and transfer the water of cleansing from Jewish ceremonial law making it "Holy Water" in Catholic churches, and the sprinkling of babies to take the place of circumcision of the Jewish ceremonial law, just so they have tried to transfer the Jewish Sabbath which was on Saturday into New Testament practice, changing the day to Sunday.

BUT SUNDAY IS NOT THE SABBATH. THE

BIBLE NEVER ONCE SPEAKS OF IT AS A SABBATH. THE BIBLE DOES NOT COMMAND CHRISTIANS TO KEEP SUNDAY AS A SABBATH. IN FACT, THE NEW TESTAMENT DOES NOT COMMAND CHRISTIANS TO KEEP ANY SABBATH WHATSOEVER! THE SABBATH WAS FOR JEWS UNDER CEREMONIAL LAW. IT WAS FOR NO ONE ELSE. IT WAS A SPECIAL COVENANT AND SIGN BETWEEN GOD AND THE JEWS.

To be sure, New Testament Christians do well to meet on the first day of the week for worship and service to God. New Testament Christians did, as indicated in Acts 20:7 and I Corinthians 16:2. It is called the Lord's day (Rev. 1:10). But the Lord's day is not the Sabbath day. It is used primarily as a day of praise and service, not as a day of rest. Its observance is voluntary and not commanded at all in the Bible. Our Lord's day is grace, pure and simple, not law. We should encourage Christians everywhere to make much of the Lord's day as a day of special privilege and blessing and worship and praise. But never call the Lord's day the Sabbath. Sunday is not the Sabbath and never was. Do not think of it as the Sabbath.

I. SABBATH WAS CEREMONIAL LAW; NOT MORAL LAW

People generally are more familiar with the Ten Commandments than with other parts of the Mosaic law. For so long Christians have been taught the Ten Commandments that they feel the Ten Commandments are moral law while other parts of the Mosaic law are ceremonial. That is not true. Many, many times in the Mosaic law there are plain commandments on moral questions, commandments which are as fitted for

Gentiles as for Jews, and as binding in spirit upon Christians in the United States as they were upon Jews in the land of Canaan. Likewise the Sabbath part of the Ten Commandments is ceremonial and not moral law, as we will plainly show.

Seventh-Day Adventists claim that the Ten Commandments are the law of God and that the rest of the law was Mosaic law. They make a false distinction, trying to make the Sabbath commandment binding upon Christians without making circumcision and other ceremonial laws binding upon us.

Seventh-Day Adventists confuse terms when they speak of the ceremonial law as Mosaic and the Ten Commandments as the "Law of God." The Bible never makes that distinction. Sometimes the whole first five books of the Bible are called the Mosaic law. But other times the Ten Commandments are called the Mosaic law.

Get this carefully, since it is very important. Hebrews 10:28 says, "He that despised Moses' law died without mercy under two or three witnesses." Now check the Scriptures and you will see that no Jew was ever stoned except for breaking some of the Ten Commandments. Any sin worthy of death would come under the Ten Commandments and so this Scripture calls these Ten Commandments "Moses' law." The law of God and the law of Moses was the same.

Likewise, in Nehemiah 8:1 the Pentateuch is called the law of Moses, and in verse 8 of the same book it is called the law of God. The law of Moses and the law of God are the same. All of the first five books of the Bible were given by God to Moses, including the Ten Commandments.

To call the Ten Commandments God's law and the rest of the books Moses' law is a deceitful wresting of Scripture which men have done to deceive the people. Those who say that God's law is the moral law and the Mosaic law was ceremonial law are absolutely wrong. God's law was given by Moses and all the Mosaic law was God's law. The Ten Commandments are only a part of the law, a summing up of the law, both the moral law and the ceremonial law.

1. The Sabbath Was Ceremonial Law and for Jews Only Because It Was Not Known Before Mount Sinai

Adam never heard of it. Enoch, Noah, Abraham, Isaac, and Jacob all lived and died without ever once keeping the Sabbath. The Sabbath is not even mentioned in connection with the stories of their lives. They were never commanded to keep the Sabbath and did not keep it. The proof of this is in Nehemiah 9:13,14, where we are plainly told that on Mount Sinai *God made known His holy Sabbath.*

"*Thou camest down also upon mount Sinai, and spakest with them from heaven, and gavest them right judgments, and true laws, good statutes and commandments: And madest known unto them thy holy sabbath, and commandedst them precepts, statutes, and laws, by the hand of Moses thy servant.*"

Exodus 16:1 tells us how ". . . all the congregation of the children of Israel came unto the wilderness of Sin, which is between Elim and Sinai. . . ." They were then on the west side of Sinai, near by. There, Exodus 16:23-30 tells us, God made known to them the Sabbath, which they had never before observed. Then in Exodus 19:1, Israel moved to the other side of Mount Sinai, and God gave Moses the whole Ten Commandments listed in Exodus 20.

Notice also that all these laws, including the Sabbath, were made known "by the hand of Moses thy servant." The Sabbath then was first made known to mankind at Mount Sinai. Up to that time no living person had ever heard of it. God had, in his own mind, sanctified the seventh day at the close of creation (Gen. 2:3), but this wasn't made known to man till Mount Sinai, and that verse in Genesis 2:3 wasn't written by Moses until after that. Before Mount Sinai, the moral law was in effect but the Sabbath law was not.

For instance, when Cain killed Abel, it was murder and God put a curse on Cain for it. And that isn't all; Cain knew he had sinned and tried to lie out of it, saying, "Am I my brother's keeper?" The Sabbath, never known before Sinai, could not be moral law binding on the whole race.

2. The Sabbath Is Ceremonial Law Because It Was Commanded as a Special Covenant Between God and Israel

That is what the Lord plainly said in Exodus 31:12-17,

"*And the Lord spake unto Moses, saying, Speak thou also unto the CHILDREN OF ISRAEL saying, Verily my sabbaths ye shall keep: for it is a sign between me and YOU throughout YOUR generation; that ye may know that I am the Lord that doth sanctify YOU. Ye shall keep the sabbath therefore; for it is holy unto YOU: every one that denieth it shall surely be put to death: for whosoever doeth any work therein, that soul shall be cut off from among his people. Six days may work be done; but in the seventh is the sabbath of rest, holy to the Lord: whosoever doeth any work in the sabbath day, he shall surely be put to death. Wherefore the CHILDREN OF ISRAEL shall keep the sabbath, to observe the sabbath throughout THEIR generations, for a perpetual covenant. It is a sign between me and the CHILDREN OF ISRAEL for ever: for in six days the Lord made heaven and earth, and on the seventh day he rested, and was refreshed.*"

A careful study of that passage shows beyond any possible doubt that the Sabbath was a sign between God and the nation Israel. He set them apart or sanctified them as a chosen nation, separate from the Gentile races, and gave the Sabbath as a sign.

Notice in the above Scripture this statement about the Sabbath: "Whosoever doeth any work therein, that soul shall be cut off from among his people." What is the penalty of Sabbath-breaking? It was to be death, yes, but that was to be a means of separating him from the Jews as a chosen people. Repeatedly about ceremonial law Jews are warned that they should be cut off from the covenant given Israel if they broke these laws. The Jews were sanctified or set apart as a separate chosen nation and were given ceremonial laws as a sign of this. Circumcision was such a sign, and the Sabbath was such a sign also.

The same thing is expressly stated again in Ezekiel 20:12:

"*Moreover also I gave them my sabbaths, to be a sign between me and them, that they might know that I am the Lord that doth sanctify them.*"

Note also Ezekiel 20:20 which repeats the statement.

Now ceremonial laws may be commanded to one group of people and not commanded to others, but the moral law is for all alike. The law against murder is certainly true for everybody, but the law commanding circumcision is only for the Jews. Therefore, it is ceremonial law. Likewise the law that Jews should keep the Sabbath is a ceremonial law because it is expressly given as a sign between God and Jews to set them apart from others. Any command that is restricted to a particular group of people and is not given to others is thereby proven to be a ceremonial law.

The Ten Commandments are given in two places in the Mosaic law, in Exodus, chapter 20, and in Deuteronomy, chapter 5. And here in Deuteronomy 5:15, following the commandment to keep the Sabbath, are the plain words which show that it was a ceremonial law commanded for Jews only:

"*And remember that thou wast a servant in the land of Egypt, and that the Lord thy God brought thee out thence through a mighty hand and by a stretched out arm: therefore the Lord thy God commanded thee to keep the sabbath day.*"

Notice that God says that, since He had brought the children of Israel out of Egypt, "therefore the Lord thy God commandeth thee to keep the sabbath day." It is clear here, as elsewhere, that there was a special meaning in the Sabbath for Jews. In the midst of the Ten Commandments God selected the commandment about the Sabbath and stated that it was for Jews because He had brought them out of the land of Egypt, setting them apart as a chosen nation in Canaan. The Sabbath is ceremonial law because it was commanded as a special covenant between God and Israel.

3. The Jewish Sabbath Is Ceremonial Law Because It Is Not Written in the Heart, and Moral Law Is Always Written in the Heart and Conscience

Romans 2:14, 15 shows that Gentiles have the moral law of God written in their hearts or consciences and that God will hold Gentiles accountable for that moral law even when they do not have a Bible. That Scripture says,

"*For when the Gentiles, which have not the law, do by nature the things contained in the law, these, having not the law, are a law unto themselves: Which shew the work of the law written in their hearts, their conscience also bearing witness, and their thoughts the mean while accusing or else excusing one another.*"

Heathen savages in Africa who never saw a Bible know that it is wrong to steal and to kill or to lie or to commit adultery. God has given savages a conscience, and that conscience has been enlightened by the Spirit of God regarding moral law. But God does not enlighten the conscience about ceremonial law.

For instance, no savage in Africa who never saw a Bible would instinctively know that it is all right to eat beef and wrong to eat pork. He could not know unless he was taught that it was all right to eat fish with scales but not right to eat catfish which have no scales. When God prohibited Jews from eating pork or catfish, it was a ceremonial law and that ceremonial law is not written in the heart.

A heathen savage could not feel any responsibility to circumcise his baby boy if he had not been taught to do that by others or by the Bible. Circumcision, being a part of the ceremonial law, is not written in the heart and conscience of men by the Holy Spirit.

Just so, we know that the Sabbath is a ceremonial law. Surely a heathen savage would not instinctively know that it was right to work on certain days and on the Sabbath it would be wrong to work. That is not written in the heart. For instance, even a devoted Jew or Seventh-Day Adventist, if he, through a period of unconsciousness, lost track of the days of the week and had no way of finding out from other men, could not instinctively know which day was the Sabbath, the Jewish day of rest. He would have to find out from other people or records since that ceremonial law is not written in the heart.

4. The Sabbath Is Certainly Ceremonial Law and Applied to Jews Only Because the Enforcement of It and Literal Fulfillment of It Was Possible Only to Jews in Palestine Under the Theocracy or Personal Rule of God

(1.) The death penalty was commanded for all who broke the Sabbath. Exodus 35:2 plainly commands this.

"*Six days shall work be done, but on the seventh day there shall be to you an holy day, a sabbath of rest to the Lord: WHOSOEVER DOETH WORK THEREIN SHALL BE PUT TO DEATH.*"

The most ardent Seventh-Day Adventists now do not ask that the government put Sabbath-breakers to death and they do not attempt to put to death even members of their own congregations who fail in this matter. This command, that people be put to death for failure in religion, would not be in order except in a country where God ruled in person as He did in Israel during the theocracy in Palestine.

(2.) To really observe the Sabbath there must be no fires in the houses whatsoever on the Sabbath day. Exodus 35:3 commands:

"*Ye shall kindle no fire throughout your habitations upon the sabbath day.*"

That command was given to Israel only, and it is obvious that others do not observe it. In cold countries it would be a terrible hardship to have no fire in the houses throughout the day, but Palestine is not a cold country. And any Seventh-Day Adventist who has a fire in his home either for heat or for cooking or heating water on Saturday then violates the plain law regarding the Sabbath and he does not keep the Sabbath, however much he may pretend to do so. God gave the

Sabbath to Israel under the theocracy in Palestine and it was issued to them and not to others from whom it was not commanded. If Seventh-Day Adventists should ever take seriously their claim that the Sabbath is binding on Christians today and start out killing everybody who broke the Sabbath by having a fire in the house on Saturday, it would bring an end to their foolish and unscriptural teaching.

(3.) If one goes west around the world, returning to the starting point, he gains an entire day. When ships cross the international date line, arbitrarily set by men (not by God) in the Pacific Ocean, they either jump ahead, skipping one day of the week or they go back over the same day the second time to keep step with the rest of the world. So if a Jew or a Seventh-Day Adventist really works six days and then rested the seventh, then when he went around the world once he would have a different Sabbath from other Jews and Seventh-Day Adventists. Clearly when God says that he gave the Sabbath as a sign to the Jews in mark of their separation, we see how fitting it is. The Sabbath fits Jews in Palestine under the theocracy and wasn't given to Christians and not meant for Christians around the world in this age.

(4.) The Sabbath given in Mosaic law was not for church-going and religious activities. The Sabbath commandment says nothing about assembling for public worship or service. There were not even any synagogues in existence when the Sabbath was given nor till the captivity of the Jews. Instead, the Sabbath command in Exodus 16:29 is: "See, for that the Lord hath given you the sabbath, therefore he giveth you on the sixth day the bread of two days; abide ye every man in his place, let no man go out of his place on the seventh day."

So the weekly Sabbath command has nothing to do with going to church, assembling for preaching or teaching. On the contrary, the people were plainly commanded to "abide... every man in his place." They were to stay in their own homes; they were not even to light a fire. Such commands were suitable under the ceremonial law for Jews in Palestine. They were not commanded for Christians in New Testament times.

5. The Proof That the Jews' Sabbath Was Ceremonial Law and Not Intended for New Testament Christians Is This Remarkable Fact: Not Once in the Entire New Testament Is Any Christian Ever Commanded to Keep the Sabbath

All the moral law is repeated again and again in one form or another. Christians are commanded not to kill, not to steal, not to lie, not to covet, not to be adulterers, to honor fathers and mothers; but never once in the New Testament are we commanded to observe the Sabbath!

This is a startling truth. The question of the Sabbath came up again and again in the personal ministry of Christ as recorded in the four Gospels — Matthew, Mark, Luke and John. The Jews later rebuked Jesus for healing on the Sabbath day. They rebuked His disciples for rubbing out handfuls of wheat and eating it on the Sabbath day. Jesus discussed the matter many times and never one time did He command that we keep the Sabbath. If He had intended for us to keep the Jews' Sabbath, surely He would have said so, but He did not say so.

In the book of Acts we find the missionary journeys of Paul. Paul went to many lands and yet never once did he command the new converts to keep the Sabbath. The question of whether or not the new converts must keep the ceremonial law came up repeatedly and finally a council was called at Jerusalem and recorded in the fifteenth chapter of Acts. The question was thrashed out by the apostles and it was fully decided that the new converts need not keep the ceremonial law and need not be circumcised; neither then nor later was it decided or ordered that Christians should keep the Sabbath.

In the epistles of Paul and Peter and James and John every kind of duty is mentioned again and again and every kind of sin. Christians are commanded not to lie, not to steal, not to kill, not to take God's name in vain, not to commit adultery or fornication, not to be guilty of idolatry, to honor fathers and mothers. Every one of the Ten Commandments is repeated in definite words except the command about the Sabbath. Not once in the New Testament is there a single command about the Sabbath. In all the lists of sins, not once is Sabbath-breaking mentioned in the New Testament.

Likewise we are not commanded in the New Testament to be circumcised, not commanded to abstain from pork. The New Testament does not give Christians commandments to keep the ceremonial law. Therefore, the Sabbath is not commanded to Christians but is a part of the ceremonial law, was nailed to the cross, as we are told in Colossians 2:14-17. There the Sabbath is particularly mentioned with other ceremonial laws.

6. We Know That the Sabbath Is Ceremonial Law Because God Plainly Tells Us So in Colossians 2:16,17

Colossians 2:16,17, says,

"*Let no man therefore judge you in meat, or in drink, or in respect of an holyday, or of the new moon, or of the sabbath days: Which are a shadow of things to come; but the body is of Christ.*"

God says of these ceremonial laws, including that of the Sabbath, that they "are a shadow," that is, a type or ceremonial with a spiritual meaning but that Christ is the body which is foreshadowed by these ceremonial laws. We are explicitly commanded here not to be judged or not to be held accountable for these ceremonial laws concerning meat, drink, holyday, new moon, or Sabbath.

Be sure to note that God here speaks of "the sabbath" and the word "days" is not in the original Greek, because it is printed in italics in your Bible. The Sabbath, as part of the ceremonial laws, is simply a shadow that was fulfilled when Christ came and died. Who, then, could possibly doubt that the Jewish Sabbath was for Jews only and was ceremonial law?

The book of Galatians was practically written by the Apostle Paul to warn the Galatian Christians against depending on keeping the law for salvation. And one of the things that grieved Paul particularly was that these Christians were still trying to keep the days and months and times and years of the Mosaic ceremonial law. In Galatians 4:9-11 he says:

"*But now, after that ye have known God, or rather are known of God, how turn ye again to the weak and beggarly elements, whereunto ye desire again to be in bondage? Ye observe days, and months, and times, and years.*"

These Galatian Christians were trying to observe these special *days* of the Old Testament, that is, the Sabbath days, once every week. They observed *months,* that is, the special ceremonies of the new moon each month. They observed *times,* that is, the annual feast periods of the Old Testament including, I suppose, the Passover and Feast of Unleavened Bread, the Feast of Tabernacles and the Feast of Pentecost. They observed *years,* that is, every seventh year was a Sabbath year and the land must rest according to Jewish ceremonial law. (The Sabbath year and the Sabbath day must properly go together. If one is binding, so is the other as you see from Leviticus 25:1-6.) But Paul feared that he had "bestowed. . . labour in vain" upon these Christians at Galatia who did not realise that the cross of Christ was the end of the ceremonial law and still tried to observe the Old Testament Sabbath!

The New Testament plainly teaches that we are not to observe nor be held accountable for the Jewish Sabbath which is ceremonial law.

II. The Ceremonial Meaning of the Sabbath and That of the Lord's Day Contrasted

The ceremonial law was law given with a symbolical meaning. For instance, circumcision was a symbol meaning that a Jew was a marked man, separate from the Gentile world. Circumcision was simply a type of conversion. Jews were not converted when they were circumcised but the spiritual meaning to a thoughtful and spiritually minded Jew was that each Jew should have a changed heart and be essentially different from the heathen men about him. In Deuteronomy 30 we are told how the Jews will be regathered at Christ's second coming and then in verse 6 is this promise:

"*And the Lord thy God will circumcise thine heart, and the heart of thy seed, to love the Lord thy God with all thine heart, and with all thy soul, that thou mayest live.*"

Circumcision thus was a type of regeneration, of being born again, of having a change of heart.

Thus all ceremonial law had a spiritual meaning. Much of it pictured the separation which a Christian should observe. A Jew was not to yoke together an ox and an ass. A Jew was not to put on a mixed garment, part wool and part linen. A Jew was not to sow two kinds of seed in the same field. All this teaches that a true child of God should come out and be separate from unbelievers. The ceremonial law is not for us but the spiritual lesson is for us.

So in the matter of the Sabbath there are beautiful lessons for us and these spiritual lessons make it utterly impossible that Christians should be required to keep the ceremonial Sabbath on Saturday. This you will plainly see if you study prayerfully the following facts.

The Sabbath is a type of Heaven. Seven in the Bible is God's number, the perfect or complete number. So the seventh day, a day of rest, would stand for that perfect rest in Heaven. But six is man's number, imperfect and less than God's number. The law commanded, "Six days shalt thou labour, and do all thy work." That command is really a command for perfection. If a man works perfectly and does everything he ought to do, literally all of his work, then he has earned a day of rest. And if a human being works all of his life doing literally everything that he ought to do, with no sin and no failure, then that person deserves Heaven. All the Mosaic law sets a perfect standard. If anybody had perfectly kept the law, then he would have salvation by his good deeds. Romans 10:5 tells us:

"*For Moses describeth the righteousness which is of the law, That the man which doeth those things shall live by them.*"

Anybody who perfectly kept the law would be saved by the law. One who never did wrong would need no forgiveness, need no Sabbath, need no change of heart. You see that the Jewish Sabbath, following six days of labor, is a perfect picture of salvation by works, salvation by keeping the law.

The only trouble about that is that it never did work.

The law is good but man is sinful and therefore no man ever was saved by keeping the law. Romans 3:20 says, "Therefore by the deeds of the law there shall no flesh be justified in his sight: for by the law is the knowledge of sin." No one was ever saved by the law and so no one ever really earned his Sabbath. The law was given to give us a knowledge of sin, to show us our failure. Therefore, when God completed His plan of salvation by giving His Son to die on the cross for us, saving men by grace and not by works, then the ceremonial law was all fulfilled and out of date. Now we do not need a Sabbath to picture Heaven earned by good works. We need something to picture free salvation received by faith without works. Of course even in Old Testament times the only way people were saved was by faith, but the law stood as a constant reminder that men were sinners.

Hebrews, chapter 3 and 4, give us this interpretation and meaning to the Sabbath. Twice in chapter 3 the "rest" (literally Sabbath) of God is mentioned, and eight times in chapter 4. Hebrews 4:9 and 10, says:

"*There remaineth therefore a rest to the people of God. For he that is entered into his rest, he also hath ceased from his own works, as God did from his.*"

In the margin of my Bible the word rest is translated "keeping of a Sabbath." It is my recollection that the Greek word here is *sabbatismos,* elsewhere translated Sabbath.

A blessed Sabbath of rest awaits the people of God. Some of us have already entered into God's rest and have peace and rest, a Sabbath in the heart. This is for those of us who have ceased from our own works and depended wholly on the work done by Jesus Christ. God finished His work in the creation of the world and rested and we enter into God's riches by resting with God. Christ lived a perfect life, wholly without sin, and then paid for the sins of the whole world on the cross. Then He cried, "It is finished" (John 19:30) and died.

Thus any poor sinner, who realizes that Jesus has done all the work necessary and so quits depending upon his own works and trusts wholly in the finished work of Christ, may now enter into that sweet rest. Those of us who quit depending upon our good deeds, quit depending upon keeping the law and so receive Christ alone as our righteousness, have heaven in our hearts today!

Here comes in, then, the blessed meaning of our Lord's day, Sunday, the first day of the week. If a Jew, after six days of hard work trying to keep the law, trying to save himself by good works, rested on the seventh day, Sabbath, picturing Heaven earned by a righteous and perfect life, then what kind of a day should Christians have? Jesus arose on the first day of the week. So every child of God whose salvation is already finished on the cross, everyone who is not depending upon himself by depending upon the blood of Christ to pay for sin and on the righteousness of Christ, ought to picture his rest on the first day of the week. I rest on the first day of the week to show that I am already saved without works, saved by grace. I rest on the first day of the week to show that I have already ceased from my own works. Then I work the rest of the week to show that I am working for Christ out of love and because He has already saved me. I am not working to get saved, I am working because I *am already* saved.

Now the observance of the Lord's day, Sunday, is not a matter of command. New Testament Christians did it voluntarily. If we observe the Lord's day, we too should do it voluntarily, not as a matter of law or command, not as a Sabbath like the Jews had when a man would be stoned for picking up sticks and when it was sin to even build a fire in the house on Saturday. For New Testament Christians the only real Sabbath we have is in the heart.

In the Old Testament the Jewish Sabbath was primarily a day of physical rest. It was not especially a day of worship or praise. But our Lord's day, Sunday, the day Christ arose from the dead to justify all who believe in Him, is not primarily a day of physical rest but primarily a day of worship and praise, a day of spiritual rest and blessing.

I believe it is proper for Christians to make Sunday a holy day as far as possible, not a day of law but a day of grace. But the real keeping of Sunday which is pleasing to God is that in the heart we should rejoice, ceasing from our own works and depending wholly on Christ for salvation.

We see then how, beyond any doubt, the Old Testament Sabbaths, the ceremonial Sabbaths, were nailed to the cross of Christ. They were, Colossians 2:16,17, tells us, "a shadow of things to come." The thing which they fulfilled was Christ and the salvation that He brings. In that sense, in His life and death Christ fulfilled all the ceremonial law.

One who trusts in Christ enters into rest now, ceasing "from his own works" (Heb. 4:10). We who have trusted wholly in Christ have heaven now in our heart. We are already entered into sweet rest in the spirit.

Yet Hebrews 4:9 says, "There remaineth therefore a rest to the people of God." There is another rest awaiting the child of God: there is a very real and blessed Heaven where the saints shall rest from their labors.

This double rest, rest in the first of life by trusting in Christ, and then the blessed rest at the close of life in Heaven, is beautifully pictured by two special Sabbaths of the Jewish ceremonial law. I refer to the two Sabbaths of the Feast of Unleavened Bread described in Exodus 12:15,16:

"*Seven days shall ye eat unleavened bread; even the first day ye shall put away leaven out of your houses:*

for whosoever eateth leavened bread from the first day until the seventh day, that soul shall be cut off from Israel. And in the first day there shall be an holy convocation, and in the seventh day there shall be an holy convocation to you; no manner of work shall be done in them, save that which every man must eat, that only may be done of you."

Just preceding this passage is given in detail the *ordinance* of the passover lamb. A male lamb of the first year, without spot or blemish, was to be killed in the afternoon and the blood was to be placed on the doorposts and the lintels of the doors of the houses where the Jews dwelt in Egypt. Then the lamb was roasted over the fire and after sundown (when the Jewish day began) they were to eat that lamb, eat all of it. If any remained it was to be burned. Then the death angel was to pass over Egypt that night and in any house where there was no blood upon the door, the first-born son must die! God said, "When I see the blood, I will pass over you."

That passover supper was given as an ordinance to the Jews to be observed annually. The passover lamb pictures Christ. First Corinthians 5:7 says, "For even Christ out passover is sacrificed for us." The blood on the door pictured a sinner safe behind the blood of Christ. To partake of the passover lamb pictured receiving Christ as Saviour. The lamb roasted with fire pictured Christ suffering for our sins. It was eaten with bitter herbs, picturing the sorrows of our Saviour in Gethsemane and on the cross. The lamb was roasted without water picturing that there was no alleviation of Christ's sufferings even as there is no water in Hell. And not a bone of the lamb was to be broken. Because Christ was to be crucified and not stoned, He was to have no bone broken.

The night the passover lamb was eaten, then began the Feast of Unleavened Bread mentioned above. As the passover lamb pictured Christ our Saviour, our atoning substitute, even so the unleavened bread pictured Christ our daily food, our strength, our "bread from heaven." One needs to be saved just once, but one needs daily strength and sustenance every day.

Notice the two Sabbaths in that week. As soon as they ate the passover lamb they entered into a Sabbath the first day of the seven. Exodus 12:16 says, "In the first day there shall be an holy convocation... no manner of work shall be done in them, save that which every man must eat, that only may be done by you." Just so when a believer has received Christ, God's passover lamb, and is safe under the blood, he enters into a sweet rest. He does no work for salvation but he rests, depending wholly upon Christ.

Here again the first six days of the seven picture man's life. In the first day of the six man enters into a rest, a heaven in the heart. Then at the end of the week, the seventh day brings another Sabbath. That pictures the two rests that await all who have trusted in Christ. We enter into rest when we receive Christ. Then all of our lives, after receiving Him, we should feast on the unleavened bread, enjoying Christ's strength and blessing. And at the end of life we enter into that sweet rest that remains for the people of God!

Don't you see that the ceremonial law of the Sabbaths has for us a beautiful spiritual meaning? And don't you see that after Christ has been nailed to the cross and has risen again on the first day of the week it becomes impossible for a Christian to properly keep the Jewish Sabbath of Saturday which pictured a rest earned by good deeds, Heaven gained by keeping the law?

The only people who would have you keep Saturday as a Sabbath according to the Jewish ceremonial law are those who do not understand the sweet and blessed teaching of the New Testament that salvation is by grace. The Galatian Christians to whom Paul wrote had fallen from the doctrine of grace and believed that they must be saved by keeping the law, such as circumcision and observing days, the Sabbath.

In a revival at Sherman, Texas, a dear woman came to talk with me. For many years she had been striving earnestly to keep the Sabbath on Saturday. In fact, she had been trying to keep all the law. With trembling lips and with tears in her eyes she told me, "Brother Rice, I just can't do it. I am afraid I never will make it. I do the best I can. I try to do everything right, but I'm always falling short somewhere and I have no peace. I just don't see how I can ever make it!"

I told her that I thanked God she had come to see that she herself could not earn salvation. I told her that Jesus Christ had already earned salvation for us and that now if she wanted to enter into rest she must cease from her own work and trust in Christ.

She begged me to come to her home. I did. She gathered about her her husband, grown sons and daughters and their husbands and wives, and for some hours I taught them the Scriptures showing that "Christ is the end of the law for righteousness to every one that believeth" (Rom.10:4). How happy she was when she saw that she could now enter into sweet rest by trusting in Christ. Later I baptized her and thirteen of her family, who found that rest.

My dear reader, "Let no man therefore judge you in meat, or in drink, or in respect of an holy day, or of the new moon, or of the sabbath days: Which are a shadow of things to come: but the body is Christ" (Col. 2:16,17). The shadows and types are already fulfilled. Christ has come, has died, and has risen again. Do not take the shadows but take the body they pictured; take Christ Himself!

And if there is one who reads this who does not have sweet peace, then you may have it the moment you believe in Christ. You may enter into the rest of God.

All you have to do is to "cease from your own works," that is, quit depending on your own righteousness and depend wholly on Christ. He died for you on the cross. If you receive Him, trust Him, then through Him you are counted as righteous and as having fulfilled all the law. Thus you have now a Sabbath in your heart, sweet rest, and you will have a part in that rest that remains later for the people of God!

Let us sum up what the Bible clearly teaches about the Sabbath day. I must repeat some things clearly taught in the Bible.

1. The Sabbath was made known at Mount Sinai (Neh. 9:14). There is no room for speculation when God says it. If you will read Exodus 16 again you will find that the Israelites were camped near Mount Sinai when the incidents there given took place. But why should any Christian not believe what the Bible clearly states, that the Sabbath was made known at Mount Sinai?

2. It is clear also that the account in Genesis 2 was not written until Moses wrote it down in the wilderness after the law was given.

3. It is clear that not a single person is ever reported to have kept the Sabbath before Exodus 16. Not Abraham, not Noah, not Adam, not any other saint of God! You have no right to read into the Bible what is not there.

4. And Colossians 2:13-17 says that the Sabbath is part of the ceremonial law ("shadow of things to come") and thus nailed to the cross of Christ, and that no Christian is now to be judged concerning the Jewish dietary laws or feast days or Sabbaths.

5. The Bible clearly and expressly states that the Sabbath was a special sign between God and Israel and the Israelites were to keep the Sabbath (Exod. 31:13-17). The Sabbath is a special sign setting the Israelites

apart from others. So the Scripture expressly states.

6. Not one time in the entire New Testament is anybody commanded to keep the Sabbath. Remember, not one time!

7. The Lord Jesus Christ Himself "broke" the Sabbath. "Therefore the Jews sought the more to kill him, because he not only had broken the sabbath, but said also that God was his Father, making himself equal with God" (John 5:18). Notice the Bible does not say that the *Jews* said Jesus had broken the Sabbath, but says that He *had* broken the Sabbath.

2. Help for a Seventh-Day Adventist

Christians, Get Out Your Bibles and Learn as You Read

We answer questions raised in a letter from an Adventist friend.

"When Was Sabbath Changed to First Day of the Week?"

The answer is that the Sabbath was never changed from the seventh day to the first day of the week. The Sabbath was Saturday, the seventh day. It was first made known at Mount Sinai as a part of the Mosaic law (Neh. 9:14). It was a special sign between God and Israel only (Exod. 31:12-17). No one was ever commanded to keep the Sabbath before the Mosaic law was given. And no one was ever commanded to keep it after Christ came. There is not a single command in the New Testament for any Christian to observe the Sabbath. Rather, the Bible expressly commands that now no Christian is to keep the Sabbath (Col. 2:14-17).

The Lord's day is an entirely different day. It is not a Sabbath day, not given to the same people nor for the same purpose. The Sabbath was a day of rest, not necessarily a day of worship.

Jesus Did Not Keep the Sabbath but Broke It

You say, "Jesus observed the Sabbath command." I am sorry, but I must point out that the Bible expressly says He did *not.* John 5:17,18 proves conclusively that Jesus did not keep the Sabbath (Saturday, the Old Testament Sabbath), as follows:

"*But Jesus answered them, My Father worketh hitherto AND I WORK. Therefore the Jews sought to kill him because he not only HAD BROKEN THE SABBATH, but said also that God was his Father, making himself equal with God.*"

"He. . . had broken the sabbath," says the Scripture! And Jesus said about what He did that Sabbath, "My Father worketh hitherto, and I work." The way to keep the Sabbath was to *rest,* simply that and nothing more. The way to break it was to *work.* The command in the Ten Commandments is not to work. Exodus 20:10 says, "But the seventh day is the sabbath of the Lord thy God: *in it thou shalt not do any work* . . . ." When Jesus worked on the Sabbath, as He plainly said He did, He did not keep the Sabbath. And the next verse expressly says He broke the Sabbath. Notice, it does not say that the Jews *thought* He had broken the Sabbath, but that He "had broken the sabbath." He made the Sabbath, so He was Lord, that is, Boss of the Sabbath, and had the right to break it as He did.

Now you must never say again that Jesus observed the Sabbath, for He said He did not.

You forget what the Bible commands as the way to observe the Sabbath. It did not command to keep the Sabbath day by going to church, by worship, by teaching or preaching. No, none of these were commanded for Jews on their Sabbath. Rather, they were simply to *rest,* not to do *any work at all!* They were not even to build a fire on that day (Exod. 35:3). They could not even pick up sticks on the Sabbath, and one who did was stoned by God's command (Num. 15:32-36). They could not even pick up off the ground manna which fell from Heaven (Exod. 16:27,28). They were even forbidden to leave their home on the Sabbath: "abide ye every man in his place, let no man go out of his place on the seventh day" (Exod. 16:29). That is not tradition, but the Mosaic law. And Jesus did not keep that.

So you do not keep the Sabbath if you go out of your place, if you have a fire in your home, if you pick up food or sticks for a meal. Going to church is not keeping the Sabbath. The Sabbath was commanded as a day of *rest*, not as a day of worship. So Jesus did not keep the Sabbath.

And that proves, too, that the Old Testament Sabbath was ceremonial law, not moral law. Certainly Jesus never broke any moral law of right and wrong. He had a right to leave off any ceremony when its purpose was fulfilled as was true of the Sabbath (Col. 2:16,17).

Paul Preached in Synagogues Where a Crowd Would Be Assembled but Did Not Keep the Sabbath

You say, "Paul very definitely observed the Sabbath," and give references where Paul went to the synagogue to preach to Jews who met on Saturday then, as they do now. In the same paragraph you say, "It was Christ's custom to go into the synagogue on the Sabbath (Luke 4:16)."

So I answer, sure, both Christ and Paul went to the synagogues. Other New Testament preachers, too, went to Jewish synagogues many times and preached to the Jews assembled there on that day. For the same reason, I used to hold most of my street meetings on Saturday because I could preach to the larger crowds that assemble. But by doing that I am not keeping the Sabbath, and neither was Paul nor Christ! Paul definitely *did not* keep the Sabbath, as I have already shown Christ did not.

Where did you get the idea that going to church was keeping the Sabbath? The Bible never suggests such a thing. The Sabbath means *rest.* Jews were commanded that both men and beasts were to rest and do no work at all. Not once in the Bible was anyone commanded to assemble for worship on the Sabbath day. No special offerings were made on Saturday. Attending the synagogue is never mentioned in the Old Testament as a Sabbath duty, and, of course, not in the New Testament. Those who went did so because they wanted to worship, or for other reasons, but not as a way of keeping the Sabbath holy. To *rest* was to keep the Sabbath. To *work* broke it.

You argue that Paul and the saints of Troas met and broke bread on Monday. Why not take the simple Word of God that it was on the first day of the week, as Acts 20:7 says? Their day began at sundown. The first day of the week began at sundown, then Paul and others gathered, with many lights in the chamber, we are told, and he preached till midnight. Later, the same day, Sunday, they broke bread. Is it hard to believe what God says?

Neither Rome Nor Constantine Started the Observance of Sunday

It amuses me when one quotes Seventh-Day Adventist writers to mean that Emperor Constantine started Christians observing Sunday as a day of worship and rest. He did not. He simply followed the counsel of bishops who had long taught that Christians should observe Sunday as the Sabbath. It is not *the Sabbath,* but the Lord's day and should not be observed as a Sabbath.

But from the days of the apostles the first day of the week had been the special day of meeting by Christians in the church, as you see from Acts 20:7 and I Corinthians 16:2. If you would study the old church fathers and church history and "reliable ancient history," as you say, and not so much Adventist literature, you would see that what I have said is so.

You say that the only record you have is that Rome forced Sunday on the church. If that be so, then it seems clear that the only record you have is the Seventh-Day Adventist record. As a student for many years (once a college teacher), I know that there is not a single record in all church history of Rome changing the Sabbath from Saturday to Sunday. Seventh-Day Adventists say they did, and some Roman Catholics, anxious for the honor, say they did. But all Roman Catholics mean is that the apostles in New Testament times met on the Lord's day, Sunday, and churches adopted the plan of meeting on that day. That much certainly is clear from the New Testament records, if you study it with an open mind.

Catholics, of course, say that Peter was the first pope and therefore that the Catholic church did whatever the apostles did. Manifestly, that is false.

Methodist and Baptist pastors have made a great mistake in trying to teach that the Sabbath has been changed from Saturday to Sunday, and calling Sunday the Sabbath. Sunday is not the Sabbath and never was. It is "the Lord's day" instead, a different day with a different meaning. Sunday school is not the Sabbath school.

Yes, Sunday is named for the sun, but Saturday is named for the planet Saturn. It is simply not historically true that Christians began to worship on the first day of the week to please the sun worshipers. Nor did Jews begin to worship on Saturday to please Saturn worshipers. You have been deceived.

In the Millennium Jews Will Again Observe the Mosaic Law Picturing the Saviour Already Come

You say, "Jesus expected the prophecies to be observed when He gave the prophecies of Matthew 24," and that, "Sabbath will be observed in the new earth (Isa. 66:22,23)."

I am glad you mentioned those two Scriptures together, for they go together.

You remember that the Lord plainly said that the Sabbath is a sign, a special covenant between Him and Israel, a covenant that sets them apart from other nations. That is the statement of Exodus 31:12-17 and of Ezekiel 20:12. Now since Israel is to be restored to Palestine as a nation and is to start again observing the ceremonial laws which set them apart from Gentile Christians in this day, naturally they will again observe the day of rest, Saturday, which is the Jewish Sabbath.

Jesus in Matthew 24:20 certainly speaks of the time when Jews will again be in Jerusalem observing the Old Testament sacrifices, and observing the ceremonial oblations which for us New Testament Christians are already passed away. Look carefully at verse 20 where the Sabbath is mentioned. Then the next verse tells us plainly, "For then shall be great tribulation." It is the Great Tribulation that comes after the rapture of the saints and just before the Saviour brings us back to reign. Now look above verse 20 to verse 15, and see that it is the time of the "abomination of desolation, spoken of by Daniel the prophet."

It is Daniel 9:27 that tells us of the abomination of desolation, and the same verse tells how many of Daniel's people, the Jews, will be given a treaty, or covenant, by the prince, the Man of Sin, or Antichrist, allowing them to return to Jerusalem and start again their sacrifices and oblations. Then, in the midst of the week of years, he will stop the sacrifices and oblations, and according to II Thessalonians 2:4 he will enter the Temple (which Jews will rebuild for their Old Testament sacrifices) and claim to be God. With this in mind, Jesus leaves word for the Jews of that day to pray that their flight may not be on the Sabbath day, when a Jew really keeping the Saturday Sabbath was commanded to "abide ye every man in his place, let no man go out of his place on the seventh day" (Exod. 16:29). In that case Jews would be killed, since they could not run away and still observe the strict Jewish Sabbath.

Isaiah 66:22 and 23 tells us that both the new moons and the Sabbaths will be observed by Jews as a nation after their regathering, in the millennial reign of Christ. Note also that it is for Jews only, that their Levites and priests will be restored (vs. 21), and that Jewish ceremonial law forbidding swine's flesh, etc., will be enforced (vs. 17 in same chapter). But we know that Christians are plainly forbidden to keep these ceremonial laws about priests, sacrifices, diet, new moons and Sabbath days. See again Colossians 2:14-17.

No, the Pope Is Not Antichrist

You say, as you read in a Seventh-Day Adventist book, that the pope is the Antichrist, that his title, *Vic Arius, Filii Dei,* meaning "Vicar of the Son of God," shows his number to be 666. You do it thus:

VIC	ARIUS	FILII	DEI
5-1-500	1-5	1-50-1-1	500-1

Then you add all the above numbers and come to 666. But to do so, notice, you have to count "u" as "v," and have to violate all the rules of Roman numerals. You have IC to mean 501 when it would clearly mean 499 in Roman numerals. You have IV in the second word to mean 6 when it always means 4. Roman numerals are never counted that way. Always if smaller numbers are before larger ones it means the larger number less the smaller. IV means one less than five, for example.

By such farfetched methods do false cults try to prove what is not in the Bible. The purpose is to say that the Catholics changed from Saturday to Sunday, that the pope is the Antichrist, and so all who worship on Sunday take the "mark of the beast" and are lost! If you would read the Bible more, and prayerfully, and check up on the Scriptures here given, you would soon clear your mind of much rubbish. Second Thessalonians 2:7,8 says that the Man of Sin, the Son of Perdition, that Wicked one, has not been revealed, will not be till after the rapture, when the Holy Spirit who restrains him is taken out of the way. However bad his teaching and influence may be, the pope could not be the Antichrist. Nor could Sunday observance be the "MARK OF THE BEAST," since the beast has not appeared.

It Is Wrong to Accept as Inspired the Writings of Mrs. White

You say, rightly, "Let us study prayerfully, accept all the light Jesus unfolds to us, try the spirits to see if they speak according to the Word of God and accept only that which we know is inspired of God."

Now, if we accept only what we know is inspired of God, we must reject the writings of Mrs. White, officially claimed to be inspired of God. Maybe you did not know that, but you can verify that she, one of the first leaders and founders of the Seventh-Day Adventist movement, claimed to have, and others accepted the claim, writings inspired like the Bible. That puts the cult with Mormons, who claim the Book of Mormon is inspired. It puts Seventh-Day Adventists on the same plane with Christian Scientists, so-called, who claim Mary Baker Eddy's writings were inspired. It brings the curse on all who accept anything else as inspired besides the Bible, as you see from Revelation 22:18.

Try Seventh-Day Adventist teaching by the Bible. Do they teach salvation by works, or by grace alone? By works, of course; by Sabbath-keeping, by tithing, by law and commandments. But that is not the plan of John 3:16 or of Ephesians 2:8. It is the heresy Paul condemned so strongly in the Galatians, when he said they had fallen from grace in doctrine, and now taught salvation by the law. He said in Galatians 4:9,10:

"*But now, after that ye have known God, or rather are known of God, how turn ye again to the weak and beggarly elements, whereunto ye desire again to be in bondage? Ye observe days, and months, and times, and years.*"

That is the sin of Seventh-Day Adventism.

3. Hidden Heresies of Seventh-Day Adventists

A friend sent me a card, "What Seventh-Day Adventists Believe," and said, "The enclosed card seems orthodox and supported by biblical references. I would not call them heresies. Wherein do they err?"

I am glad to give you a brief analysis of the position of Seventh-Day Adventists stated on that card.

Unfortunately, heresy always presents itself in deceitful form. False doctrine has always involved some moral guilt also. So in II Corinthians 11:13-15 God warns us:

"*For such are false apostles, deceitful workers, transforming themselves into the apostles of Christ. And no marvel; for Satan himself is transformed into an angel of light. Therefore it is no great thing if his ministers also be transformed as the ministers of righteousness; whose end shall be according to their works.*"

So Satan makes sure that heresy always appears like orthodoxy. Wolves put on sheep's clothing, as Jesus said about false prophets in Matthew 7:15. And the worst heresies in the world pretend that their doctrine is founded on Scripture and they give Scripture references, though the Scriptures themselves do not always teach what the false doctrines try to teach.

I call your attention to some things in this statement of faith of Seventh-Day Adventists which a good Christian should question.

Truly Converted People Are Saved and Kept by Grace

In article 9 it says, "That those who are truly converted and love God will diligently study, and give heed to, His Word." And they give eight Scripture references and none of them say anything like that. The simple truth is that people who are converted do no always "diligently study" the Bible and do not always obey it in many matters. This is a part of the doctrine of salvation by works which they teach, and that one may keep saved by keeping on working.

Our Bodies Are Mortal, but Contrary to Adventist Teaching the Soul Lives Forever

Then article 11 on this card by Adventists says that man "is 'mortal' and must 'seek' for immortality." It would be good for you to check those references. Job 4:17 says, "Shall mortal man be more just than God?" Of course, we all know that man dies physically, and that "it is appointed unto men once to die" physically. But that is not what Seventh-Day Adventists mean by the statement.

It is true that I Corinthians 15:53 says that "this mortal must put on immortality" at the resurrection, to give a body that lives forever. But Seventh-Day Adventists use this kind of an innocuous and ambiguous statement in article 11 on this card to excuse the fact that they preach that the soul itself passes out of existence —that the soul sleeps and the body goes to the grave, and then the soul of lost people passes out of existence forever without eternal torment.

In article 13 Adventists say "that 'the dead know not any thing,'" referring to Ecclesiastes 9:5. But what Solomon meant in his reasoning recorded there in Ecclesiastes is that a dead body knows nothing. It had no reference to the state of the soul. On the contrary, the Bible clearly teaches that the rich man in Hell was conscious, and that Lazarus in Abraham's bosom was conscious and that Abraham was living. So they would pervert the Scriptures to teach that heresy and keep away from the Bible doctrine of eternal Hell.

So in article 14 they say "that the wicked will finally be utterly destroyed." But the Scriptures they give have to do with the destruction of the body and of torment in Hell and do not mean annihilation as Seventh-Day Adventists teach.

A False Division Between Ten Commandments and Rest of Bible, to Teach Keeping of the Jewish Sabbath

Other statements of their faith are sometimes incidental, teaching things that the Bible says nothing about, as in article 17 which teaches that we should have public footwashing services before partaking of the Lord's Supper. New Testament Christians never had footwashing as a public service or an ordinance of the church. The apostles did not so understand it and it is never commanded in the Scriptures.

Again, article 22 says "that God's moral law, written with His own finger, will 'stand fast forever and ever.'" But only the Ten Commandments were written with God's own finger physically. So what they are teaching is that the Ten Commandments is moral law, including the Sabbath, and that other commands in the Old Testament are not moral law. Both are false. The Sabbath is not moral law but ceremonial law which New Testament Christians are plainly commanded in Colossians 2:14-17 not to be judged by. And there are other clear moral standards in the Old Testament which are still binding today and repeated in the New Testament.

But the strict Seventh-Day Adventists' principle is that

the Ten Commandments are God's law and the rest is the law of Moses. So they go to that extreme to try to prove that the Jewish Sabbath ceremonially is still commanded for us today and is moral law. And so with article 23 "that the seventh day of creation week is God's 'perpetual' Sabbath." But in the Scriptures, the only place where the seventh day God rested is mentioned, nothing is said about it being perpetual or about identifying that with the Sabbath that Seventh-Day Adventists observe, in that passage referred to.

It is true that Hebrews 4:4 refers to this, that "God did rest the seventh day from all his works," but does not there discuss any perpetual Sabbath as a day. But it is talking about the rest and peace in Christ and the eternal rest. Verses 9 and 10 say, "There remaineth therefore a rest to the people of God. For he that is entered into his rest, he also hath ceased from his own works, as God did from his."

But our Seventh-Day Adventist friends do not give that reference because it doesn't refer to a Sabbath day and because they do not teach the eternal blessedness of those who have trusted in Christ and have eternal salvation and cannot be lost.

Article 26 says "that the personal, visible coming of Christ 'is near, even at the doors.'" But the only Scripture that says that is Matthew 24:33, which speaks of the regathering of Israel by the angels after the tribulation period (as vs. 29 above says), and has no reference to the present time before the rapture.

You see, Seventh-Day Adventists, like other false cults, put on a good front, but they deceive about what they teach.

A False Cult in Taking Mrs. White's Writing as Inspired

Summing it up, they are wrong in insisting that we

keep the Jewish Sabbath, wrong in teaching that Hell is not eternal torment, wrong in teaching that one can figure when Christ will return, and, of course, wrong in teaching a number of other matters.

Worst of all, I think, is they take the writings of Mrs. White as inspired like the Scriptures and base many of their teachings upon what she said, not on what the Scripture says. They teach with Mrs. White for example, a so-called "investigative judgment," which is said to have begun in 1844. And in this investigative judgment (said to be going on now), God will determine whether people are good enough to go to Heaven!

So we call Seventh-Day Adventism seriously wrong and unscriptural in doctrine.

4. Seventh-Day Adventist's Protests Answered

1. **Do Adventists Teach Tithing Essential to Salvation? Yes and Much More**
2. **Have They Claimed the 144,000 of Revelation 14 Are the Seventh-Day Adventists? Yes, They Claim They Are the Group Pictured in Chapters 12 to 17.**
3. **Has It Been the Deliberate Policy of Seventh-Day Adventist Preachers and Publishers to Keep Their Identity Secret, to Pose as Orthodox Christians and So Deceive?**

In a letter from an Adventist pastor concerning my pamphlet, *Sunday or Sabbath,* he begins: "Either the author was careless in his investigation or he was downright dishonest." Good men do not have to talk or write that way. And the character and maturity of any man would be questioned who starts out on that basis, speaking about a serious, scriptural, and widely accepted Bible teaching such as that pamphlet.

Teach Tithing as a Duty, and All Known Duty Essential to Salvation

1. He says, "We do not teach tithing is essential to salvation, or that SDA's are the 144,000." In the first place, many Seventh-Day Adventist teachers and preachers have taught and preached that tithing is essential to salvation. In that they only carry to its logical end the regular creedal position of all Seventh-Day Adventists. That position is, that when one is saved it is only "past sins" that are forgiven. They do not believe that anybody is now saved forever, has already everlasting life in the absolute sense. Mrs. White, the "prophetess" of Seventh-Day Adventists, is quoted in their book, *Answers to Objections,* by Francis D. Nichol (published by the Review and Herald Publishing Association, Washington, D.C.), page 402, as saying:

> Those who accept the Saviour, however sincere their conversion, should never be taught to say or to feel that they are saved. This is misleading. Every one should be taught to cherish hope and faith; but even when we give ourselves to Christ and know that He accepts us, we are not beyond the reach of temptation. . . . Only he who endures the trial will receive the crown of life.

Then Nichol comments on that on page 403:

> We accept all that the Bible says about our being saved here and now from past guilt and thus standing justified through the blood of Christ. But we accept also all that the Bible says about the dangers that beset us on the heavenly path upon which our feet have been placed, and of the need of constant watchfulness unto prayer if we are to reach the heavenly goal.

On page 409 Mr. Nichol says, speaking officially for Seventh-Day Adventists:

> Thus we escape, on the one hand, the false doctrine of Universalism; and on the other, the equally false doctrine

> of claiming full and final salvation for a man before he has endured "unto the end."

And for this reason Seventh-Day Adventists teach that the atonement is not completed, so that on page 408, Nichol says:

> Of those who charge us with teaching strange doctrines because we believe that Christ's work of atonement for sin was begun rather than completed on Calvary....

Now Seventh-Day Adventists clearly teach tithing as a duty, and that one can finally be saved only by doing his duty in everything that he knows. Nichol says on page 243:

> Here is our position: Only those will be saved who, having been redeemed by the grace of Christ, walk in obedience to all the light that God sheds on their way.

So they clearly teach repeatedly. And remember this is the official Adventist position. Since they teach that tithing is right, and required, a part of the law, and still binding, then when one has the Adventist teaching on the matter of tithing, he must "walk in obedience to all the light that God sheds on" his way, to be saved. And that would include tithing, of course. This is salvation by works, and besides, the official Seventh-Day Adventist position.

On page 119, again, Nichol, in the official statement of the Seventh-Day Adventist group, says:

> It is surely unfortunate that so many Christians remember only one portion of the statements of Christ. They preach much about the passive side of Christianity --of accepting Jesus Christ as a Saviour. But there is an active side as well, for Christianity embraces much more than the saving of a man from his *past* sins. It has to do with his living a sinless life. There is for the Christian a *doing* of God's will, a *keeping* of God's commandments, and a certain *working out* of his own salvation....

Teach That Revelation, Chapter 12 to 17, Specially Refer to the Seventh-Day Adventist Church

2. Your Seventh-Day Adventist preacher says, "We do not teach... that SDA's are the 144,000." Many Seventh-Day Adventists have taught it very expressly. For example, in *The Truth About Seventh-Day Adventism*, by Walter R. Martin, there is an extended chapter on "The Heart of Adventist Theology," endorsed November 4, 1959, by H. W. Lowe, Chairman of the Biblical Study and Research Group of the General Conference of Seventh-Day Adventists, Takoma Park, Washington 12, D.C. He says, "His presentation of our doctrines and prophetic interpretations as found on pages 47-86 is accurate and comprehensive." This statement is on page 15 of Martin's book. And on page 79 Martin quotes from a new book of Seventh-Day Adventists themselves, saying:

> XIV-2. "We believe that the prophecy of Revelation 12-17 points to the experience and work of the Seventh-Day Adventist Church...."

On page 80 he says:

> XIV-4. "Following as we do the principles of this historical school of prophetic interpretation, it is our conviction that the events portrayed in Revelation 14 to 17 are in process of fulfillment, or are about to meet their fulfillment."

At the bottom of page 79 he says:

> XIV-3. "Seventh-Day Adventists believe there are special truths for today we have been called of God to give. We definitely feel that we must emphasize certain neglected truths, must restore others that most Protestant bodies no longer stress and must continue the work of the Reformation...."

That is quoting from the most recent Adventist book,

Seventh-Day Adventists Answers to Questions on Doctrine. Note the official position is that Revelation, chapters 12 to 17, point to the experience and work of the Seventh-Day Adventist church, and that part in chapters 14 to 17 is in process of fulfillment now. So when a Seventh-Day Adventist preacher, preaching from that passage about the 144,000, in Revelation 14, says that represents Seventh-Day Adventists, he is simply saying what this official book really means. And an honest Seventh-Day Adventist ought not to dodge that question.

Now the pastor who wrote can find those statements on pages 178-190 in the book, *Seventh-Day Adventists Answers to Questions on Doctrine.*

Why Seventh-Day Adventist Preachers and Publishers Hide Their True Identity

He says, "On p. 21 about the Voice of Prophecy hiding its identity,—the speaker is clearly mentioned as a Seventh-Day Adventist on every broadcast and has been for many years. I listen. This is true of our TV broadcast, in fact, I know of none of our programs that hide our identity."

Well, some of us have made such a loud protest that some Seventh-Day Adventists are now beginning to announce who they are on some of their programs, not all of them, but there was a well-planned and intentional way of hiding their identity, and their preachers were openly taught to do so.

In the book, *Answers to Objections,* by Francis D. Nichol, published by the Review and Herald Publishing Association of Washington, D. C., Mr. Nichol says on page 421:

> It should not be difficult, therefore, for any reasonable person to see why Adventist ministers through the past years have sought first to cause people to see them simply as Christian preachers before announcing their Adventist connection.

On the same page, in the last paragraph, he says:

> It has undoubtedly been true in years past that Adventists could not have gotten a crowd out to hear them in certain cities, at least, if they had revealed their identity at the outset.

And on page 422 he says:

> In more recent years our activities have become so much better known that in many places the former distorted picture has been largely corrected. Accordingly, we are increasingly following the plan of announcing at the outset the Adventist sponsorship of the public meetings.

And what are the publishing firms named that publish Seventh-Day Adventist propaganda everywhere? They are the Review and Herald Publishing Association, the Southern Publishing Company, and others—never frankly and openly "The Seventh-Day Adventist Press" or "Seventh-Day Adventist Publishing House." Because our wide protest has caused some change in their plans, this does not change the fact that they were deliberately deceptive on that matter, and are often, still, and on purpose.

You may get *The Truth About Seventh-Day Adventism,* by Walter R. Martin, which is put out by Zondervan Publishing House, 1415 Lake Drive, S. E., Grand Rapids, Michigan 49506 *(out of print).* This book is really very generous to Seventh-Day Adventists, and the statements of their doctrines are exact quotations and with their approval. It shows that Seventh-Day Adventists have somewhat modified their teaching now and is more favorable but factual and comprehensive. Or you may get the book, *Answers to Objections,* by Francis D. Nichol, from the Review and Herald Publishing Association, Washington, D.C., or the newer book, *Seventh-Day Adventists Answers to Questions on Doctrine* (their official statement). For further reading, I suggest *The*

Seventh-Day Adventism Renounced by D. M. Canright, a classic, Baker Book House, (out of print).

And Seventh-Day Adventist leaders still call Mrs. White a prophetess who had the gift of prophecy and say that her writings were inspired, despite their many contradictions and obvious mistakes. And they still teach an "Investigative Judgment" going on since 1844, by which, they say, God checks over Christians to find out whether they are good enough to get to Heaven or not. And they still say the scapegoat in the Old Testament pictured Satan. They say that in 1844 there began a period of last days just before Christ's second coming.

5

The Tongues Heresy

1. Questions and Bible Answers About Speaking in Tongues
2. Letters on Tongues Question
3. Tongues Propaganda Inaccurate, Ignorant
4. Are Tongues People the Only Good Christians?

1. Questions and Bible Answers About Speaking in Tongues

"*And when the day of Pentecost was fully come, they were all with one accord in one place. And suddenly there came a sound from heaven as of a rushing mighty wind, and it filled all the house where they were sitting. And there appeared unto them cloven tongues like as of fire, and it sat upon each of them. And they were all filled with the Holy Ghost, and began to speak with other tongues, as the Spirit gave them utterance. And there were dwelling at Jerusalem Jews, devout men, out of every nation under heaven. Now when this was noised abroad, the multitude came together, and were confounded, because that every man heard them speak in his own language. And they were all amazed and marvelled, saying one to another, Behold, are not all these which speak Galileans? And how hear we every man in our own tongue, wherein we were born? Parthians, and Medes, and Elamites, and the dwellers in Mesopotamia, and in Judaea, and Cappadocia, in Pontus, and Asia, Phrygia, and Pamphylia, in Egypt, and in the parts of Libya about Cyrene, and strangers of Rome, Jews and proselytes, Cretes and Arabians, we do hear them speak in our tongues the wonderful works of God.*" —Acts 2:1-11.

There are good people who say that the gifts of the Spirit as named in I Corinthians 12:8-11 are no longer given as they were in New Testament times. More often men say simply that the gift of tongues particularly is no longer given.

I think, however, that they are greatly mistaken in two ways. First of all, they misunderstand what the gift of tongues, literally the gift of languages, was in Bible times. They think it was some ecstatic utterance of some heavenly language, given for enjoyment of the individual perhaps, a language which no one understood, neither the speaker himself nor anyone else. But they are mistaken. There was no such gift even in Bible times. The gift of tongues was the power, like that at Pentecost, to preach the Gospel to people who understood, in their own language but not the native language of the speaker. So he was given power to speak to them in their own tongue or language. That, I think, we can prove here.

And those who say that the gift of tongues is now passed away and is not given today as in the New Testament times, place a wrong interpretation on I Corinthians 13:8. That verse says, "Charity never faileth: but whether there be prophecies, they shall fail; whether there be tongues, they shall cease; whether there be knowledge, it shall vanish away." Such good people, even scholars, sometimes say that when the canon of Scripture was completed, there was no more need for this gift of tongues. But that is not what that chapter speaks of. It speaks of the time when we in resurrection bodies all speak the same language, and all the prophecies of God are fulfilled, and when our partial knowledge shall vanish away, replaced by perfect God-like knowledge in the resurrection.

Yes, all the gifts of the Spirit may be given as God Himself decides in these days, as they were when needed in New Testament times. God answers prayer now as He did then. People are saved by the supernatural work of the Holy Spirit now as then. Christian workers need to be filled with the Holy Spirit for soul-winning power and witnessing now as then.

However, in order not to be led away by false doctrine and foolish, unscriptural fanaticism, we need to understand what the Bible teaches about the scriptural gift of tongues. We need to go by the Bible instead of tradition or feeling. We need to have the power of God, not some rite or practice which we may enjoy but which does no good but often harm.

We believe that the simplest, clearest way to give the Bible teaching about what is called "speaking in tongues" may be to ask principal questions about it and give the answers from the Bible.

I. WHAT IS THE ONE CLEAR CASE OF MIRACULOUS GIFT OF TONGUES IN THE BIBLE?

It is: In the case at Pentecost as described above. Several facts stand out about this clear case.

1. The "other tongues" are simply foreign languages. The Greek word *glossa* is regularly used in the New Testament for language, as it is here.

Here people filled with the Spirit were given the power to speak to others so that "every man heard them speak in his own language." And there were others who said, "How hear we every man in our own tongue [or language], wherein we were born?" And in verses 9,10, and 11, about sixteen languages are named. Tongues in the Bible means languages. "Other tongues" simply means foreign languages.

2. In this case the ability to speak these foreign languages was clearly miraculous, that is, was a gift, the gift of "tongues" or the gift of languages. Here unlearned, uneducated Galileans spoke in other languages which they did not know, to these foreign-born Jews from various countries.

They spoke miraculously "as the Spirit gave them utterance" (vs. 4).

3. The reason for the gift of tongues here is obvious. Thousands of Jews from other countries were in Jerusalem who could not understand the native Aramaic which Jews spoke there. But Christians had been commanded to set out to preach the Gospel to every creature and had earnestly prayed, tarrying in Jerusalem until they were endued with power from on High, as they were commanded (Luke 24:49). There was no meaningless jabber, no useless ecstasy. They witnessed in the power of God to these unsaved people. Surely honest hearts can see the reason that God gave the gift here. There was a need for it.

4. God used these people, who preached the Gospel in various languages, to win three thousand souls that day, as we see in Acts 2:41. These Spirit-filled people were simply fulfilling the Great Commission to get out the Gospel.

5. It is important to notice that the foreign languages were incidental. They were not promised to these apostles and others who waited in the Upper Room. The apostles were simply promised enduement with power from on High, and they were given that. They were not waiting for tongues, not waiting for signs but for power and to preach the Gospel with power.

Now, if anybody claims to be "pentecostal," he ought to mean having soul-winning power as they had at Pentecost. And if anyone wants the "gift of tongues," or foreign languages, as it was in the Bible, he should mean what it meant at Pentecost.

II. DID NOT CORNELIUS AND HIS FAMILY AND FRIENDS SPEAK WITH TONGUES?

Yes, those saved of Cornelius' household spoke with

languages. The Bible does not say it was a miraculous gift of tongues but they did speak in more than one language. Acts 10:44-46 says:

"*While Peter yet spake these words, the Holy Ghost fell on all them which heard the word. And they of the circumcision which believed were astonished, as many as came with Peter, because that on the Gentiles also was poured out the gift of the Holy Ghost. For they heard them speak with tongues, and magnify God.*"

Now examine the Scripture carefully and do not read into it what God did not put into it.

1. They spoke in tongues, that is, when the Holy Spirit came upon them they witnessed in more than one language. Since the Bible does not say that it was miraculous nor give any divine reason to suppose it was miraculous, we should not say so.

2. The people here were people of more than one language, so it would be natural for them, in time of great blessing, to speak in more than one language. Cornelius and his soldiers were "of the Italian band," that is, from Rome, and they spoke Latin. Servants and friends who were natives of Palestine spoke the native Aramaic language, as did all the Jews. But the cultivated people among them also spoke Koine Greek too, which the Greek people, ruling the world before Rome, had spread all over the then known world. Thus all the New Testament was written in the Greek language. Paul preached everywhere in the Greek language.

In the Chicago area, in the midst of a great revival, many of the Swedish people praising God and testifying lapsed into their own native and beloved Swedish language, their mother tongue.

4. There is no need for people here to be given a miraculous gift of tongues. They could all understand Peter, so we need not list this case as one of miraculous gift of tongues.

It is important to notice that Peter and the Jews who were with him understood what these people said "for they heard them speak with tongues [languages], and magnify God." And when Peter told back in Jerusalem about the wonderful conversion of these people and their praises, "they held their peace, and glorified God, saying, Then hath God also to the Gentiles granted repentance unto life" (Acts 11:18). Their praises were understood and were evidence that they were saved.

III. DID NOT SOME MEN AT EPHESUS SPEAK IN TONGUES, WHEN PAUL BAPTIZED THEM AND LAID HIS HANDS UPON THEM?

Yes, we read in Acts 19:1-7 that at Ephesus Paul came and found certain disciples who had not understood about the blessed fullness of the Spirit. They had been taught by Apollos, who won them to Christ (see the preceding chapter). Apollos was from Alexandria. He had not been at Jerusalem at Pentecost, we suppose, so did not understand about the fullness of the Spirit until Aquila and Priscilla took him aside and taught him more perfectly (Acts 18:26). And when these believers understood that they should be wonderfully filled with the Spirit, they were baptized again. "And when Paul had laid his hands upon them, the Holy Ghost came on them: and they spake with tongues, and prophesied" (Acts 19:6).

However, the facts seem quite clear here that this was not a miraculous gift of tongues.

1. The Scripture does not mention "a gift of tongues." There is no mention in the context of a miracle.

There was no special need as at Pentecost to speak to people in their own language to get them saved.

2. These Spirit-filled people "prophesied," and that was the thing that the Apostle Paul urged upon Chris-

tians *instead of speaking in foreign languages.* First Corinthians 14:1-3 says:

"*Follow after charity, and desire spiritual gifts, but rather that ye may prophesy. For he that speaketh in an unknown tongue speaketh not unto men, but unto God: for no man understandeth him; howbeit in the spirit he speaketh mysteries. But he that prophesieth speaketh unto men to edification, and exhortation, and comfort.*"

So they did not speak in any language not known among them; they did witness for the Lord in the power of the Spirit.

3. Ephesus was a great cosmopolitan city, a center of the tremendous statue to the idol goddess Diana of the Ephesians. People of many nations passed through this city and so they would speak not only the Koine Greek and the Aramaic spoken by Jews there, but other languages. It is not surprising that with the wonderful enduement of power upon them they witnessed in the various languages known among them, in the power of God.

But why add to what God has said? If God did not say a gift of tongues, did not say it was miraculous, why should we say so? We had better keep the example clearly given at Pentecost to define the miraculous gift of tongues. We know we will be right regarding that example as a miraculous gift from God at Pentecost.

IV. DOES GOD EVER GIVE THE GIFT OF TONGUES TODAY?

I think the Bible is very clear on this matter on the following points.

1. The gift of the Holy Ghost, that is, the enduement of power to win souls, is promised to all in Acts 2:38,39,

". . . and ye shall receive the gift of the Holy Ghost. For the promise is unto you, and to your children, and to all that are afar off, even as many as the Lord our God shall call." The command of Ephesians 5:18, "And be not drunk with wine, wherein is excess; but be filled with the Spirit," certainly is for every Christian.

2. The various gifts of the Holy Spirit may be given at the discretion of the Lord, at any time, all through the ages, to people differently according to their need and God's will. In I Corinthians 12:7-11, we have this clear teaching:

"*But the manifestation of the Spirit is given to every man to profit withal. For to one is given by the Spirit the word of wisdom; to another the word of knowledge by the same Spirit; To another faith by the same Spirit; to another the gifts of healing by the same Spirit; To another the working of miracles; to another prophecy; to another discerning of spirits; to another divers kinds of tongues; to another the interpretation of tongues: But all these worketh that one and the selfsame Spirit, dividing to every man severally as he will.*"

Everybody may have some gifts of the Spirit. No one has all these gifts. But the Holy Spirit Himself divides "to every man severally as he will," not as men seek.

In the same chapter of I Corinthians 12:29 and 30, we read: "Are all apostles? are all prophets? are all teachers? are all workers of miracles? Have all the gifts of healing? do all speak with tongues? do all interpret?" The obvious answer is no. God did not intend for every Christian to work miracles, to have the gift of healing and speak in foreign languages.

3. It is only honest and fair to say that God mentions the gift of tongues and the interpretation of tongues, that is, the gift of foreign languages and the interpreta-

tion of foreign languages as the least and last of the gifts of the Spirit.

4. It is also important to notice that the gift of languages was very rarely given even in Bible times and we may suppose that the occasion for it in these days would be rare also.

5. It is also important to notice that no one is commanded to seek the gift of tongues or seek to "speak in tongues."

V. SHOULD NOT ALL CHRISTIANS BE BAPTIZED WITH THE SPIRIT LIKE AT PENTECOST?

1. Let us say we should have what God commanded them to have, the enduement of power from on High or, if you want to call it, the fullness of the Spirit, or baptized with the Spirit, or the gift of the Spirit, or the pouring out of the Spirit, or the anointing of the Spirit. Certainly the enduement of power from on High is for every Christian.

2. However, it would be foolish to expect the incidental miracles which happened at Pentecost. There was a great cyclonic "sound... of a rushing mighty wind, and it filled all the house where they were sitting" (Acts 2:2). Again "there appeared unto them cloven tongues like as of fire, and it sat upon each of them" (vs. 3). These miraculous manifestations were incidental. They were not promised to these Christians and were not expected. They did not happen to other Christians filled with the Holy Spirit in Bible times. There is no reason to suppose that we should expect that kind of experience today.

Then why should we talk in the sixteen different languages that people were given to talk in that day? Then that was a way to win people to Christ when without the gift of languages there would be nobody to hear and understand in their own tongue in which they were born. At other times conditions are not the same as at Pentecost. Since the circumstances are not the same, the language in which we speak the Gospel to them need not be the same. The essential thing is the enduement of power from God for witnessing.

3. We should want earnestly what they wanted, what they waited for those ten days, and what they had—the power to win souls. The great distinguishing mark at Pentecost was the power of God that helped them to win three thousand souls, as they started out to obey the Great Commission and get the Gospel to every creature possible. That is exactly what we should seek today.

VI. DOES NOT I CORINTHIANS, CHAPTER 14, DISCUSS THE GIFT OF TONGUES?

No, it discusses the use of unknown, foreign languages in the services.

1. The "gift of tongues" is not mentioned as being used at Corinth. There is no indication that what these people were doing at Corinth which needed some limitation and some rebuke, was the use of the miraculous gift of tongues. The Bible does not say so, therefore, we do not say so. They were simply using foreign languages.

2. One proof that these were natural languages, not miraculously given, is that Paul here soundly rebukes the way they used them. God never does give a miracle and then rebuke it. In many hundreds of cases of miraculous healings in the Bible, no one is ever rebuked for using that miraculous power. When God reproves a thing it is not miraculous. And so what was going on in the church at Corinth, as discussed in I Corinthians 14, was not the miraculous gift of tongues.

3. Paul referred to a natural language when he said in verse 18, "I thank my God, I speak with tongues more than ye all." Actually, in the original Greek it is not plural but singular—"a tongue." Paul was saying, "I speak in a foreign language more often than any of you." That foreign language was Koine Greek which Paul used in preaching all over the Roman Empire. It was the Greek language in which he wrote all his epistles and in which all the New Testament was written. Paul's native language was Aramaic, spoken by all the Jews in Palestine, but he regularly used this other language in preaching the Gospel. But he explained to these people, "Yet in the church I had rather speak five words with my understanding, that by my voice I might teach others also, than ten thousand words in an unknown tongue," that is, in a foreign language they did not understand. Paul speaks here of natural languages, not of the miraculous gift of tongues.

4. It was natural languages at Corinth which are discussed and rebuked in I Corinthians 14 because we are told that it was the "unlearned" who would not understand them. And verse 16 argues, "Else when thou shalt bless with the spirit, how shall he that occupieth the room of the *unlearned* say Amen at thy giving of thanks, seeing he understandeth not what thou sayest?" Paul was insisting that they speak in a language that people can understand when they give thanks so that the uneducated who do not know other languages can understand them and say amen.

Again in verses 23 and 24 he is further saying, "If therefore the whole church be come together into one place, and all speak with tongues [foreign languages, mind you], and there come in those that are unlearned, or unbelievers, will they not say that ye are mad?" Not heavenly languages but languages simply that *unlearned* people would not understand. And the next verse says, "But if all prophesy, and there come in one that believeth not, or one unlearned, he is convinced of all, he is judged of all." Even an uneducated man who would speak only his own native language would be convinced and blessed if one spoke in the power of the Holy Spirit in his own language.

Then this passage discusses natural languages and says unknown foreign languages should not be used in the church lest the unlearned people would lose the blessing or would think that you were crazy.

No, we do not undertand that the people at Corinth then were exercising a miraculous gift of tongues. Paul rebuked them and they are not a model we should pattern after.

So in verse 9 they are exhorted to use "words easy to be understood" in the church so others may understand and be blessed. And the rebuke of the heresy at Corinth ought to be a warning for any heresy in modern times on the tongues question.

VII. BUT ARE NOT ALL CHRISTIANS TO HAVE A GIFT OF TONGUES AS "THE INITIAL EVIDENCE OF THE BAPTISM OF THE HOLY SPIRIT"?

No, they are not.

1. The gift of foreign languages at Pentecost was not given as an evidence of the fullness of the Spirit. It was given so that people could hear the Gospel in their own language in which they were born and be converted. It served its purpose. The purpose was not as "an initial evidence of the baptism of the Holy Spirit."

2. The Bible never anywhere says that speaking in tongues is an evidence of the Holy Spirit power nor that it is to be the "initial evidence." That is a doctrine made

up by men without a particle of command to that end in the Bible.

3. We have many cases in the Bible of Christians filled with the Holy Spirit, where it is evident they did not speak with tongues. John the Baptist was "filled with the Holy Ghost, even from his mother's womb," as we learn in Luke 1:15 and the result was that "many of the children of Israel shall he turn to the Lord their God." Soul winning is the only evidence mentioned there.

In Luke 1:41 we find that "Elisabeth was filled with the Holy Ghost," but she talked in her usual language and the words she spoke are plainly given to us. She did not speak in any foreign tongue, any unknown tongue.

In the same chapter, in Luke 1:67, after the birth of John the Baptist, we read, "And his father Zacharias was filled with the Holy Ghost, and prophesied, saying . . . ," and the words of his prophecy are given, wonderful, Spirit-filled words, but they were in his regular language, not in any unknown tongue or jabber.

In Luke 3:21, 22, when Jesus was baptized and was first filled with the Holy Spirit, there is not a hint that He spoke in tongues.

In Acts 8:17 we read how the apostles came and laid hands on the new converts won by Philip in Samaria: "Then laid they their hands on them, and they received the Holy Ghost." But there is no hint that they talked in any foreign language or any unknown tongue.

In Acts 9:17 we find that Ananias came to the new convert, Paul, laid his hands on him and said, "The Lord, even Jesus . . . hath sent me, that thou mightest receive thy sight, and be filled with the Holy Ghost." And Paul received his sight, was baptized and set out to preach but there is not a hint that he spoke in some foreign language or unknown tongue or had any "initial evidence" of language at the time.

4. In human history, the greatest soul winners, the

most Spirit-filled, mighty men of God, have had soul-winning power when the Holy Ghost was on them, but they did not speak in some miraculous gift of tongues or unknown tongue.

There was Luther, Spurgeon, Wesley, Finney, Moody, Torrey, Chapman, Billy Sunday, and others who won their thousands and hundreds of thousands. They did not seek, they did not have, they never claimed to have any special sign of "tongues." No, it is illogical, unscriptural and untrue to facts to say that one should have "speaking in tongues" as the "initial evidence of the baptism of the Holy Ghost." It simply is not true in the Bible nor in human experience and is not taught in the Scriptures.

VIII. WHAT RULES ARE GIVEN IN I CORINTHIANS 14 LIMITING THAT HERESY OF FOREIGN LANGUAGES AT CORINTH?

1. The real gift of tongues, the miraculous gift of languages, is not for all, as clearly taught in I Corinthians 12:29 and 30. But the Holy Spirit divides "to every man severally as he will" (I Cor. 12:11). The gift of tongues is the last mentioned and least of all the gifts.

2. If one could speak with all the languages of men and angels without Christian love and anxiety to bless others he would be as sounding brass and a tinkling cymbal (I Cor. 13:1). Even two chapters before the fourteenth chapter Paul was approaching their heresy and confusion on this matter of foreign languages.

3. People are to "desire spiritual gifts, but rather that ye may prophesy" (I Cor. 14:1). Witnessing for Jesus in the power of the Holy Spirit is the thing we should seek, not to talk in some foreign language.

4. Five words understood are better than ten thousand words not understood (vs. 19).

5. All the speaking and witnessing and the use of heavenly gifts are for the purpose of teaching others and blessing others and so they should be in "words easy to be understood" (vs. 9).

6. It would be silly to play a harp or organ or trumpet without an understandable tune. So it is silly to speak words in a language that people present do not understand (vss. 7-10). Speaking things that only God understands because it is in some foreign language is here plainly forbidden.

7. Speaking in foreign languages that people do not understand makes one seem like a barbarian (vs. 11), and makes it so uneducated people cannot understand and say amen (vs. 16). And so unsaved people and uneducated people will think you are crazy (vs. 23).

So the plain order is given, "If any man speak in an unknown tongue [an unknown language], let it be by two, or at the most by three, and that by course; and let one interpret. But if there be no interpreter, let him keep silence in the church." If he cannot speak the language of people present, "let him speak to himself, and to God."

8. And on this matter evidently women have more temptation than men, so the Lord in this connection says, "Let your women keep silence in the churches: for it is not permitted unto them to speak; but they are commanded to be under obedience, as also saith the law" (vs. 34).

In conclusion, let me say it seems shocking that all of us have a tendency to be interested in the incidental and secondary things instead of in the one great business of getting people saved. When people think of Pentecost they are not even concerned that three thousand people were saved. People speak of "the baptism of the Holy Ghost," and they do not want or do not get an enduement of power from on High.

IX. HOW DO YOU EXPLAIN THE MANY PEOPLE WHO CLAIM AN ACTUAL EXPERIENCE OF SPEAKING IN UNKNOWN TONGUES?

ANSWER: Yes, thousands do claim such an experience. They claim that something takes over and they speak words they do not understand; they have an emotional experience and they think that is "the initial evidence of the baptism of the Holy Ghost, or the gift of tongues."

Many say that we have never experienced "the blessing" they claim, and thus cannot judge on this matter whether it is right or wrong.

1. However, that argument is silly. I have never been drunk, but I know by the Bible that, "Wine is a mocker, strong drink is raging: and whosoever is deceived thereby is not wise" (Prov. 20:1). I know by the Bible that, ". . . nor drunkards. . . shall inherit the kingdom of God" (I Cor. 6:10). Bible Christians are not to go by an emotional experience or feeling but by the plain Word of God. Our emotions are to go along with the Bible and we are not to twist the Bible to go along with our emotional experiences.

2. The experience of those who "talk in tongues" condemns the doctrine. Often shameful confusion in such services leads to mockery by the unsaved and scandal before the public. Women preachers are prominent often among those who "talk in tongues," and they disobey the plain command of the Bible. And how often has some woman preacher argued with me about tongues when her own husband is unsaved.

Many good Pentecostal people preach and witness

and win souls, but those who stress tongues the most win the fewest souls. The doctrine that God wants to give perfect healing and health to all prominent in the tongues movement is belied by the multitude of frustrated people who have heard them and prayed, yet were not healed. The experience does not prove their doctrine that all should "talk in tongues," but rather condemns it.

3. It is a sad commentary on the Pentecostal movement that the actual spiritual results at Pentecost are not repeated in the Pentecostal services. At Pentecost there was the mighty power of God; those who were filled with the Spirit spoke to people in their own language in which they were born; they got three thousand people saved. That is not what happens in the "speaking in tongues" in Pentecostal circles. So what happens is not "pentecostal" in the factual Bible sense and should not be called that.

4. But how do we explain the experience that some people have?

Well, some are intentional frauds. A friend of mine, a preacher, who had been active in the Pentecostal movement, demonstrated to me how he had done it. And he said that many others did it the same way, deliberately pretending to speak in an unknown language.

Others, very sincere, have it drummed into them for hours and sometimes weeks and months, so they become so brainwashed that they subconsciously begin to repeat the jumble of sounds they have heard. When the mental controls are released and relaxed, the subconscious takes over and they think that they are saying something wonderful though they have no idea what.

On the other hand, some, after being delivered, have told me that they were influenced by demons.

Many doubtless are sincere but look for and get the psychological reaction they have been taught to expect.

5. The one final answer is that the present-day experiences of talking in tongues are not what they had in Bible times. There is not a single record of any such service in the Bible and not a single command that we should seek such an experience.

2. Letters on Tongues Question

We Need New Testament Power, Not Some Uncommanded Tongue

Dear Brother A————:

Thank you for your letter. You have written kindly and at length and I am grateful for it.

"Praying in the Spirit" Does Not Mean Foreign Languages

However, Ephesians 6:18, "Praying always with all prayer and supplication in the Spirit," has nothing to do with foreign languages and no Bible commentator through the years, as far as I know, has thought so. It would not even come to the mind of any Christian who knows what it is to pray in the Spirit or pray with the Spirit's leading and help as all Christians can and sometimes do. You see, you start out with the thing already settled in your mind and then you, without being conscious of it, twist Scriptures around to fit what you already have in your mind.

Likewise, in I Corinthians 14:13-15 Paul is plainly saying that when he prays he will not only be praying in the Spirit but praying so people can understand him at the same time, and he will not only sing with the Holy Spirit but will sing so people can understand it at the same time. There is not a word there nor anywhere else in the Bible to indicate that people ought to sing or pray in a tongue unknown to them. The gift of the Spirit is very plainly described in a case at Pentecost when people spoke to others in their own tongue in which they were born and thus gave them the Gospel and three thousand were saved.

And again, even a most casual reading of I Corinthians 14 shows that Paul was rebuking talking in a foreign language which people could not understand and forbidding them to speak in any foreign language unless someone would tell them what was said.

We Want New Testament Blessings but Not What God Never Commanded or Promised

Now you say, "I am also aware that many will state that these things were fine for that day, but they say we don't believe that they apply now . . . ." But I say nothing like that. I say we need all of New Testament Christianity, but, not what they never had.

And you need not argue with me that God often heals the sick in answer to prayer. Rather, you should have read my book on *Prayer—Asking and Receiving* where I tell many remarkable and wonderful cases of healing in answer to prayer. I am for New Testament Christianity. I am not for imitation, a fake, different from what they had then.

And you say, "Don't you think it is time we started believing?" Yes, I certainly do.

I think we ought to come back to putting first things first. And the first thing in the Great Commission is to get the Gospel out and get people saved. And the baptism of the Holy Spirit is plainly promised as "an enduement of power from on high" for witnessing (Luke 24:46-49 and again in Acts 1:8). And I have been wonderfully baptized with the Holy Ghost, have been endued with power from on High, I have seen tens of thousands of people saved, I do believe the Bible, I have seen marvelous, wonderful answers to prayer, hundreds of them. And I do not like for some Pentecostal people, some of whom never did win souls much, to run down Bible-believing, soul-winning, Spirit-filled preachers who do far more for God than they do in some cases, just because we do not talk in tongues.

Such Pentecostal people will find it very hard to be accepted as good Christians as long as they maintain a proud and haughty attitude, a "holier-than-thou" attitude toward other Christians who are obviously as good Christians as they are. And in many cases they suffer more for Jesus, have more answers to prayer and win more souls than many of the most bitter-talking Pentecostal people.

Again thank you for writing, dear friend, and thank you for being kind.

In Jesus' name, yours,
John R. Rice

Soul Winning Is the Bible Evidence of the Fullness of the Spirit

Dear Brother P————:

Thank you for your good letter just received. I am glad to hear from you, and I thank God for your devotion to Christ.

I have gone over your letter carefully, and I think that I can answer your questions in a way that will help to clarify the issues in your mind. You say, "I heartily agree the church's greatest task is soul winning and also that the Holy Spirit is given for that purpose, yet how can we judge one's spiritual depth or commitment on this basis... ?

"Nowhere does the Scripture say to my knowledge they knew they were filled with the baptism of the Holy

Spirit for they won many souls. You would not want to state it that way, would you?"

But you see, while you really say that you agree with me that the church's greatest task is winning souls, you do not actually believe that the first duty of every Christian is to win souls, that what God is most concerned about is seeing people saved, and that the fullness of the Spirit is given particularly for soul-winning power. If you ever got that straight in your mind and believed it, then the importance of the so-called "evidence" of talking in tongues would fade away.

Soul winning is the thing that God is most pleased with and the thing that He commands the most plainly of every Christian. Then, why would not the Lord be more pleased for you to win souls than for you to talk in tongues without winning souls? Why would not the man be a better Christian who won more souls, even if he did not talk in tongues? You see, you do not really believe that soul winning itself is the main thing, or you have not made it so in your own plans or you could not put the matter of talking in tongues the better evidence of pleasing God than soul winning.

Again, you have neglected a good many Scriptures, I think, or you would see that the Lord Himself put soul winning as the inevitable result of the fullness of the Spirit. He said in Acts 1:8, "But ye shall receive power, after that the Holy Ghost is come upon you: and ye shall be witnesses unto me both in Jerusalem, and in all Judaea, and in Samaria, and unto the uttermost part of the earth."

Here Jesus plainly said that the result of the coming of the Holy Spirit upon the disciples would be witnessing for Christ in power. He did not promise tongues, but He did promise power in that verse. So, when the people got the power to win souls and witness for Jesus with soul-saving results, they did not need any other evidence.

That is what Jesus said also in Luke 24:46-49:

"*Thus it is written, and thus it behoved Christ to suffer, and to rise from the dead the third day: And that repentance and remission of sins should be preached in his name among all nations, beginning at Jerusalem. And ye are witnesses of these things. And, behold, I send the promise of my Father upon you: but tarry ye in the city of Jerusalem, until ye be endued with power from on high.*"

Now, see carefully that Jesus said that repentance and remission of sins should be preached, but that they should first have the power of God to do it, and then they would witness for Him. So, they waited in Jerusalem until the power came and then they witnessed. Isn't that saying that the one great direct purpose of the fullness of the Spirit was to win souls?

About John the Baptist, the Scripture says, "He shall be filled with the Holy Ghost, even from his mother's womb. And many of the children of Israel shall he turn to the Lord their God" (Luke 1:15,16). Doesn't the Lord here connect the fullness of the Spirit with soul winning? Not one time does the Bible ever promise that people would talk in tongues when they were filled with the Spirit, but it does clearly promise that they will win souls when they are filled with the Spirit. So why could not disciples today be like those in Bible times and so seek what the Lord commanded them to seek, that is, power from on high to witness for Him, and be content with that? If I need the power to speak in some other language to win souls, then, of course, God could give it today, just as He did it at Pentecost. But again, what He had in mind was winning souls, and that is what we ought to have in mind. And there would be no other reason in the Bible for talking in foreign tongues, except as there was somebody who needed the Gospel in such tongues.

Again, in Acts 11:24 the Bible says about Barnabas, "For he was a good man, and full of the Holy Ghost and of faith: and much people was added unto the Lord." Doesn't that Scripture plainly say that because Barnabas was filled with the Holy Ghost and had faith, much people were saved?

No, the Learned Preachers Would Not Have the Better Evidence

You say that if soul winning is the greatest thing with God, "Preachers would sure have the advantage, wouldn't they? Wouldn't the laity who perhaps live in sparse areas have only a small evidence; while well trained preachers have much evidence in mass meetings?"

My dear brother, are you trying to excuse yourself for not winning souls? You should remember that the Great Commission is not primarily given about preaching in a pulpit. In Mark 16:15 the Great Commission says, "Go ye into all the world, and preach the gospel *to every creature.*" So, the best way of soul winning is to individuals, and the simple truth is that many lay people win more souls than most preachers do.

I knew a good woman in Dallas, Texas, a little seamstress, who won 360 souls in one year, and many of them were adult men and women; some were hardened sinners. My wife wins more souls than most preachers do, often one or two or three a week, without ever speaking in public to lost sinners—just visiting in poor homes. I know a farmer who for two years won from 1 to 23 people every single week. One day a man sent in 14 decision slips from my pamphlet, "*What Must I Do to Be Saved?*" He had gone out in personal work, gotten these people saved, and then gotten them to read the pamphlet and sign the decision form in their own handwriting, and then he had sent them in.

And so, the theological training or preaching to big

crowds is not the easiest and the best way to win souls in every case. And if a preacher has mighty power and wins many souls, God will give him greater opportunities to win more souls. And so with a layman. One ought not to argue about the proposition that the one thing Jesus came for was to win souls, and the one thing He commanded His disciples the most clearly is the Great Commission, that is, to go out and preach the Gospel to every creature and get people saved. And it is abundantly clear from the clear statements of Jesus that what the fullness of the Spirit was for was to enable them to do what He commanded them to do about soul winning.

Why Should We Seek Some "Experience" Instead of the Power Promised?

You say, "Do you believe that in Acts 2 they waited to see if they were going to win souls before they accepted the fact they were baptized with the Spirit?" You say, "You state your filling is scriptural, but your evidence takes time, which was immediate in the Bible accounts."

But your trouble, dear brother, is that you start out with a proposition that you are seeking an experience. The disciples started out with the proposition that they were commanded to win souls and they were eager to get at it, and as soon as God opened the door and led them, they started to work at it. You see, you have made so much of the matter of speaking in tongues as an experience that your primary thought is about that itself. God has in mind power for witnessing. You have in mind some experience of feeling or emotion or assurance or some gladness or something else you can talk about, but the Bible never taught anybody to seek that experience and you are off the track of New Testament Christianity that far when you seek an experience after you are saved instead of seeking to have God's power to do God's business—soul winning.

At Pentecost, why should it matter to Peter and others whether they had some mighty evidence? They had been commanded to tarry until they be endued with power. They were promised that they would then be witnesses in the power of God. Now, at the day of Pentecost Jerusalem was filled with people. They were clearly led to begin their preaching and they did. The power of God was obvious. There were other signs. There was the supernatural sound of a rushing mighty wind that filled the house. There were visible tongues of fire that sat on the people. There were such incidental miracles, but God had not promised them; they were not always repeated. They were incidental to Peter and they ought to be to us, just like the matter of tongues was incidental then, and it ought to be incidental now. If there is some reason for God to have me talk in tongues in a foreign language to somebody who could not understand English, I would be glad to speak in a foreign language to him if God would give me the power. I see no reason to seek it, if there is no earthly use of it, and if it is not commanded in the Bible, as it certainly is not.

Some people seek an experience which they call "sanctification," but they are wrong in calling any such experience the baptism of the Holy Spirit in the Bible pattern. Instead of seeking an experience, they ought to be seeking the power of the Holy Spirit to witness for Jesus. Other people think of talking in tongues and they seek the tongues. They ought to be seeking for the power to win souls as the Lord commanded.

You say, "Your evidence takes time." Well, I am willing for the evidence to wait as long as people are saved. That is all I want, and that is all I think God wants. At least, that is the main thing with God and it ought to be the main thing with me. If I have waited on God and He gives me leadings where to go and gives me the message, I can trust Him to give the power. So I wait on Him for His enduement, and I do what He said the best I can.

Why Not Rejoice in Scriptural Soul Winning Instead of Liturgical Churches Speaking in Tongues?

You say, "I have read the Episcopal clergyman's book, *Tongue Speaking*, by Morton T. Kelsey. I rejoice in God pouring out His Spirit in this manner in so many of the major denominations." But again, you are not talking about what God is talking about. That Episcopal rector is not talking about what the New Testament is talking about. The Lord Jesus was talking about a mighty supernatural power that led three thousand souls to Christ in one day. The Rector is talking about signs and wonders, while he goes on sprinkling babies and while he goes on with the formal church services. I remember that the Episcopal rector in Wheaton, Illinois, where I lived, who had the article in the *Saturday Evening Post,* had dances in his church on Saturday night, and had healing meetings Sunday morning. That may give you great rejoicing, but it does not give me rejoicing.

You say, "We sincerely yearn for all of Christendom to become alive with the flame of baptism of the Holy Spirit and fire that John the Baptist spoke regarding." Then you ought to be rejoicing in the men with whom I associate who have won thousands of souls year after year. For example, my good friend, Dr. Lee Roberson, and the Highland Park Baptist Church in Chattanooga, has baptized over a thousand converts a year every year for eighteen years (1970). That is like New Testament Christianity. Dr. Jack Hyles, pastor of First Baptist Church in Hammond, Indiana, had over twenty-five hundred public professions of faith last year (1970), over fifty a Sunday in His church. And he wins them day after day, week after week, in house-to-house soul winning, and so do many, many others. And may I speak modestly: everywhere I go in these conferences on soul winning and revival, we hear the most wonderful stories of people saved, of prayers answered, often of people healed, and of other wonderful works of God. New Testament Christianity is not for people to go on in their modernism and go on in their formalism and go on in their unscriptural sprinkling of babies and their unconverted church membership while they talk in tongues. God's plan is for us to simply have God's power to do God's business and set out to win souls.

Now, I will tell you what I think you ought to do. You set out to win at least a hundred souls to Christ this year. That is not very many. I know a number of my office workers who win that many. But you get your mind on that and work primarily at that, do a lot of house-to-house personal soul winning, and then you write to me and I will be much more impressed about your genuine understanding of the baptism of the Spirit.

Nowhere in the Bible Is Speaking in Tongues Given as "Evidence"

Oh yes, another thing. You say, "I am sure you agree in all instances they had immediate evidence." You mean that in Bible times, always, when people were filled with the Holy Spirit they talked in tongues? That certainly is not true. It was not true of John the Baptist in Luke 1:15 and 16. It was not true of all the disciples in Acts 4:31. It was not true of Barnabas, as far as we know, as we see from Acts 11:24. It was not true about Paul the apostle, who was filled with the Holy Spirit in Acts 9:17. At Pentecost, there was a reason for talking in foreign languages to people who could understand foreign languages. In Cornelius' household there were men of different nationalities. Cornelius himself was of the Italian band and his soldiers were Italians. His servants, evidently Jews in the land of Israel, spoke Aramaic. In fact, when they talked in foreign languages it may not have been supernatural at all, but each one in his own language praising God because he had been saved. The Bible does not say it was a miracle, does not say it was a gift of tongues. We do not know that they were filled with the Spirit as soon as they were saved, and that is well and good. But the tongues are not said to be miraculous, and you and I ought not to speak boldly about it where the Bible does not speak.

And so with those disciples in Acts 19:1-7. They talked in foreign languages, and whether it was supernatural or not we do not know; the Bible does not say. You see, you have an idea and the word "tongues" means to you a certain supernatural manifestation, but in the Bible it simply means languages. And in I Corinthians 14 we have clear instructions showing that they had a false use of tongues which was not supernatural which Paul rebuked. I agree that at Pentecost when there was a reason for it, in order to preach the Gospel to the people in their own language, they spoke in foreign languages and not in "tongues" as you mean it. Since there is no occasion for me to talk in a foreign language when I have been filled with the Spirit, I have not, of course. So I say if your experience is like that at Pentecost and you preach to people in their own language in which they were born, that would be scriptural. If you talked some foreign language and nobody understood it, that was not scriptural and certainly not Pentecostal. In my case, mine clearly was Pentecostal because I received power to witness for Jesus exactly like the Bible promised.

Again, thank you for your letter.

In Jesus' name, yours,
John R. Rice

3. Tongues Propaganda Inaccurate, Ignorant

Someone sent me a pamphlet, *Baptists and the Baptism of the Holy Spirit,* put out by the Full Gospel Businessmen's Fellowship International. Now it is true that Christians ought to have New Testament Christianity with its gifts and power and blessed soul-winning results today. It is true that many groups, Baptists and others, have formal, cold, powerless services when they ought to be filled with the Spirit and ought to have the joy and power and blessing which New Testament Christians had. Many miss the blessing of Holy Spirit power. Many fail to pray for healing when needed. I know it is not always God's will to heal the sick; I know it often is. It is always right to pray.

However, Pentecostal people and those promoting the tongues heresy have capitalized on this lack, to lead spiritually immature but earnest Christians into the foolish, unscriptural business of "talking in tongues."

The Bible is very clear as to the meaning of the fullness of the Spirit. Jesus plainly said in Acts 1:8, "But ye shall receive power, after that the Holy Ghost is come upon you: and ye shall be witnesses unto me both in Jerusalem, and in all Judaea, and in Samaria, and unto the uttermost part of the earth." So when the fullness of the Spirit came at Pentecost, they had three thousand people saved and baptized.

It is true that some there talked in foreign languages.

They were known foreign languages, and God gave some people the miraculous power to speak in those languages for the very sensible reason of getting out the Gospel. So people who heard them said, "And how hear we every man in our own tongue, wherein we were born?. . . we do hear them speak in our tongues the wonderful works of God" (Acts 2:8,11). But the Spirit-filled preaching and witnessing at Pentecost with thousands of people being saved is entirely different from the fanatical, unscriptural "talking in tongues" so widely promoted among Pentecostal people and by which they mislead many earnest but ignorant Christians.

The unscriptural and often foolish, ignorant, and irresponsible teachings of these ardent proselyters are evident in this little pamphlet, *Baptists and the Baptism of the Holy Spirit.* We call your attention to some of the indefensible statements in the book.

It Says That "Dwight L. Moody, Charles Finney, and Others Testify to Speaking in Tongues as They Received the Baptism of the Holy Spirit"

Under Foreword, page 2, Jerry Jensen, compiler of the book, says,

> From the vivid accounts of the mighty moving of the Holy Spirit in the Book of Acts, through the great revivals of yester-years when Dwight L. Moody, Charles Finney and others testified of speaking in other tongues as they received the Baptism with the Holy Spirit, we are brought today, to another mighty outpouring of the Spirit of God on people of all denominations.

Now anybody who wanted to know could know whether or not "Dwight L. Moody, Charles Finney and others testified of speaking in other tongues as they received the Baptism with the Holy Spirit." And the above statement in regard to Dwight L. Moody and Charles

G. Finney is simply absolutely false, utterly untrue.

I have read every book available on the life of D. L. Moody, including the famous *Life of D. L. Moody* by his son, including *D. L. Moody a Worker in Souls* by Gamaliel Bradford, including *Moody Still Lives* by Moody's son-in-law, A. P. Fitt, including Goodspeed's *The Wonderful Career of Moody and Sankey in Great Britain and America.* I have the biography of Sankey by Charles Ludwig, titled: *Sankey Still Sings;* the life of Mrs. D. L. Moody; I have a book of reminiscences by Farwell; I have the large book by J. Wilbur Chapman, a close associate of Moody, on his life. And I have the most thorough and complete annotated bibliography concerning D. L. Moody by Dr. Wilbur M. Smith. Anyone who wants to know can know that Moody told plainly when he was filled with the Spirit in Wall Street, New York, and there is not a mention by Moody nor by any of his reputable biographers, nor in the discussions by his associate, R. A. Torrey, to indicate that he ever spoke in tongues. That is simply untrue. The statement is surely made in willing ignorance, not, we hope, in intentional deceit.

One writer, Boyd, casually speaking of how young men in Great Britain went out to win souls and witness for Jesus, compared their witness to the preaching at Pentecost and used the word "tongues" for languages as it is meant in the Bible. He did not indicate, and he did not believe, that these converts talked in any so-called heavenly language as used by the Pentecostal people in the tongues movement. Moody himself never did. It seems to me inexcusably deceitful and immoral to say that Dwight L. Moody "testified to speaking in other tongues" as he "received the Baptism of the Holy Spirit." And if anybody doubts about that, he should read the amazing wealth of material in print on the life of D. L. Moody, should read D. L. Moodys' own sermons on the Holy Spirit. No, Moody did not "speak in tongues" nor did he teach others to do so.

It is equally false that Charles G. Finney "testified to speaking in tongues." One of the books that has greatly influenced my life is the biography of Charles G. Finney. There he himself wrote in great detail of his conversion, of his "baptism of the Holy Ghost," of his wonderful revival career through the years. I have read with blessing his *Revival Lectures.* And neither in his own story of his life (his story of his conversion, the story of the "baptism of the Holy Ghost") nor in his *Revival Lectures* nor in his book of *Systematic Theology,* does Finney report that he talked in tongues or teach that anyone else should talk in tongues in the Pentecostal fashion, in connection with the fullness of the Spirit. How can one who would make such unfounded claims be trusted as a writer or teacher in spiritual matters?

From time to time ignorant and fanatical "tongues" people have published that this writer spoke in tongues. Not long ago I had a letter asking if it were true, as Pentecostal people were saying, that Evangelist Hyman Appelman spoke in tongues. He did not, of course, and does not believe in it. I have on my desk a recent sermon which he sent to me, on the question of the fullness of the Spirit, and I know his position intimately and well. It has been widely stated by some of these people that Billy Sunday talked in tongues; and of course, he did not. Such false statements are inexcusable. To deceive those who do not have access to a great store of historical material is sinfully wrong.

I have made a careful study of the lives of great soul winners, and I particularly sought for Bible-based material on the fullness of the Holy Spirit and the power of Pentecost. In my large book, *The Power of Pentecost,* one full chapter is on "How Great Men of God Were Filled With the Holy Spirit," and there I give in detail the personal testimonies of Moody, Torrey,

Chapman, Spurgeon, and Billy Sunday—their own statements on the matter of the Holy Spirit's fullness. The great soul winners of the ages have not "talked in tongues," did not teach it, did not believe it. The people who have given the best evidence of being "baptized with the Holy Ghost" have been those who had the Bible evidence, that is, "Ye shall receive power, after that the Holy Ghost is come upon you: and ye shall be witnesses unto me," as Jesus said (Acts 1:8).

There Is a Careless Twisting and Misinterpretation of Scriptures to Fit Their Tongues "Experience"

In II Peter 1:20 and 21 the Scripture says, "Knowing this first, that no prophecy of the scripture is of any private interpretation. For the prophecy came not in old time by the will of man: but holy men of God spake as they were moved by the Holy Ghost."

In other words, God has a divinely given meaning in the Scriptures and as the Scofield center reference note says, no Scripture is of "its own interpretation; i.e. not isolated from all that the Word has given elsewhere." So no one has a right to take a Scripture out of its context and make it mean something besides the honest and face-value meaning the Scripture itself gives. And II Peter 3:16 speaks of Scripture "which they that are unlearned and unstable wrest, as they do also the other scriptures, unto their own destruction."

Our Pentecostal friends, at least those who are "unlearned and unstable," wrest the Scriptures, twisting them to fit their own "experiences" or opinions. That is wrong and dangerous. And, unfortunately, in this pamphlet, *Baptists and the Baptism of the Holy Spirit*, put out by the Full Gospel Businessmen's Fellowship International, that is what happens.

For example, in the first of these articles by Baptists, printed to promote "talking in tongues," Rev.

John H. Osteen gives a fantastic interpretation of Ezekiel's valley of dry bones (Ezek. 37:1-14). The article is headed, "This Southern Baptist Preacher Wept, Shook and Listened as HE HEARD GOD SPEAK." He quotes in detail the passage mentioned, about the dry bones. But this Baptist pastor ignored the Bible context which explains in detail the vision that God would raise up Israel as a nation, as the following Scripture says: ". . . and I shall place you in your own land: then shall ye know that I the Lord have spoken it, and performed it, saith the Lord" (vs. 14). And then the Lord in the context immediately following tells how one stick for Judah and one stick for Israel were to be bound together since the divided nation was to be reunited. And then verses 21 and 22 explain: "And say unto them, Thus saith the Lord God; Behold, I will take the children of Israel from among the heathen, whither they be gone, and will gather them on every side, and bring them into their own land: And I will make them one nation in the land upon the mountains of Israel; and one king shall be king to them all: and they shall be no more two nations, neither shall they be divided into two kingdoms any more at all." And the Scripture goes on to tell about the conversion of Israel and Christ's reign on earth as King of Israel.

Now no one has a right to put on this passage a private interpretation meaning something else, when God Himself explained His own Scripture as definitely as He had in this case. But our Brother Osteen, this former Southern Baptist pastor who talks in tongues, says God appeared to him in a vision and explained that Scripture as meaning Ezekiel would bring a revival in Israel and that likewise he, Rev. Mr. Osteen, would bring revival in America. Osteen says:

> I wanted to go to the heathen, but the power of God came upon me, and the shaking came, and I heard a

> Voice. And God said unto me, "Thou shalt not go. Thou shalt stay and be as Ezekiel unto me." And He said, "As Ezekiel marched up and down the valley, and the bones began to make a noise, and to come together, so shall you march up and down the valleys of America until my people begin to make noise, and to come together, so shall you march up and down the valleys of America until my people begin to make a noise, and until my people come together!"

Then he says,

> You ask, "What is it that's going across the land, and around the world, that we are reading about? What is this strange phenomenon of speaking in tongues?" I'll tell you what it is. It's the rattling of the bones. It's the shaking in the valley! God is saying, "I have seen the affliction of my people. I know their sorrows! I have heard their cry! I have come down!" It's just like a vision to me. I see under many nets denominational groups held down by traditional teaching.

Now if God has really called our brother to go across America and get everybody talking in tongues, which I doubt, that still is not "the rattling of the bones" of Ezekiel 37. It is not the shaking in the valley of which God spoke in Ezekiel. And I am convinced that God did not tell Brother Osteen a false interpretation of that Scripture. Truth that is of God is not twisted truth, is not wrested Scripture, is not Scripture of some private interpretation contradicting the context and God's own interpretation. The tongues people thus twist Scripture to fit their "experiences" and visions.

In the introductory chapter, "What Is the Baptism of the Holy Spirit?" by Jerry Jensen, managing editor of the Full Gospel Businessmen's *Voice*, this same custom of using the Scripture by twisting it appears. Under a subhead, "*Why the Baptism of the Holy Spirit and Speaking in Tongues?*" he ignores the one plain reason Jesus gave in Acts 1:8, "But ye shall receive power, after that the Holy Ghost is come upon you: and ye shall be witnesses unto me both in Jerusalem, and in all Judaea, and in Samaria, and unto the uttermost part of the earth." Mr. Jensen says this experience was given so that "God might speak supernaturally to men."

Well, God does speak to men through men when He puts His power upon men, but that is not what the brother is talking about. He is talking about a jabber in "heavenly" languages that have no meaning to men but which he thinks gives some rapture to the one who thus talks. He says, "What a blessed experience to have God speak to us through His Word, but what a miraculous experience to have Him speak to us supernaturally by this miraculous gift of tongues." That is not what God talks about in the Scripture at Pentecost, as any careful reader could learn. The Christians witnessed and preached to lost people in their own, though foreign, languages at Pentecost and so three thousand were saved; but that is not what our friend wants for himself and not what he is teaching here.

Again he said, "In turn, the gift was also given that *men may speak to God supernaturally.*" And he uses I Corinthians 14:2 as if it taught that, "For he that speaketh in an unknown tongue speaketh not unto men, but unto God: for no man understandeth him; howbeit in the spirit he speaketh mysteries." But what he ignores is that in I Corinthians 14:2 Paul is using this as a reason why *there should not* be any talk in foreign languages in the services unless someone present should interpret it. Read for yourself the first seventeen verses of that 14th chapter of I Corinthians and you will see that it is all a rebuke of the kind of talking in foreign languages that they had at Corinth, and for the very reason that when they talked in a foreign language in the services only God would understand it, but the others would not. So Paul says,

"*What is it then? I will pray with the spirit, and I will pray with the understanding also: I will sing with the spirit, and I will sing with the understanding also. Else when thou shalt bless with the spirit, how shall he that occupieth the room of the unlearned say Amen at thy giving of thanks, seeing he understandeth not what thou sayest? For thou verily givest thanks well, but the other is not edified."* — I Cor. 14:15-17.

Why should Pentecostal people approve that which the Scriptures plainly disapprove in the same passage?

Again, Mr. Jensen says, "A vital purpose for speaking in tongues is *that we might edify ourselves.*" And he quotes I Corinthians 14:4, "He that speaketh in an unknown tongue edifieth himself; but he that prophesieth edifieth the church." But Paul is saying there that one's testimony should be given so people could understand it and so that others could be edified; and Paul complains: "For thou verily givest thanks well, but the other is not edified" (vs. 17).

Again the brother is using the Bible to say the opposite of what the Scripture he quotes plainly means. And so he says, "When we speak with tongues *we magnify* God," ignoring the fact that in Acts 10:46, which he quotes ("For they heard them speak with tongues, and magnify God"), we are plainly told that they understood what was heard, for it was in their own languages in which they were born!

And he says, "Speaking in tongues is used so that *our spirits might pray—as distinct from our understanding.*" But that is exactly the opposite of what Paul commanded in I Corinthians 14—we are supposed to pray both with understanding and in the Spirit. No Scripture ever praises anybody for praying in some ecstatic language he doesn't understand, and there is no such case spoken of in the Bible. And so our brother all through his article twists Scriptures out of their context meaning. Any doctrine or practice that must wrest Scripture out of its plain meaning to prove itself is wrong, of course.

The Bible nowhere teaches that people should seek to talk in tongues (languages). It is the least of all the gifts, and in the Bible the gift of tongues was never just a heavenly language, but was simply the power to speak on a given occasion in some language other than his native tongue, to people who could understand it and thus hear the Gospel in their own tongue, when otherwise they could not understand it. And so tongues people, to fit their visions and "experiences," twist the Bible to make it mean what it nowhere says. That is wrong. The Bible never indicates that "speaking in tongues" is the evidence or the initial evidence of the fullness of the Spirit. Men say so, but the Bible never does.

These Who Use the Bible So Carelessly Make Much of Feelings, Emotions, Experiences, Visions, Dreams, in Teaching the Tongues Business

This is a favorite argument of those who promote speaking in tongues: "I know because I have had this experience myself." I have heard Pentecostal preachers sneer at the greatest soul winners in the world because they did not "speak in tongues," though they have won thousands to Christ and manifestly had the power of the Holy Spirit upon them.

And the favorite rebuke they have for those of us who go to the Bible to prove what the fullness of the Spirit is, is that "you are not capable of teaching on this matter because you don't have 'the baptism,' you have never talked in tongues."

Actually the great emphasis on "experiences," on visions and dreams, is a retreat from the Word of God itself.

There is a fatal danger in putting anything up alongside the Word of God as authority. With the Roman Catholic the Bible is claimed as authority but it is the Bible modified or interpreted by "the Church," the traditions, the councils. So it turns out that actually they ignore the Bible, which has nothing to say whatever about the sacrifice of the Mass, about prayers to Mary, about confessing sins to a Catholic priest, about the pope.

Our Seventh-Day Adventist friends use the Bible plus the revelations of Mrs. White, so it turns out that they have doctrines that violate the Scriptures. Christian Scientists have the Bible, but only as it is interpreted and added to by Mrs. Mary Baker Eddy, and so they turn away from the Christ of the Bible, the new birth, the fact of sin, regeneration, etc. And our Pentecostal friends, while intending, I am sure, to follow the Bible, get so obsessed with experiences and feelings and emotions and visions that they go beyond the Bible, beyond its plain teaching.

For example, in this little pamphlet, *Baptists and the Baptism of the Holy Spirit,* the first article (by a Baptist preacher, John H. Osteen) is headed, "He Heard God Speak." And in the article he says:

> I say to you without any equivocation whatsoever, "I have heard God's Voice." I do not say that in any egotism, but I know when I hear the Voice of God. I have been sent forth by the Lord; for it was in a little hotel room after my Baptism that I saw Jesus, and I could hardly believe my eyes. I saw His lips begin to move, and He said, "I am your Savior, and have sent you forth to do this work."

And the story goes on: "Electricity" he says, pulled him back down to his knees, he saw the vision again. Then Jesus told him to stretch forth his hands toward the vision "and suddenly, like two bolts of lightning, a million volts of electricity hit my hands as though God took them. And they bent, and surged, and I wept as I listened, and shook as God spoke to me. Away with money, and fame, and prestige! I have heard God speak!"

Yes, and he might as well have said, away with the plain teaching of the Bible—to visions and experiences.

Later the same man woke up in the night, he says, and "I saw a ball of light, and in that light was a Man.... When I leaped up, the bubble burst." And then Jesus told him, he says, that explanation of Ezekiel 37:1-14, which purported explanation contradicts the explanation given in the chapter itself.

The second article by a Baptist preacher starts out with the subhead, "Cold Chills Went Up and Down My Body. I Began to Think...." He tells us that he had a prayer meeting in his church and "Cold chills went up and down my body." Then he said, "Some of the men began to tell of a numbness they felt in their bodies."

It is suggestive that no address, no pastorate of these two men is mentioned. They are simply described as "Spirit-filled Baptist Minister" and "Baptist Pastor Filled With the Holy Spirit." The editor avoids the fact that one of them is now not a Baptist at all, after causing division and strife and resigning.

How we need to remember that God is jealous for the authority of His Word. In Jeremiah 23:25-29 God says:

"*I have heard what the prophets said, that prophesy lies in my name, saying, I have dreamed, I have dreamed. How long shall this be in the heart of the prophets that prophesy lies? yea, they are prophets of the deceit of their own heart; Which think to cause my people to forget my name by their dreams which they tell every man to his neighbour, as their fathers have forgotten my name for Baal. The prophet that hath a dream, let him tell a dream; and he that hath my word, let him speak my word faithfully. What is the chaff to the wheat? saith the Lord. Is not my word like as a fire? saith the Lord; and like a hammer that breaketh the rock in pieces?*"

In verse 32, in the same chapter, God says, "Behold, I am against them that prophesy false dreams, saith the Lord. . . ." And we ask in the words of Scripture, "What is the chaff to the wheat?" Let those that have dreams and visions preach their dreams and visions. Let the prophet of God teach what the Word of God says.

There Is a Carnal Appeal to Human Influence to Persuade People

You will note this pamphlet I mentioned in *Baptists and the Baptism of the Holy Spirit.* Their intent is not to prove the Scripture but to teach that some Baptists have talked in tongues and that therefore, presumably, it is proper and scriptural for Baptists to do so.

John R. Osteen is simply named as a "Spirit-filled Baptist Minister." No address, nothing about his church, no story of soul winning is given—just his visions and experiences and opinions. And the subtitle, "This Southern Baptist Preacher Wept, Shook and Listened As. . . ." But the editor does not mention that Rev. Osteen is no longer a Baptist pastor. He calls Osteen a "Southern Baptist pastor," which he is not now.

Then there is a dishonest effort to use the famous names of the past. The Foreword falsely says, ". . . Dwight L. Moody, Charles Finney and others testified of speaking in other tongues as they received the Baptism with the Holy Spirit. . . ." Untaught Christian people, who have heard of Finney and Moody, will not know enough to check up and see that the account is false. And probably even the man who wrote it had never studied the lives of these men or he would not have said such a thing. But it is a carnal effort to use names of famous men to prove what they cannot prove by the Bible.

Then there is an article by Billy Graham. He came to speak, I understand, at a Full Gospel Businessmen's Fellowship meeting. Billy Graham did not speak in tongues and did not advocate speaking in tongues, though naturally he tried to please them and said, "And people, people that ten years ago would have made *fun* of you are now engaged in the *same* type of meetings that you're engaged in, and we believe that *there is a move of the Spirit of God!*" They know that just as he spoke for the Pentecostals and did not rebuke their "tongues," so he spoke before the Protestant Council in New York and did not rebuke their infidelity, so he spoke in Bishop Pike's Cathedral and had that blaspheming Episcopalian on the committee for his San Francisco campaign and to lead in prayer in his meetings. So he had the Catholic bishop on the platform in Brazil to bless the converts as they came forward. So he attended President Johnson's dance in July 1964. It is obvious that Billy Graham goes to any platform where he can get some notoriety and some hearing, and our Pentecostal friends, who do not agree with Billy Graham, use his name as if he favored the tongues movement.

In this pamphlet one article is "by M.G. 'Pat' Robertson, Son of Senator A. Willis Robertson, Founder of Christian Broadcasting Network."

Tragically, These Promoters for Tongues Miss the Great Lesson of Pentecost: Soul Winning!

In the Bible the great emphasis about the fullness of the Spirit or the baptism of the Spirit is soul-winning power. Not so with our Pentecostal people as represented by the Full Gospel Businessmen's Fellowship International. Jesus said, "But ye shall receive power, after that the Holy Ghost is come upon you: and ye shall be witnesses unto me. . . ." Instead they teach as if it said, "And ye shall talk in unknown tongues."

In Luke 24:47-49, Jesus told the disciples that "repentance and remission of sins should be preached. . . among all nations," and that they were witnesses, but commanded them, ". . . tarry ye in the city of Jerusalem, until ye be endued with power from on high." But our Pentecostal friends would interpret that as meaning that Christians are to tarry till they talk in tongues!

The Scripture says in Luke 1:15 and 16 about the ministry of John the Baptist that "he shall be filled with the Holy Ghost, even from his mother's womb. And many of the children of Israel shall he turn to the Lord their God." These tongues advocates have no such message.

In all the talk about Pentecost, in this pamphlet, it is never once mentioned that they had three thousand people saved and baptized at that time! The salvation of souls is mentioned, I think, two or three times in the whole pamphlet, but only incidentally. The great emphasis all the time is on talking in tongues, seeing visions, raising the hands in public praise, etc.

And now let me earnestly lay on the heart of every reader this central truth: We can have, we ought to have, the mighty power of God upon us for witnessing, for soul winning, for preaching the Gospel. I am not against the fullness of the Spirit; I am against false substitutes for the fullness of the Spirit.

I believe that Christians ought to have great joy, ought to have answered prayer, ought to have sweet fellowship. And all that we can have, and honor Christ better, by following the Bible instead of dreams, visions, "experiences," and the opinions of men.

Every reader might do well to read my pamphlet of 79 pages on *Speaking With Tongues,* in which this subject is dealt with scripturally and kindly and conclusively, we believe. But it would be better yet if you could get the large book, *The Power of Pentecost,* 441 pages, which deals exhaustively with the tremendous question of the fullness of the Spirit in Bible times, what it means, how to have this power and blessing now.

and packing and order from The Sword of the Lord, Box 1099, Murfreesboro, Tennessee 37130. The pamphlet on *Speaking With Tongues* is $1.50, plus 70 cents for postage.

4. Are Tongues People the Only Good Christians?

Dear Brother J———:

Your letter arrived November 9th, and I thank you for your temperate and kindly expressions.

I do not object to the fact that you differ with me on some matters, and I hope you will not object to the fact that I, as a Christian brother, differ on some matters of interpretation of the Bible.

Some Essentials All Good Christians Agree on

But, at least, you and I ought to agree on the deity of Christ, the blood atonement, the virgin birth, the bodily resurrection, the verbal inspiration of the Bible, the need to be born again, Heaven and Hell, and such matters. And since my strong and carefully stated position, again and again through the years, is that Christians need to be filled with the Holy Spirit, need the enduement of power from on High, and a Christian ought to have New Testament power, New Testament gifts and blessings, it seems to be that you and I ought not to fall out over the lesser matter of "tongues" as the evidence of the power of God. Suppose you do not agree with me and I do not agree with you. We still are agreed on the main things and we can be brethren, and of course I feel that way.

I have many, many friends among the Assembly of God brethren. I was a guest speaker in the publishing house at Springfield some years ago, and in my big tent meeting there I had twenty-six Assembly of God ministers on the platform one night, and others night after night. So, though you may feel very keenly our difference about tongues, you ought to feel equally keenly, it seems to me, our unity on the need to be filled with the Spirit, to have the power of God daily, and the joy and the answered prayer and the results of New Testament Christianity.

Why Do Pentecostal People Slander the Best Soul Winners Who Do Not Agree on Tongues?

And now, may I remind you as a Christian brother that you are not really the one to be offended, but I am and others like me, at the viewpoint you express in your letter and as other Pentecostal people do express it again and again in much more vigorous language than you do. I say, in effect, that speaking in tongues is not the Bible evidence of the fullness of the Spirit, and that Christians may be wonderfully filled with the Spirit and have the enduement of power and New Testament joy and gifts and results, without necessarily talking in tongues. But you go much further, and simply say that when I do not talk in tongues, you deny that I have the power of God or the baptism of the Holy Spirit, and you even accuse me "that while hundreds of others in many denominations are receiving this infillment of power and others are earnestly seeking God in their hearts concerning this thing, you seem to be on a personal vendetta against it."

You see, the attack is on your part and that is what makes it difficult for good Christians, Spirit-filled, soul-winning Christians, sacrificial Christians who risk all for Jesus Christ, to get along with the Pentecostal people, who make speaking in tongues the one criterion of being filled with the Spirit, and who slanderously accuse others of us of not having the power of God, not wanting the power of God, of fighting God, and worse, that that is because we do not talk in tongues. That makes you good people hard to get along with because you are in that matter not only unkind but unreasonable in your charges.

I have said plainly, and said it in the articles published in THE SWORD OF THE LORD, that I sought most earnestly to be filled with the Spirit of God and that God wonderfully, again and again, has answered the prayer. I said that I have been baptized with the Holy Ghost. I sought what Jesus promised in Luke 24:49, to "be endued with power from on high." I received it. I sought most earnestly that which Jesus plainly offered and promised in Acts 1:8: "But ye shall receive power, after that the Holy Ghost is come upon you: and ye shall be witnesses unto me both in Jerusalem, and in all Judaea, and in Samaria, and unto the uttermost part of the earth." Yet you have what the Bible certainly does not plainly say is the evidence of the baptism of the Spirit, and then you accuse me, who sought and found what God promised, and say I do not have the baptism of the Holy Spirit and that I fight it and carry on a fight against it!

Now, a good Christian ought to welcome plain, honest talk from another well-meaning Christian. And I do not see any basis of fellowship between you and me as long as you put it on the basis that you are "holier-than-thou," that you have the power of God and I have not, that you are sincere and I am not, that you have New Testament Christianity and I am fighting New Testament Christianity, that you have the power of the Holy Ghost and I resist the Holy Ghost.

Your letter is milder than many others I receive from Pentecostal people, but your claim in essence is the same.

You have it and I haven't. You are a better Christian than I am. You have the power of God and I have not. You are willing to take what God gives and I fight what God offers. That is your position, is it not?

The "Tongues" People Put Tongues Before Soul Winning and Dedication

Now, you are impatient because I say that I have the fullness of the Spirit and I have not talked in tongues. So I say that not only according to the Bible, which I think is clear, but according to my abundant experience, I have been baptized with the Holy Spirit and have been filled with the Holy Spirit with the results plainly promised in the Bible, and I didn't talk in tongues. I do not know any way to have peace with you on such a basis unless I can see that the only people in the world who are right are Pentecostalists.

You wave aside the fact that God has given me tens of thousands of souls. You wave aside the fact that, as anyone could well know, I have gladly offered and given up and have lost the things most dear to most men, in order to be true to Christ. I have lost the friendship of thousands. I suffered abuse and slander. I have done it gladly. I would do it again in order to be true to Christ and the Bible. And so now you cannot fellowship with me because I do not agree that you are better than I am, that you have what I don't have, that you are following the Bible and I am not, that you have the power of God and I do not!

You say, "I would ask you to remember that most Pentecostal people are conscientious, dedicated people, and I have never known anyone who had the Holy Spirit as we teach it that did not live for God and try to win others to the Lord." Oh, but brother, that I freely admit and I always have. And I am glad of the growth of the Pentecostal churches and soul winning.

(Of course I am sorry that many, many Pentecostal churches spend their principal efforts in getting people out of other churches instead of getting people saved.) But I am glad that Pentecostal people win many.

Dear brother, that is not really what your claim involves. Your claim involves that your people have the enduement of power to win souls and that others who do not talk in tongues do not have that power of God promised in Acts 1:8 and Luke 24:49! If you say that some Pentecostal people have won as many souls as I have, I gladly admit it. But that is not really your contention. That fits what I am saying, that the talking in tongues is not the essential matter and does not necessarily go with the baptism of the Holy Ghost, which I have and which D. L. Moody had, and Billy Sunday and R. A. Torrey and Dr. Bob Jones and Sam Jones and other great soul winners had. But your contention is that you have the power and I have not! In fact, you say that I not only do not have the power but that I seem to be in a personal fight against it.

You see, for Pentecostals to be right in that they are the only ones who have the baptism of the Holy Ghost, then they must prove not that they win as many souls as some others but that they win far more than anybody else. Otherwise you pervert the whole meaning of the baptism of the Holy Spirit and entirely lose sight of the promise of Jesus in Luke 24 and Acts 1:8 and lose sight of what happened at Pentecost, when three thousand were saved, and elsewhere through the book of Acts.

Now if you could prove that Pentecostal people are the only ones who have the power of the Holy Spirit, then you could talk sense to me. Until you do, it is rather unreasonable for you to expect everybody to agree with you in your attack on the best soul-winning Christians in the world who do not talk in tongues and who say that that is not an essential evidence of the fullness of the Spirit.

The Experience of the Greatest Soul Winners Prove That "Tongues" Is Not "The Evidence of Holy Spirit Enduement"

You say concerning "the baptism of the Holy Spirit with the initial evidence of speaking with other tongues as the Spirit gives utterance, this is a doctrine in which I believe, have personally experienced, and have seen thousands of others with the same experience." Oh, but while you make so much of your experience, why would you wave off the experience which I have so clearly and wonderfully had, the enduement of power that has enabled me, a poor, unworthy and frail human being, to win tens of thousands of souls? My experience is as important as your experience. And why would you sneer at the experience of Charles G. Finney and D.L. Moody and R. A. Torrey and Billy Sunday and Gypsy Smith and Sam Jones and Dr. Bob Jones and Hyman Appelman? Why is your experience so much better than the experience of those who win more souls and do more good for God than you do? (I mean in such cases, of course, the famous soul winners mentioned; I do not mean to compare myself with you.)

Now, the fact of experiences is against you. And I do not mind your interpreting your experience in your own way, provided it does not mean a slander and abuse of all the rest of us who have the power of God and who are used of God to win thousands and who are willing to suffer any reproach for Jesus, to be true and to manifest New Testament Christianity, but who never did talk in tongues and do not find it promised nor commanded for us.

Now, I have written you in brotherliness and I hope you will read it the same way. Of course the easy way would be simply never to have any contact with anybody who differs with you and who didn't have your experience. Then always you could draw your holy robes around you and say that you have what everybody else has not. But, of course, you and I know that that is not the honest way and the proper way for a Christian to deal with a scriptural matter, a doctrinal matter.

Now I give you the right to talk in tongues. What I do not concede is that you have a right to slander me and accuse me of not having the power of God because I do not talk in tongues. The facts speak more eloquently than words in that matter. Now you may not want to read what I understand the Bible to teach on this question, but you have no right to take for granted that you have the power of God and I have not, you are sincere and I am not, you have listened to the Spirit of God and I have not. So, if you want fellowship with Bible-believing Christians, then some brotherly kindness and consideration and charity, and some proper Christian humility are in order, it seems to me.

In Jesus' name, yours,
John R. Rice

For further reading see *The Power of Pentecost,* 441 pages, by Dr. John R. Rice, Sword of the Lord Publishers. Has some 70-odd pages on the tongues question and is the most comprehensive scriptural teaching available on the whole matter of the fullness of the Spirit.

6

Hyper-Calvinism--
A False Doctrine

Hyper-Calvinism — a False Doctrine

Through the years there has been a conflict between the doctrine of eternal salvation by grace through faith, not of works, and the doctrine of salvation partly by God's grace and partly by man's works or by deserving it or by faithfulness. We know that all false religions teach salvation by good works, character, human merit, or rites, not the free salvation given instantly to penitent, believing sinners, wholly by grace. But many Christian groups tend to include works or mourning or faithfulness as the way to get saved and the price of keeping saved. Those who believe men must "hold out faithful" to keep saved and think they will never be surely eternally safe until they reach Heaven are of what is called the Arminian position because it was so insistently taught by Arminius. Wesley and his followers held to this position, as do all who think a saved person can be lost.

I. WHAT IS HYPER-CALVINISM?

Those who believe in eternal salvation wholly of grace are usually called Calvinists simply because, in the Protestant Reformation, Calvin strongly emphasized that doctrine long contradicted under the Roman heresy of salvation by merit and church rites. So any person who is not Arminian in faith but rather believes in eternal security of the believer is likely to describe himself as a Calvinist. Or where Calvinism has not been carried to its more unscriptural, unevangelistic, arrogant extreme, one might probably call himself a "moderate" Calvinist. Most of those who might be called Calvinists do not believe in a limited atonement, for example, nor do they believe that some are foreordained by unconditioned election to go to Hell and so could not be saved, that salvation was never provided for nor offered for them. But they do believe in eternal salvation by grace, the principal truth Calvin emphasized.

Those who do believe a doctrine of God's limited love, limited grace, limited atonement, and unchangeable plan to damn millions who could not be saved, are called hyper-Calvinists.

These extreme doctrines were first taught somewhat by Augustine. Then for about a thousand years no one found them in the Bible, of course, till Calvin developed such a theology. Adopting the theory men then persuaded themselves that they find it in the Bible.

Salvation by grace, eternal salvation, without works, is a Bible doctrine. I believe hyper-Calvinism is not a Bible doctrine but is a perversion by proud intellectuals who thus may try to excuse themselves from any spiritual accountability for winning souls.

II. EXAMINE THE DOCTRINE OF HYPER-CALVINISM

Those whom we call hyper-Calvinists usually outline their doctrinal position as represented by the letters *TULIP*:

T for *Total Depravity* of the sinner.

U for *Unconditional Election.*

L for *Limited Atonement.*

I for *Irresistible Grace.*

P for *Perseverance* of the saints.

1. Sinners Are Depraved, Cannot Be Saved Unless God Calls, but All Have Some Light, Some Calling

The hyper-Calvinist says sinners are totally depraved and so incapable of repentance except as God calls some selected individuals, and leaves others He has predestined for Hell, unable to repent.

Now the doctrine that all are sinful, incapable of being saved or doing good without God's help, is true. But it is certainly not true that some never could repent, that God leaves some intentionally without light or calling. Consider these Scriptures:

a. "God...now commandeth all men every where to repent" (Acts 17:30). Can anyone accuse God of commanding people to do what He has made it impossible for them to do?

b. The apostle said, after hearing of Cornelius' conversion, "Then hath God also to the Gentiles granted repentance unto life" (Acts 11:18). God granted repentance to the Jews; now they see repentance is granted "*to the Gentiles*"—not to a few selected individuals, but to the Gentiles, as to Jews.

c. In John 1:9 we are told about Jesus, "That was the true Light, which lighteth every man that cometh into the world." So every man in the world has light from God and from Christ, and so could be saved.

d. In John 12:32,33, Jesus said, "And I, if I be lifted up from the earth, will draw all men unto me. This he said, signifying what death he should die." When Jesus draws "all men" unto Him, then any one of "all men" could be saved.

e. Romans 1:18-21 says that after the flood, the races became heathen, idolators, barbarians, and are without excuse because the truth of God was manifiested unto them. It says:

"*For the wrath of God is revealed from heaven against all ungodliness and unrighteousness of men, who hold the truth in unrighteousness; Because that which may be known of God is manifest in them; for God hath shewed it unto them. For the invisible things of him from the creation of the world are clearly seen, being understood by the things that are made, even his eternal power and Godhead; so that they are without excuse: Because that, when they knew God, they glorified him not as God, neither were thankful; but became vain in their imaginations, and their foolish heart was darkened.*"

f. Psalm 19:1-4 tells us,

"*The heavens declare the glory of God; and the firmament sheweth his handywork. Day unto day uttereth speech, and night unto night sheweth knowledge. There is no speech nor language, where their voice is not heard Their line is gone out through all the earth, and their words to the end of the world. In them hath he set a tabernacle for the sun.*"

So there is a speech in nature to turn men to seek God. It speaks in all the world and every man is therefore accountable to God for it.

g. Romans 2:11-16 says,

"*For there is no respect of persons with God. For as many as have sinned without law shall also perish without law: and as many as have sinned in the law shall be judged by the law; (For not the hearers of the law are just before God, but the doers of the law shall be justified. For when the Gentiles, which have not the law, do by nature the things contained in the law, these, having not the law, are a law unto themselves: Which shew the work of the law written in their hearts, their conscience also bearing witness, and their thoughts the mean while accusing or else excusing one another;) In the day when God shall judge the secrets of men by Jesus Christ according to my gospel.*"

Does that not mean that every person in the world is warned from God, either by the Word or by God speaking through the law He has written in their hearts, that is, their consciences?

And God, in this matter, has "no respect of persons," we are told here, giving every man alike a call to be saved. All who seek more light find enough light even as Cornelius did in Acts 10.

Man's sinfulness does not mean some men could not be saved.

h. We are told that "the gospel of Christ...is the power of God unto salvation" (Rom. 1:16). And again Hebrews 4:12 says, "For the word of God is quick, and powerful, and sharper than any twoedged sword, piercing even to the dividing asunder of soul and spirit, and of the joints and marrow, and is a discerner of the thoughts and intents of the heart." Does not that Scripture surely mean that the Scriptures themselves call men to repentance? And would you say, like the neo-orthodox teachers who do not accept the Bible as objectively the Word of God, that it becomes the Word of God to individuals only as it affects them? No, the very nature of the powerful Word of God, "sharper than any twoedged sword, piercing even to the dividing asunder of soul and spirit, and of the joints and marrow," means that it acts upon all who hear it. And again, we read in I Corinthians 1:21 that "it pleased God by the foolishness of preaching to save them that believe." And that means, of course, the preaching of the Gospel of the Word of God. The Word of God itself has supernatural power to affect the lost sinner, and it needs only to be "mixed with faith" (Heb. 4:2) to save the sinner.

So every lost sinner is in some sense lighted by Jesus

who "lighteth every man that cometh into the world" (John 1:9), is somewhat moved by his conscience, is preached to by the creation about him, and when he hears the Word of God he is called by that. Then the fact of the depravity of every lost sinner does not mean there are some sinners who cannot be saved.

2. "Unconditional Election" Is Not Bible Doctrine

It is true the saved are God's elect, "chosen. . . in him before the foundation of the world," as Ephesians 1:4 tells us. But it is wrong to make this election a whim of God whereby He saves some, compels them to be saved, and damns some whom He has decided He does not wish to save. No, election is not "unconditional." It is simply that God knows who will trust Him when they hear the Gospel and chooses them to be carried through till they be "conformed to the image of his Son."

Romans 8:28-30 tells us so; thus:

"*And we know that all things work together for good to them that love God, to them who are the called according to his purpose. For whom he did foreknow, he also did predestinate to be conformed to the image of his Son, that he might be the firstborn among many brethren. Moreover whom he did predestinate, them he also called: and whom he called, them he also justified: and whom he justified, them he also glorified.*"

God gives the order of things here. First, foreknowledge, then predestination, then calling, then saving, then finally, at the resurrection, glorifying. To ignore or to change the inspired, divine order is false doctrine.

Again, I Peter 1:2 says that the saints addressed were "Elect according to the foreknowledge of God the Father." That is a flat contradiction of so-called "unconditional election." Election is based on God's foreknowledge of who will trust Christ. So salvation depends upon personal faith in Christ.

3. The Term "Limited Atonement" Really Means Limited Love, Limited Grace of God, and So Slanders God, and Is Unscriptural

The heart of hyper-Calvinist doctrine is the "Limited Atonement" claim, that Christ did not die for all men, made no provision for them so they could possibly be saved. It really claims that God did not love all men enough to have Christ die for all, that His grace is limited, so is finite instead of infinite. But this is contradicted by many plain Scriptures.

a. John 3:16 says that "God so loved *THE WORLD,* that he gave his only begotten Son"—that it was so that "whosoever" could believe on Him and be saved. No limited love or atonement in John 3:16!

b. In John 1:29 we read the inspired statement of John the Baptist about Jesus, "Behold the Lamb of God, which taketh away the sin of the world." Since Christ atoned for "the sin of the world," not just part of the sin of the world, it could not be a limited atonement.

c. First John 2:2 plainly says, "And he is the propitiation for our sins: and not for our's only, but also for the sins of the whole world." No limited atonement there!

d. Romans 5:20 says, "Where sin abounded, grace did much more abound," Does not that mean God has grace for all the sin in the world, and even a great surplus? So the total number of people who will ever be born on the earth is a *finite* counted number that God knows. But the grace of God is infinite, much more than for those who will be saved, even much more than for all the sins of all the people in the world, so says the plain Word of God. Romans 5:20 leaves no limit on the atonement.

e. First Timothy 4:10 tells of "the living God, who is the Saviour of all men, specially of those that believe." To those who believe, Christ is a *special,* personal, accepted Saviour. But to all who have not believed He is potentially and intentionally a Saviour. When God says in the Bible that He has provided a "Saviour of all men," what an arrogant wresting of Scriptures it is to say He did not provide and offer salvation for all!

f. Colossians 1:20 tells us that Christ, "having made peace through the blood of his cross, by him to reconcile all things unto himself; by him, I say, whether they be things in earth, or things in heaven." Note that that verse speaks, not of all accepting Christ, but of atonement for all, amnesty offered every rebel, a peace treaty prepared to end the war between God and the sinner. If Christ, "through the blood of his cross," intended "to reconcile all things unto himself," as that verse says, who dares put a limit on that atoning blood, so offered for all?

4. God's Grace Is Not Irresistible; Some Are Not Compelled to Be Saved Unconditionally, Others Compelled to Be Damned

The fourth part of the doctrine of hyper-Calvinism, represented by the letter "I" in TULIP, is "Irresistible Grace," by which it is meant that all who are elected to be saved will be saved, that they cannot resist this special grace limited to them but will be saved when God calls. It would necessarily follow, first, that those not elected are irresistibly damned, cannot be saved; and, second, that since God works irresistibly to save or damn, Christians cannot affect the salvation or damnation of sinners and need feel no responsibility or burden about it. But this is wrong, unscriptural, and no doubt Satan uses this doctrine of "Irresistible Grace" to lull Christians to disobedience and lack of compassion and burden to get people saved.

Consider these Scriptures which prove sinners can and do resist God's grace and many are lost who could be saved, and refuse Christ.

a. In II Peter 3:9 we read, "The Lord is not slack concerning his promise, as some men count slackness; but is longsuffering to us-ward, not willing that any should perish, but that all should come to repentance." Then God desires all men to besaved. And as we showed in section 1, all are enlightened to some degree, and called.

So many resist the grace of God.

b. We are commanded to pray for "all men," says I Timothy 2:1, and verses 3 and 4 tell us, "For this is good and acceptable in the sight of God our Saviour; Who will have ALL MEN to be saved, and to come unto the knowledge of the truth." We should pray for all men because God our Saviour "will have all men to be saved." So God would have all saved, but some will not be saved. So God's grace may be resisted.

c. We are told that Jesus wept over Jerusalem and told the sadness of His heart that His love and grace were refused. He said, in Matthew 23:37, "O Jerusalem, Jerusalem, thou that killest the prophets, and stonest them which are sent unto thee, how often would I have gathered thy children together, even as a hen gathereth here chickens under her wings, and ye would not!" Jesus said, "I would," "and ye would not." So His grace was rejected. It was not irresistible.

d. In Proverbs 1:24,25, we have a clear statement that God, personified as Wisdom, calls and men refuse. That Scripture says, "Because I have called, and ye refused; I have stretched out my hand, and no man regarded; But ye have set at nought all my counsel, and would none of my reproof." And the context plainly teaches that the refusal is final and those who so refused God's wisdom and "did not choose the fear of the Lord" went to destruction. Surely, then, people do reject the call of God and resist His grace.

e. Paul says in Galatians 2:21, "I do not frustrate the grace of God." That clearly shows then that those Galatian teachers who teach salvation by the law do frustrate the grace of God. Grace is not irresistible.

And did not you, my reader, long resist God's grace? Only very few were saved the first time they heard the Gospel at the first conviction of sin they felt! Did you not for a time resist God's grace? One who resists one time may resist the last time. And so many continue to resist and are lost forever.

f. In fact, the unpardonable sin is surely the sin of a lost man or woman, greatly enlightened and convicted, who comes to a final and irrevocable choice so that God's Spirit gives him up. Genesis 6:3 says, "My spirit shall not always strive with man." He does strive—resisted to a certain point He sometimes strives no more, so the sin is unpardonable. If the Spirit who strives, then when men resist, may cease forever striving, then grace is not irresistible.

Hebrew 6:4-6 says, I think, the same thing:

"For it is impossible for those who were once enlightened, and have tasted of the heavenly gift, and were made partakers of the Holy Ghost, And have tasted the good word of God, and the powers of the world to come, If they shall fall away, to renew them again unto repentance; seeing they crucify to themselves the Son of God afresh, and put him to an open shame."

The term "partakers of the Holy Ghost," Dr. Scofield

says, here is "Gr. *metochous, going along with.*" So the Scripture here speaks of one not born of the Spirit but one who is followed, warned, convicted by the Holy Spirit going along with him. He has felt or "tasted" the "powers of the world to come," we are told; has "tasted the good word of God," but refuses Christ, still falls away from that conviction and, after coming to the verge of repentance, turns from it; it is impossible to renew such an one to repentance. So it is with those who, called, convicted, brought to the very crisis of decision, decide finally, eternally against Christ. Oh, every sinner who commits the unpardonable sin does resist the grace of God to the last. So we think did Pharaoh, Judas and, we think, those Pharisees of Matthew 12:24-32 who said Jesus cast out devils by Beelzebub but in heart knew better and blasphemously fought the Holy Spirit who convicted them. God's grace is not irresistible.

5. The Saints Do Finally Persevere

The P in TULIP stands for final "Perseverance" of the saints. In this, all Bible believers must agree if we mean simply that those who are saved have everlasting life. I think a better way to say it is the Preservation of the saints. I do not believe Christians always do right. They do not get salvation by works and they cannot keep it by works. So our righteousness is the righteousness of Christ who died in our place, paid for all our sins, and gives us eternal life freely when we believe on Christ. So John 5:24 says plainly, "Verily, verily, I say unto you, He that heareth my word, and believeth on him that sent me, hath everlasting life, and shall not come into condemnation; but is passed from death unto life."

So in John 10:27-29 Jesus said, "My sheep hear my voice, and I know them, and they follow me: And I give unto them eternal life; and they shall never perish, neither shall any man pluck them out of my hand. My Father, which gave them me, is greater than all; and no man is able to pluck them out of my Father's hand."

And Paul the apostle could say by infallible inspiration, "...for I know whom I have believed, and am persuaded that he is able to keep that which I have committed unto him against that day" (II Tim. 1:12).

III. WHY FOLLOW MEN?

Do you follow Arminius? or Wesley? Then you are certain to be wrong wherever those good but frail men were wrong. Do you follow Calvin? Then whatever doctrine Calvin formulated or invented will be wrong for you as for him.

Charles Spurgeon, great and blessed London preacher, was a Calvinist though he spoke against "hyper-Calvinism," and called it that; and his hyper-Calvinist friends criticized him for preaching that "whosoever will" may come.

In his sermon on Sunday morning, March 24, 1861, on Isaiah 1:18, Spurgeon said:

OUR TEXT ADDRESSED TO SINNERS OF THE DEEPEST DYE

Some of my brethren are greatly scandalized by the general invitations which I am in the habit of giving to sinners, as sinners. Some of them go the length of asserting that there are no universal invitations in the Word of God. Their assertion, however, is not so forcible an argument as a fact, and we have one here. Here is most plainly an invitation addressed to sinners who had not even the qualification of sensibility. They did not feel their need of a Saviour. They had been scourged and flogged till the whole body was a mass of sores, and yet they would not turn to the Hand that smote them, but went on sinning still. A more accurate description of careless, worthless, ungodly, abandoned souls, never was given anywhere. We have in the context one of the most graphic descriptions of human nature in its utterly lost and godless estate. There is not a single gleam of light in the midst of the thick darkness. The man is bad--bad--bad from the beginning to the end. Nay, he is all the worst, and the worst is come to its worst. There is not a ray of promise in their nature, not a glimmer of anything good in the description of the persons to whom this text is addressed.

So Spurgeon did not really believe all the points of hyper-Calvinism, did not believe that some sinners are not called or could not repent.

In the same sermon, he says,

Furthermore, I think that in giving this description, I shall be better preaching the Gospel than during the other parts of the sermon. Let me remind you that the invitation of the text is sent to men who appeared to have been *totally depraved from the sole of the foot even to the head.* [The emphasis is Spurgeon's.]

Again, in the same sermon, Spurgeon said,

Yes, Mercy Offered to "Every One of You"

I have a big net this morning--Oh, that we might all be caught in its meshes! There is not one of us today who can be exempt from this invitation; not even that poor soul yonder who shivers in his shoes because he fears that he has committed the unpardonable sin,--

None are excluded hence, but those
Who do themselves exclude;
Welcome the learned and polite,
The ignorant and rude.

"Repent, and be baptized every one of you," said Peter. As John Bunyan puts it--one man might have stood up in the crowd and said, "But I helped to hound Him to the cross!" "Repent, and be baptized *every one of you.*" "But I drove the nails into His hands!" saith one. "*Every one of you,*" says Peter. "But I pierced His side!" said another. "*Every one of you,*" said Peter. "And I put my tongue into my cheek and stared at His naked-

> ness and said, 'If He be the Son of God, let Him come down from the cross.'" "*Every one of you,*" said Peter. "Repent, and be baptized every one of you." I do feel so grieved at many of our Calvinistic brethren; they know nothing about Calvinism, I am sorry to say, for never was any man more caricatured by his professed followers than John Calvin. Many of them are afraid to preach from Peter's text, "Repent, and be baptized every one of you." When I do it, they say, "He is unsound."
>
> Well, if I am unsound on this point, I have all the Puritans with me--the whole of them almost without a single exception. John Bunyan first and foremost preaches to Jerusalem sinners; and Charnock, you know, has written a book, *The Chief of Sinners, Objects of the Choicest Mercy.* But I do not care for that; I know the Lord has blessed my appeals to all sorts of sinners, and none shall stay me in giving free invitations as long as I find them in this Book. And I do cry with Peter this morning to this vast assembly, "Repent, and be baptized every one of you in the name of Jesus Christ.... For the promise is unto you, and to your children...even as many as the Lord our God shall call."

So Spurgeon was a Calvinist and said so, but he did not accept all the doctrines of hyper-Calvinism, and he said so.

In truth, the false doctrines of hyper-Calvinism would not do so much harm if they were emphasized as little as Spurgeon emphasized them, and particularly, if those who advocate them worked unceasingly to win souls as Spurgeon did.

But why follow Spurgeon? He was human. He was an amazing preacher, an evangelist. Some think he was the greatest preacher since the Apostle Paul. But when he was wrong he was wrong. He plainly said he did not know enough about the return of Christ to preach on it. No man is perfect. It would be as foolish to follow Spurgeon in whatever part of the false doctrine of hyper-Calvinism he believed as to follow him in smoking cigars. He saw the error of smoking a little while before he went to Heaven, and I am sure he saw the errors of hyper-Calvinism, besides those he himself criticized, as soon as he reached Heaven. Why not just follow the Bible instead of Arminius or Calvin or Wesley or Spurgeon?

IV. GOD NEVER IS PARTY TO SIN, NEVER ARRANGES SO ONE MUST SIN

Did God plan every evil, every sin that men have ever committed? Did God predestine Adam and Eve to sin? Did He plan and bring about the rebellion of Satan, once Lucifer, an angel of light; and did He bring about the fall of the angels that fell? We must agree that God knew all the future, but can we say that all the sin really originated in the heart and planning of God? No! Surely such a thought is abhorrent to every spiritual mind. The Bible does not teach it.

God planned and elected much in the lives of all men, but not the sin. Men themselves do not have to sin. They sin because they are sinful and can choose to sin, or choose the path that leads to sin.

A man cannot choose the date of his birth, nor the place he is born, nor his parents. He cannot choose the color of his eyes, the shape of his face, the talents or limitations with which he may be born. Many of the things that happen to one he cannot control, but on moral issues, issues of right and wrong, man can choose and must choose. Election does not settle the choice anyone makes about sin or salvation.

Four great truths show that man is not coerced to sin, that sin and rejection of Christ are moral issues in which man always has a choice.

1. There Are God's Commands Which Men Can Obey or Disobey

God never commands a man to "be born in Chicago

on June 30th." God settles that, with the person affected having no choice, no responsibility to obey or refuse. But on moral matters, right and wrong are clearly set forth in God's commands. The "Thou shalt not's" of the Bible show that on moral issues men have a choice to make and do make a choice.

2. God Gives Man a Conscience to Tell Him Right and Wrong

The Scripture says, "The spirit of man is the candle of the Lord, searching all the inward parts of the belly" (Prov. 20:27). On other matters men must decide; with no moral issue involved, a man does not have inward light always. Should he buy this house at this price? Should he have a Ford car or a Chevrolet? Conscience has no answer. One may ask God for wisdom and have help, but conscience says only, "This is right" or "That is wrong." So "that little spark of celestial fire called conscience" proves God gives inward light so one can choose right on issues of moral and spiritual duty. Men are not so predestined that they must sin or must reject Christ.

3. A Way of Escape From Sin Always Provided

Has God made man so, and provided circumstances so that a man can not avoid sinning in a given instance? No, for we are plainly told in I Corinthians 10:12,13,

"*Wherefore let him that thinketh he standeth take heed lest he fall. There hath no temptation taken you but such as is common to man: but God is faithful, who will not suffer you to be tempted above that ye are able; but will with the temptation also make a way to escape, that ye may be able to bear it.*"

So if one takes heed he need not fall. Always a way of escape is provided. God is faithful to not only allow one to take heed and choose not to sin, but also makes a way of escape in every case. In any particular case men may have help, may escape sin. So men are not predestined to sin or to reject the Saviour.

4. Men Come to Judgment for Their Sins, Are Accountable, So They Need Not Blame God Nor Predestination for Sins

For every idle word men shall come to judgment, Jesus said (Matt. 12:36). And Revelation 20:12 tells us that the unsaved dead will be judged "according to their works," which are meticulously recorded. Does not that prove that in moral matters man is accountable and must choose?

God chose Jacob to head a nation for Him, and rejected Esau. That was predestined before they were born (Rom. 9:11-13). But Esau, while rejected as head of a tribe through which God would bring the Saviour, was not predestined to go to Hell, and for all we know may have been saved.

Pharaoh was a wicked, murderous man, and in the matter of letting Israel go from Egypt, God had raised him up to make an example of him and kill him (Rom. 9:17,18). But there is no evidence that God predestined him to go to Hell. He could have chosen to be saved. Knowing ahead of time what Pharaoh would do, God planned to make an example of His destruction of a wicked king.

Hyper-Calvinism is unscriptural, false doctrine. It tends to flourish in intellectual pride and in neglect of soul winning, and is a symptom of moral guilt. It is Satan's effort to kill concern and compassion for souls.

(The author's book, *Predestined for Hell? No!* goes into more detail in answering this false doctrine which has brought decay and ruin to the ministry of so many. The book, 103 pages, paperbound, may be obtained from this publisher; price, $1.95 plus postage.)

7

Jehovah's Witness Errors

1. What Is a Jehovah's Witness?

By Dr. John S. Wimbish

(This message was delivered to a **large** congregation in the auditorium of the famed Calvary Baptist Church during the summer of 1953 when the international conference of the Jehovah's Witnesses was being held at the Yankee Stadium. The sermon was made available in printed form to the radio listeners of Calvary Baptist Church, where Dr. Wimbish was pastor, and has received a wide distribution.)

In the twenty-fourth chapter of Matthew we behold Jesus sitting on the gentle slope of Olivet. The shadow of the cross is upon Him. Soon He will be hanged on the ignominious tree.

The disciples have just heard the Lord Jesus predict the destruction of the Temple in Jerusalem, and they inquisitively gather about Him and ask, "Tell us, when shall these things be? and what shall be the sign of thy coming, and of the end of the world?"—that is, "the consummation of the age" (Matt. 24:3).

Then Jesus enumerates the perilous characteristics of the age—wars, universal unrest, famines, pestilences, earthquakes, and widespread persecutions.

And He went on to tell His disciples that many cults would seek to counterfeit Christianity. Notice verses 23 and 24:

"*Then if any man shall say unto you, Lo, here is*

Christ, or there; believe it not. For there shall arise false Christs, and false prophets, and shall shew great signs and wonders; insomuch that, if it were possible, they shall deceive the very elect."

And throughout the epistles we find that the Holy Spirit directed the apostolic writers to warn against the apostasy that would plague Christendom during this dispensation. Over and over again Paul and Peter and James and John lashed out against the demoniacal heresies that would seek to undermine the foundational truths of the Gospel. And in his first letter to Timothy, the great apostle said:

"*Now the Spirit speaketh expressly, that in the latter times some shall depart from the faith, giving heed to seducing spirits, and doctrines of devils; Speaking lies in hypocrisy; having their conscience seared with a hot iron.*"—I Tim. 4:1,2.

Unquestionably the false prophets prophesied by the Son of God and the Spirit of God have appeared. Down through the centuries the Christian church has been subtly and yet severely attacked by Satan. Seldom has the onslaught come from professed paganism, but rather from spurious religions which have a 'form of godliness, but deny the power thereof.'

These cultists emulate Christianity; their voluminous writings are sprinkled with biblical quotations; they talk much about Jesus and Jehovah, and claim to have the only true interpretation of the Scriptures.

Even in the days of primitive Christianity there was a noticeable falling away from the 'faith once for all delivered to the saints'; however, in recent years, especially since the latter part of the nineteenth century, there has been a decided increase of demon activity manifested by the springing up of many diabolical sects.

Foremost among these systems of error is the cult

under consideration — JEHOVAH'S WITNESSES.

At the outset, it would be wise for us to review

I. THE CREATION OF THE CULT

It is commonly known today, among informed people, as RUSSELLISM, deriving this sobriquet from Charles Taze Russell, its founder.

Now the cult—"Jehovah's Witnesses"—has had a variety of names. Back in 1874, at its inception, it was called MILLENNIAL DAWN. When it was exposed under this title, the self-styled "Pastor" Russell changed the name to WATCHTOWER AND TRACT SOCIETY. Later it was known as THE PEOPLE'S PULPIT ASSOCIATION, and to some as THE BROOKLYN TABERNACLE. And, shortly before the founder died aboard a Santa Fe train, the cult became known as THE INTERNATIONAL BIBLE STUDENTS' ASSOCIATION.

Charles Taze Russell is one of the tragedies of the Christian church. We are told that his parents were God-fearing Congregationalists. He spent his boyhood in Pittsburgh, Pennsylvania, where, during his youth, he was haunted by a great fear of Hell.

Eventually he succumbed to the teachings of an infidel who was an apostate from Christianity. This man convinced him there was no place of eternal punishment. Soon Russell was found spending his time and talents trying to convince all who would listen to him that there was no literal Hell.

It is not surprising to learn that he was one of the most brazen men imaginable. He has been called "The Great Paraphraser," so promiscuously did he alter the meaning of Scripture to suit his purposes.

To say that he employed exaggeration and subterfuge to further his ends is an understatement indeed. Once he promoted the sale of what he called "Miracle Wheat" at the exorbitant price of sixty dollars a bushel. It was supposed to grow five times as much as the average wheat and could be purchased only by the "faithful."

When his wife sued him for divorce, he admitted his improper relationship in court and later transferred his property to corporations and societies of which he himself had control in order to avoid paying alimony.

However, despite his unorthodox practices and tarnished reputation, at the convention of the Jehovah's Witnesses held in Yankee Stadium several years ago, this statement appeared in the New York press:

> When the history of the Church of Christ is fully written, it will be found that the place next to Saint Paul in the Gallery of Fame as expounder of the Gospel of the Great Master will be occupied by Charles Taze Russell.

Now, when Russell died in the fall of 1916, his funeral oration was delivered by ex-Judge Joseph Franklin Rutherford, who was destined to take up the reins of leadership.

This is what he said of the beloved "Pastor" who had taught the erroneous theory of "soul sleep," i. e., the dead sleep until the resurrection:

> Our dear brother sleeps not in death, but was instantly changed from the human to the divine nature, and is now forever with the Lord.

Now, this man Rutherford was both militant and mysterious, and was disliked by a number of his members. However, he was able to keep things going, even through the year 1925 when Abraham, Isaac, and Jacob were to have returned to set up their kingdom, as Judge Rutherford himself had foretold.

By 1931 the new leader had stopped the sale of Russell's books and had caused all mention of the founder to cease. He changed the name of the organization to "Jehovah's Witnesses," and convinced his followers that every one of them was one of the final messengers to the nations.

Rutherford died in 1942, and as yet no successor with the cunning and color of Russell and Rutherford has arisen. However, under the leadership of the current president, Nathan H. Knorr, who was elected after the "Judge's" death, and who closely follows the fallacious theories of his predecessors, the cult moves on, with its headquarters in the fabulous borough of Brooklyn.

The cult has spread with such rapidity that the property of its home base is valued at millions. It owns a large printing concern which up to this time has produced an estimated half-billion pieces of literature. It also owns a modern apartment building, spacious offices, a farm, a radio station and a Bible school. Since the school's opening in 1943, it has sent out one thousand missionaries.

Incidentally, we understand there are seventy thousand Jehovah's Witnesses who distribute literature on the streets and from door to door in New York City and its environs!

During the aforementioned convention of the Jehovah's Witnesses, I received a letter from an official of one of the leading business concerns in our city. The correspondent, who is an intelligent and informed Christian, said:

> While the Jehovah's Witnesses were in New York, I made it a point to question a few on their doctrine, and it is a wonder to me how these poor, unfortunate, seemingly sincere people, can be so gullible and misguided. They repeat their teachings in parrotlike fashion, as if they had been drilled into them, and they have expressionless countenances.
>
> Whether consciously or unconsciously, these people are doing more harm to the Christian world than the communists, primarily because they call themselves Christians. And they certainly are contributing to the cause of the enemies of our country.

Notice this sentence once again: "They repeat their

teachings in parrotlike fashion as if they had been drilled into them, and they have expressionless countenances." I have made the identical observation. Down through the years I have talked with many of these poor people, and I can truthfully say all of them seem to have been drugged by some powerful narcotic.

Now understand, we are not opposed to these deluded cultists. If there ever was a group of people on the face of the earth that needs spiritual illumination and guidance, it is these "Witnesses." However, we are definitely opposed to the evil system of teaching that has blinded them to the Truth.

Contemplate with me, if you will

II. THE CONCOCTION OF THE CULT

If ever there was a poison brewed by the Devil himself, we find it in the books and pamphlets of Russellism.

The great Bible scholar, Dr. James M. Gray, was right when he said, "Russellism contradicts almost every fundamental revelation," and Dr. William E. Biederwolf was equally right when he declared, "Pastor Russell has left scarcely one great truth or fundamental doctrine untouched with his unholy and unwarranted conclusions."

The scholarly pulpit orator of the South, Dr. A. C. Dixon, said, "Its plan of salvation is a plan of damnation," while Dr. H. A. Ironside, the late minister of Moody Memorial Church in Chicago, said, "This is indeed a sect of perdition; and its teaching is rightly labeled 'damnable heresy.' 'From such turn away.'"

Never in the history of the Christian religion has there been such a distortion of the Scriptures, such a twisting of the truth, such a devilish presentation of error.

The founder of this cult was a complete egotist. Once he made this ridiculous statement with reference to his *Studies in the Scriptures,* which statement appeared in his publication, *The Watchtower* of September 15, 1910, page 298:

> If the six volumes of "Scripture Studies" are practically the Bible, topically arranged with Bible proof texts given, we might not improperly name the volumes "The Bible in an arranged form." That is to say, they are not mere comments on the Bible, but they are practically the Bible itself. Furthermore, not only do we find that people cannot see the Divine plan in studying the Bible by itself but we see also that if anyone lays the "Scripture Studies" aside, even after he has used them, after he has become familiar with them, after he has read them for ten years --if he then lays them aside and ignores them and goes to the Bible alone, though he has understood his Bible for ten years, our experience shows that within two years he goes into darkness. On the other hand, if he had merely read the "Scripture Studies" with their references and had not read a page of the Bible as such he would be in the light at the end of two years, because he would have the light of the Scriptures.

Can you imagine anything more audacious than that! This man who said that it was better to ignore the Scriptures and study his books than to scan the Scriptures and neglect his books was constantly guilty of taking the text from the context and arriving at a pretext. And those who have succeeded him are likewise guilty.

Isaiah admonishes us, "To the law and to the testimony: if they speak not according to this word, it is because there is no light in them" (Isa. 8:20).

Well may we heed these words for, as someone has reminded us, "the only way to determine whether a system of teaching is of God is by examining the system through the lens of Holy Scripture"—that is, viewing the system in the light of the Bible, and not viewing the Bible in the light of the system.

Now, let us turn the searchlight of God's Word on some of the teachings of this cult.

First of all, what do Jehovah's Witnesses say about

1. The Holy Trinity?

Notice! "This view [the doctrine of the Trinity of the Godhead] suited well the Dark Ages, which it helped to produce." This is taken from the fifth of Russell's six-volume work, *Studies in the Scriptures,* page 166, which constitutes the basis for the dogma of this cult.

In the same volume, and on the same page, we also find the two following quotations:

> This...theory is as unscriptural as it is unreasonable.
> ...if it were not for the fact that this trinitarian nonsense was drilled into us from earliest infancy and the fact that it is so soberly taught in theological seminaries by gray-haired professors...nobody would give it a moment's serious consideration.

But what does the Bible say about the Trinity?

In Genesis 1:26 we read: "And God said, Let us make man in our image, after our likeness."

Notice "us" and "our." Here Jehovah, in speaking of creation, applies plural pronouns to Himself.

In Genesis 11:7 we read: "Go to, let us go down, and there confound their language...."

And in Isaiah 6:8 we read: "Also I heard the voice of the Lord, saying, Whom shall I send, and who will go for us?"

In the latter two verses, as in the first verse, the Holy Trinity is referred to as "us."

In Matthew 3:16 and 17 we read:

"*And Jesus, when he was baptized, went up straightway out of the water: and, lo, the heavens were opened unto him, and he saw the Spirit of God descending like a dove, and lighting upon him: And lo a voice from heaven, saying, This is my beloved Son, in whom I am well pleased.*"

Here we have the witness of the Father, Son, and Holy Ghost—the Trinity appearing together.

In Matthew 28:19 we read:

"*Go ye therefore, and teach all nations, baptizing them in the name of the Father, and of the Son, and of the Holy Ghost.*"

These are the words of the Lord Jesus, and here we have the witness of the Son to the Trinity.

Scripture is replete with references to the Trinity, and yet these poor people ignore the biblical teachings of the Triune God.

And Jehovah's Witnesses have this to say concerning

2. The Deity of Christ

Our Redeemer existed as a spirit being before he was made flesh and dwelt amongst men. At that time, as well as subsequently, he was properly known as "a god"—a mighty one. As chief of the angels and next to the Father he was known as the Archangel (highest angel or messenger), whose name, Michael, signifies, "Who as God," or God's representative.

As he was the highest of all Jehovah's creation, so also he was the first, the direct creation of God, the "only Begotten," and then he, as Jehovah's power, and in his name, created all things—angels, principalities and powers, as well as the earthly creation.—*Studies in the Scriptures,* Vol. V, page 84.

And they further comment on the deity of Christ:

Some insist that Jesus when on earth was both God and man in completeness. This theory is wrong, however. . . . It is also easy to be seen that Jesus could not be part God and part man, because that would be more than the law required; hence divine justice could not accept such a ransom.—*The Harp of God,* pages 101 and 128.

And think of this: these cultists say that "God the Father created Jesus and God has two sons—Jesus and Satan." They maintain that the Devil is the brother of

Jesus, the Lord. This information is taken from their book entitled *Creation,* pages 18 and 53.

Now, can you think of anything, anywhere, that is more blasphemous than that?

But what does the Bible say concerning the deity of Christ?

In John 1:1 we read: "In the beginning was the Word, and the Word was with God, and the Word was God."

Here we have three tremendous assertions:

(1) "In the beginning was the Word [*Logos*]. . . ."
This affirms the eternal existence of Jesus.

(2) ". . . and the Word was with God. . . ."
The Word being WITH God affirms the distinct personality of Jesus.

(3) ". . . and the Word was God."
This, of course, affirms the deity of Christ.

Also, we have the testimony of Jesus, Peter, Paul, and John concerning the deity of Christ:

JESUS said:

"*I and my Father are one.*"—John 10:30.

". . . *he that hath seen me hath seen the Father*. . . ."—John 14:9.

"*Before Abraham was, I am.*"—John 8:58.

You will notice He did not say, "Before Abraham was, I WAS." He said, "Before Abraham was, I AM," indicating that He has always been, from everlasting to everlasting. "Jesus Christ the same yesterday, and to day, and for ever" (Heb. 13:8).

PETER said:

"*Thou art the Christ, the Son of the living God.*"—Matt. 16:16.

PAUL said:

"*God was in Christ, reconciling the world unto himself.*"—II Cor. 5:19.

"*It pleased the Father that in him should all fulness dwell.*"—Col. 1:19.

"*In him dwelleth all the fulness of the Godhead bodily.*" —Col. 2:9.

JOHN said:

"*Who is a liar but he that denieth that Jesus is the Christ? . . . Whosoever denieth the Son, the same hath not the Father.*"—I John 2:22,23.

And then, too, Jehovah's Witnesses say this concerning

3. The Efficacy of the Blood Atonement of Christ

> One unforfeited life can redeem one forfeited life, but no more. The man Christ Jesus redeems Adam.—*Studies in the Scriptures,* Vol. I, page 133.
>
> Christ gave Himself a ransom that He might give to every man an individual trial for life. The ransom does not guarantee everlasting life, to any man, but guarantees a second chance.—Ibid., Vol. I, page 150.

The Bible has this to say concerning the blood atonement of God's Son:

"*God so loved the world, that he gave his only begotten Son, that whosoever believeth in him should not perish, but have everlasting life.*"—John 3:16.

"*Verily, verily, I say unto you, He that believeth on me hath everlasting life.*"—John 6:47.

"*Believe on the Lord Jesus Christ, and thou shalt be saved.*"—Acts 16:31.

"*Except a man be born again, he cannot see the kingdom of God.*"—John 3:3.

"*But as many as received him, to them gave he power* [or authority] *to become the sons of God. . . .*" John 1:12.

But let us consider what Jehovah's Witnesses say about

4. The Bodily Resurrection of Christ

They say that "Jesus no longer exists in human form" (*Studies in the Scriptures,* Vol. II, page 107).

They say:

> It was necessary not only that the man Christ Jesus should die, but just as necessary that the man Christ Jesus should never live again. – Ibid., Vol. V, page 454.

And they further assert:

> Our Lord's human body . . . did not decay or corrupt . . . whether it was dissolved into gases or whether it is still preserved somewhere . . . no one knows. – Ibid., Vol. II, page 129.
>
> He was put to death a man, but was raised from the dead a spirit being of the highest order of the divine nature. . . . For our Lord Jesus to have been raised a man would have implied two evils: (1) It would have implied the taking back of our ransom, which would have left us as much under sentence of death as before. (2) It would have implied to him an everlasting loss of the higher nature which he had left in order to become a man, and to be our Redeemer. . . . The man Jesus is dead, forever dead. – Ibid., Vol. V, pages 453,454.

But what does the Bible say concerning the resurrection of Christ?

In the twenty-fourth chapter of Luke we read (Bear in mind this was after the crucifixion and resurrection of our blessed Lord):

"*And as they thus spake, Jesus himself stood in the midst of them, and saith unto them, Peace be unto you. But they were terrified and affrighted, and supposed that they had seen a spirit. And he said unto them, Why are ye troubled? and why do thoughts arise in your hearts? Behold my hands and my feet, that it is I my-*

self: handle me, and see; for a spirit hath not flesh and bones, as ye see me have. And when he had thus spoken, he shewed them his hands and his feet."—Vss. 36-40.

And I am sure when Thomas was asked of the Lord to reach hither his finger that he did not brazenly put the Master to the test of physical touch but, rather, instantaneously fell to his knees and cried out, "My Lord and my God."

And in Acts 1:3 we read:

"*To whom also he shewed himself alive after his passion by many infallible proofs, being seen of them forty days, and speaking of the things pertaining to the kingdom of God.*"

Now, what do Jehovah's Witnesses say relative to

5. The Visible Return of Christ?

Their deluded founder stated that Christ "is no longer a human being. Since he is no longer in any sense or degree a human being, we must not expect him to come again as a human being" (Vol. II, *The Time Is at Hand*).

In their book, *Let God Be True,* page 185, these spiritually blind people say:

> Christ Jesus comes, not as a human but as a glorious spirit creature.

And in their devilish volume, *The Truth Shall Make You Free,* page 295, this is the bit of blasphemy that we find:

> It is a settled scriptural truth, therefore, that human eyes will not see him at his second coming, neither will he come in a fleshly body.

Now these "heavenly witnesses" actually teach that

Christ has already come—that He came in 1914! This is set forth in their volume, *The Truth Shall Make You Free,* page 300.

Now, on the basis of their assumption that Christ is a spirit, He would not be visible, and they erroneously affirm He has been here since 1914, wrestling with the forces of evil. World Wars I and II, so they say, attest this struggle.

They claim that the final conflict, Armageddon, will take place in the near future, and this will be the decisive battle between Jehovah and the Devil. At that time Christ, as a spirit creature, will not be visible, but He will lead His loyal legionnaires—the 144,000 Jehovah's Witnesses—against the hordes of Satan, comprised of Catholics, Protestants, and other unenlightened individuals.

But what does the Bible say about the visible return of Christ?

Our blessed Lord, of course, has not yet returned. But He may descend the skies at any moment to catch away His church.

You will remember the words of the celestial messengers to the disciples:

"*Ye men of Galilee, why stand ye gazing up into heaven? this same Jesus, which is taken up from you into heaven, shall so come in like manner as ye have seen him go into heaven.*"—Acts 1:11.

Notice the emphasis—"this SAME Jesus"—'shall COME AGAIN.' In other words, when Jesus came forth from the grave, it was in a literal, bodily form. He still bore the print of the nails in His hands and feet, and the mark of the spear in His side. His appearance to Thomas attests these facts.

And when Jesus comes again He will do so in a visible, bodily, human form. He will still bear the print of the nails in His hands and feet and the mark of the spear in His side.

He will come back to this earth in the same body in which He was buried, and in which He rose again from the dead.

Paul says:

"*For the Lord himself shall descend from heaven with a shout, with the voice of the archangel, and with the trump of God: and the dead in Christ shall rise first: Then we which are alive and remain shall be caught up together with them in the clouds, to meet the Lord in the air: and so shall we ever be with the Lord. Wherefore comfort one another with these words.*"—I Thess. 4: 16-18.

And in Titus 2:13, we read:

"*Looking for that blessed hope, and the glorious appearing of the great God and our Saviour Jesus Christ.*"

But what do Jehovah's Witnesses say about

6. The Eternal Punishment of Lost Sinners?

In volume I of *Studies in the Scriptures,* page 127, they say:

> Many have imbibed the erroneous idea that God placed our race on trial for life with the alternative of eternal torture, whereas nothing of the kind is even hinted at in the penalty.

And on page 128 of the same volume we find these words:

> Eternal torture is nowhere suggested in the Old Testament Scriptures, and only a few statements in the New Testament can be so misconstrued as to appear to teach it.

And in their volume, *Let God Be True,* on page 79, they call the doctrine of eternal punishment a "God-dishonoring doctrine."

Also, on page 80 of the same volume, they say:

> The doctrine of a burning hell where the wicked are tortured eternally after death cannot be true.

But what does the Bible say about the eternal punishment of lost sinners?

Actually, there are more verses in the Bible which speak of Hell than of Heaven. Any informed believer knows that if we want a God capable of love and infinite love, we must accept a God capable of wrath and infinite wrath.

The unregenerated man finds it exceedingly difficult to understand this. Naturally, a man in his sins finds it extremely distasteful to think of being judged by a holy God for those sins. Consequently, cults with a dogma similar to Russellistic "theology" have flourished, especially in these days of spiritual and moral declension.

No saved person revels in the contemplation of eternal punishment for the unsaved. The great evangelist, Dwight Lyman Moody, once said that no man should ever preach on Hell without tears in his eyes!

The Bible description of the place of everlasting torment causes all of us to shudder, but no sincere student of the Word of God will deny that the Scripture declares Hell as a literal place where those who reject Christ as Saviour will be punished forever.

Permit me to list for you some of the Scripture locations that speak of the doctrine of Hell: Psalm 9:17; Proverbs 5:5; 9:13-18; 15:24; 23:13,14; Isaiah 30:33; 33:14; Matthew 3:12; 5:29,30; 7:13,14; 8:11,12; 10:28; 13:30, 38-42,49,50; 16:18; 18:9,34,35; 22:13; 25:28-30; 25:41,46; Mark 9:43-48; Luke 3:17; 16:23-28; II Thessalonians 1:9; II Peter 2:4; Jude 6, 23; Revelation 9:1,2; 14:10,11; 19:20; 20:10,15; 21:8.

The Bible is explicit in its teaching that those who spurn the call of Christ and die without Him will spend eternity in Hell.

Space will not permit to tell more of the blasphemy of the gospel of Russellism. The teaching of Jehovah's Witnesses is so full of coarse, brutal, and devilish error that human language furnishes no vocabulary of sufficiently keen and cauterizing words or phrases whereby I might denounce it.

But notice with me, if you will,

III. THE CONCLUSIONS OF THE CULT

Suffice it to say that with such a faulty foundation their ultimate philosophy is bound to be erroneous.

I am constantly receiving literature from these poor, deluded people, and some time ago one of them wrote: "The enclosed tract presents the truth about WHAT IS A JEHOVAH'S WITNESS, and unless you present the truth regarding the Jehovah's Witnesses to your congregation, you will receive due punishment from Jehovah God." Then there followed quite a few Scriptures about lying, etc.

There you have the typical attitude of these deceived cultists. They feel that any individual, or group of individuals, who disagrees with them is of the Devil.

They are bold to state that all denominations, Protestant as well as Catholic, make up a segment of "Satan's Organization," and only those will be saved who turn to their movement and enter what they call "The Theocratic Kingdom."

However, the Bible tells us there is only one way to become a member of the kingdom of God, and that is by experiencing the new birth.

"*But as many as received him, to them gave he power to become the sons of God, even to them that believe on his name.*"—John 1:12.

"*Jesus answered and said unto him, Verily, verily, I say unto thee, Except a man be born again, he cannot see the kingdom of God.*"—John 3:3.

"*Jesus saith unto him, I am the way, the truth, and the life: no man cometh unto the Father, but by me.*" —John 14:6.

"Come unto ME," Jesus said—not to a man-made organization!

If we get no farther than the local church, we will never be admitted into the kingdom of God. We must go past the church to Jesus Christ, and in Him find forgiveness for our sins.

And the "Witnesses" also relegate all human government to "Satan's Organization." They believe all civil authority is of the Devil, and consequently, they will not salute the flag of any nation. They will not vote; they will not participate in public affairs; they will not defend their nation against aggression.

In the correspondence mentioned earlier on page 275 of this message, my informant said this:

> I asked one Jehovah's Witness if he would defend himself if a robber attacked him on the street and he said he would. I then asked him whether he would defend his country if it were attacked by a foreign power and he said no. He based his answer on the commandment, "Thou shalt not kill."
>
> I pointed out that in defending himself against the robber he was risking the chance of killing also; then he changed his mind and said he would rather have a policeman apprehend the robber if one were nearby. If not, he would still defend himself. The policeman, you see, is not supposed to believe as he does.

Now, any open-minded individual reading Romans 13:1-7, I Timothy 2:1,2, Titus 3:1 and I Peter 2:13,14 immediately sees the fallacy of Russellistic teaching in matters of human government in the light of the plain teaching of the Word of God.

And these words from the lips of Jesus alone should settle once and for all the Christian's responsibility in this matter: "Render...unto Caesar the things which are Caesar's; and unto God the things that are God's" (Matt. 22:21).

But the fact of the matter is that it is not government or commerce that is evil but rather the sinful people who comprise this sphere of human activity.

The heart of man is evil and the devilish teaching of Russellism will never do anything to cleanse the sinful heart of humankind, but will rather further blind men to the truth.

Now, another false conclusion of the cult is Judge Rutherford's foolish declaration that Jesus actually returned in 1874 and that the work of restoration began in 1878 and concluded in 1918.

It was then that the Lord was to have come "to his temple," meaning, of course, the "Witnesses" who alone were anointed to catch the significance of His presence.

It was in the year 1914 that Jesus was supposed to have ascended His throne, and the kingdoms of this world became "the kingdoms of our Lord, and of his Christ" (Rev. 11:15).

Satan's rule is said to have culminated in that year, and we are told that the judgment of the emissaries of the Devil has been under way since then.

The clergymen are said to be condemned with no chance of coming into the light.

The "Witnesses" alone are supposed to have on the "wedding garments of salvation," and all churches are said to be under the domination of corrupt politicians and ecclesiastics.

How wonderful it is to rely on the simple statements of the Word of God rather than the contradictory, confusing concoctions of the word of man. Whereas the Jehovah's Witnesses say that salvation rests in their finite organization, the Bible makes us to understand that our salvation rests alone in Jesus Christ—"...for there is none other name under heaven given among men, whereby we must be saved" (Acts 4:12).

And, whereas Jehovah's Witnesses say that Christ returned in 1914, the Bible makes it explicitly clear that when Jesus returns to set up His kingdom, wars and rumors of war will be no more. Then He will reign and rule with a rod of iron to smash into pieces, as a potter's vessel, all opposition. Then the prophecy of Isaiah will be fulfilled.

"*And righteousness shall be the girdle of his loins, and faithfulness the girdle of his reins. The wolf also shall dwell with the lamb, and the leopard shall lie down with the kid; and the calf and the young lion and the fatling together; and a little child shall lead them.*" — Isa. 11:5,6.

And this leads us to consider

IV. THE CATACLYSM OF THE CULT

In the nineteenth chapter of Revelation we read that when the Lord Jesus descends the skies with power and great glory, He will come as King of kings and Lord of lords.

And in II Thessalonians Paul says that in that day

"*. . . the Lord Jesus shall be revealed from heaven with his mighty angels, In flaming fire taking vengeance on them that know not God, and that obey not the gospel of our Lord Jesus Christ: Who shall be punished with everlasting destruction from the presence of the Lord, and from the glory of his power.*" — II Thess. 1:7-9.

The Jehovah's Witnesses know not the true God, as their teachings clearly prove. Rather than 'obeying the Gospel,' they deny practically every truth of the Gospel.

Because of this they will be among those who, in the day of manifestation and judgment, will cry out to the mountains and rocks: "Fall on us, and hide us from the face of him that sitteth on the throne, and from the wrath of the Lamb" (Rev. 6:16).

And in the twentieth chapter of Revelation, we learn further of the ignominious destiny of the devilish cult and all others who deny the faith once for all delivered to the saints:

"*And I saw a great white throne, and him that sat on it, from whose face the earth and the heaven fled away; and there was found no place for them. And I saw the dead, small and great, stand before God; and the books were opened: and another book was opened, which is the book of life: and the dead were judged out of those things which were written in the books, according to their works. And the sea gave up the dead which were in it; and death and hell delivered up the dead which were in them: and they were judged every man according to their works. And death and hell were cast into the lake of fire. This is the second death. And whosoever was not found written in the book of life was cast into the lake of fire.*"—Vss. 11-15.

What a time of confusion and consternation and cataclysm it will be for the thousands of this cult when they have to bow and confess before the assembled universe that Jesus Christ, whose deity they denied, is Lord to the glory of God the Father:

"*Wherefore God also hath highly exalted him, and given him a name which is above every name: That at the name of Jesus every knee should bow, of things in heaven, and things in earth, and things under the earth; And that every tongue should confess that Jesus Christ is Lord, to the glory of God the Father.*"—Phil. 2:9-11.

2. Beware of Jehovah's Witnesses Falsehood

Many readers will be interested in the editor's letter about a characteristic pamphlet written and spread by Jehovah's Witnesses.

My dear Brother:

Thank you for sending me the booklet, *Christendom or Christianity—Which One Is "the Light of the World"?* I looked the booklet over carefully and I find that it follows the usual Jehovah's Witness line. There are many good things in it mixed along with much that is absolute poison. Note these faults in the book:

1. The first terrible falsehood of Jehovah's Witnesses at the start of this book is on the plan of salvation itself. There is no word about personal regeneration, being born again by individual faith in Christ as Saviour, the very heart of Bible Christianity. On pages 15 and 16 is this false definition of what it is to be a Christian.

> It was Jesus' disciples or learners who were called Christians, first at Antioch, Syria, and hence a Christian is one who accepts Christ's teaching and obeys it, believing the things he believed, preaching the things he preached, and following him or copying his example in doing the will of his God and heavenly Father, even at the cost of life itself.

This teaches salvation by works, salvation by merit, and not salvation by personal faith in Christ on the merits of the shed blood of Jesus. And so Jehovah's Witnesses are a false religion and most Jehovah's Witnesses are unconverted people, not knowing what it takes to be saved, because that is not preached in any of the books of Pastor Russell or Rutherford or the Watchtower Bible and Tract Society.

2. This pamphlet teaches the usual heresy of this false cult of Jehovah's Witnesses, about the Gospel of Christ. Instead of a saving Gospel about Christ's death, burial, and resurrection, to pay for the sins of every sinner who would trust Him, this is what the pamphlet, *Christendom or Christianity,* says on page 27:

> By "this gospel" is meant the good news of God's kingdom as having been established and not as yet to come. Jehovah's witnesses are the only ones today preaching this good news, particularly since the year 1914. For then God's kingdom by Christ was established in the heavens, to bring this old world to its end and bring in a righteous new world, as Jehovah's witnesses show from Bible prophecies and its time schedule and also from the world events since A.D. 1914.

These blasphemers claim that Jehovah's Witnesses are the only true Christians.

3. On page 30 of *Christendom or Christianity* there is the following question and answer:

> QUESTION: Who are the Bible Christians today?
>
> ANSWER: Not letting ourselves be prejudiced against them by reason of the international and inter-religious hatred against them, but honestly examining the facts about them and comparing the facts with the Holy Scriptures of the Bible, we are led irresistibly to the conclusion that Jehovah's witnesses are the Bible Christians of today. They resemble their great leader and Exemplar, Jesus Christ.

The same claim in other words is found several other places in this blasphemous pamphlet of this false cult.

4. On page 14 this pamphlet scoffs at the Bible doc-

trine of the Trinity, the Bible doctrine of Hell, the Immortality of the soul.

Jehovah's Witnesses is thus a false cult, is not Bible Christianity. This kind of a booklet would do great harm. It quotes the Scriptures deceitfully, it ignores most fundamental truth and denies other fundamental truth. It develops a group of self-righteous, hard-working Pharisees who know nothing about actual regeneration and who despise true Christians and mock at true Christian doctrine.

Thank you, dear brother, for sending me the pamphlet. I trust this will help you answer the inquiries you are receiving about it.

(For further reading, see *A Christian Answers the Jehovah's Witnesses* by Charles Trombly, "A Textbook Written by a Student of Watchtower Theology for Twenty-Five Years." Includes his Christian experiences and provides the believer with a complete evaluation of their doctrines, and true-to-the-Scripture answers; published by *The Expositor,* Sarasota, Florida.)

(*Jehovah of the Watchtower,* A Thorough Expose of the Importance of Anti-Biblical Teaching of Jehovah's Witnesses, by Martin and Klann, Bethany House Publishers)

8

A Bible Answer to the Ultra-Dispensational Heresy

A Bible Answer to the Ultra-Dispensational Heresy

A young pastor writes saying:

> Sometime when you have time to write to me, would you please state the plainest Scripture and any other reason you know against O'Hair's and Stam's hyper-dispensational teaching.

The hyper-dispensationalists, or ultra-dispensationalists usually say that a new dispensation began at Acts 28:28. Before that time, they say, the Scriptures were given to the Jews, and the church as the body of Christ was not revealed. They say that the teaching of the Gospels, particularly the Sermon on the Mount, was for Jews and not for Gentiles. They say that the Gospel of grace taught by Paul in his epistles, written after his Roman imprisonment, is different from the Gospel preached by the apostles in the book of Acts and the Gospel preached by John the Baptist and Jesus. They make a distinction between the "kingdom gospel," so-called, and "Paul's gospel." There are various small differences in the doctrine of different teachers but this is the general trend of the ultra-dispensational groups.

Ultra-dispensationalism, which teaches that a large part of the New Testament is for Jews only and is not applicable to Gentile Christians in the present day, is a modernism or heresy developed somewhat by Bullinger in England, by O'Hair in Chicago, and others. Generally it is promoted by men without adequate theological training. They have done much to split churches, to arouse enmity between Christians, and to discredit much of the Bible for present use. They say, generally, that baptism has been done away with. Some say that the Lord's Prayer is not for this age; some fervently deny that the Great Commission is for us; and some have repudiated even the Lord's Supper, saying it is of law instead of grace.

I wrote the young pastor the following answer, giving Scriptures that disprove the teachings of this modern heresy.

I. The Great Commission Is the Same for the Whole Age

The Great Commission itself clearly contradicts the hyper-dispensational teachings of Mr. O'Hair. Jesus said,

"*All power is given unto me in heaven and in earth. Go ye therefore, and teach all nations, baptizing them in the name of the Father, and of the Son, and of the Holy Ghost: Teaching them to observe all things whatsoever I have commanded you: and, lo, I am with you alway, even unto the end of the world. Amen.*" —Matt. 28:18-20.

Note the following things about this commission: (a) it is expressly given to the eleven disciples, verse 16; (b) these eleven disciples were to go to all nations, making other disciples, baptizing them, etc.; (c) but every new disciple was to be taught "to observe all things whatsoever I have commanded *you*." That is, there was to be an unbroken chain, with every new convert carrying out this same Great Commission, obeying exactly the same command given to the disciples. (d) Notice the marvelous extent of this Great Commission. They were to go to "all nations," and it was to continue "even unto the end of the world."

This same Great Commission is given in Mark 16:15,16, and in Luke 24:46-49, and in Acts 1:8. Exactly the same Gospel was to be preached to all nations, and exactly the same Gospel was to be preached from the time of Christ's ascension to the end of the world. Therefore baptism and all the Great Commission is still commanded of Christians.

II. Plan of Salvation the Same in All Ages

Acts 10:43 clearly shows there has never been any dispensational change in the matter of salvation. It says, "To him give all the prophets witness, that through his name whosoever believeth in him shall receive remission of sins." Every Old Testament prophet taught exactly what Jesus taught, what John the Baptist taught, what Paul taught, and now what Peter taught: that those who trusted in Christ should be saved. That plan never varied in any dispensation. So it is foolish to say that the "kingdom gospel" is one gospel and the "gospel of grace" is another gospel. That is a distinction manufactured by men ignorant of the Bible. There is no distinction in the Bible between one gospel and another gospel, except between the true Gospel and a false gospel.

III. John the Baptist Taught the Same Plan of Salvation

John 3:36 clearly shows that John the Baptist taught exactly the same plan of salvation that Jesus taught and that Paul taught. John the Baptist said, "He that believeth on the Son hath everlasting life: and he that believeth not the Son shall not see life; but the wrath of God abideth on him" (John 3:36). You see at once that this is exactly the same plan of salvation that Jesus taught in John 3:16, that Peter preached in Acts 10:43, and that Paul and Barnabas preached in Acts 13: 38,39. So to say that the preaching and baptizing of John the Baptist was of another dispensation and is not part of the Gospel, is foolish and unscriptural.

IV. The New Testament Baptism Began With John the Baptist

Mark 1:1 clearly shows that the Gospel in the New Testament began to be preached by John the Baptist, and that John the Baptist properly belongs in the New Testament and not in the Old, and that he preached the Gospel of grace and did not preach the law. Speaking of John the Baptist, Mark 1:1 says, "The beginning of the gospel of Jesus Christ, the Son of God." Compare this with John 3:36, and you will see that it is only ignorance which would have John the Baptist baptizing people in order to save them. Anybody who interprets Matthew 3:11 as teaching that baptism went before repentance, or that baptism was essential to salvation, simply misunderstands the Scripture. Others pervert Acts 2:38 in trying to prove baptism essential to salvation, but it never was. Neither Peter nor John the Baptist nor any other Bible preacher of either the Old or New Testament ever preached that baptism is essential to salvation.

V. No New Dispensation in Acts 28:28

The ultra-dispensationalists say that a new dispensation began with Acts 28:28 when Paul said, "Be it known therefore unto you, that the salvation of God is sent unto the Gentiles, and that they will hear it." That is farthest from Paul's mind. Actually Paul was simply following his usual order, every place he went, "to the Jew first, and also to the Greek" (Rom. 1:16). The same idea was included in the Great Commission, "beginning at Jerusalem" (Luke 24:47). Jews should naturally begin with Jews.

When Jews would not hear the Gospel, Paul always turned then to the Gentiles in the same city and preached to them. That is what he did in Antioch of Pisidia. In Acts 13:46 we are told, "Then Paul and Barnabas waxed bold, and said, It was necessary that the word of God should first have been spoken to you: but seeing ye put it from you, and judge yourselves unworthy of everlasting life, *lo, we turn to the Gentiles.*"

Exactly the same thing happened in Acts 18:6 at Corinth. We are told, "And when they opposed themselves, and blasphemed, he shook his raiment, and said unto them, Your blood be upon your own heads; I am clean: from *henceforth I will go unto the Gentiles.*"

Paul did not start a new dispensation in every town he came to! And it is silly to start a new dispensation in Acts 28:28 unless you start a new dispensation in Acts 13:46 and in Acts 18:6. Quarrelsome and critical preachers, without any solid seminary training, simply jumped to conclusions and started this heresy about a new dispensation at Acts 28:28.

VI. The Church Not the Mystery but That Gentiles Would Be in the Same Body as Jews

The ultra-dispensationalists utterly misunderstand the mystery revealed to Paul, as taught in Ephesians 3:3-6. There we are told,

"*How that by revelation he made known unto me the mystery; (as I wrote afore in few words, Whereby, when ye read, ye may understand my knowledge in the mystery of Christ) Which in other ages was not made known unto the sons of men, as it is now revealed unto his holy apostles and prophets by the Spirit;*

That the Gentiles should be followheirs, and of the same body, and partakers of his promise in Christ by the gospel."

The mystery was *not* that there would be a church. No, the mystery is that "the Gentiles should be fellowheirs, and *of the same body,* and *partakers* of his promise in Christ by the gospel." The mystery was that Gentiles should be saved and in the same body with Jews.

Jews found it hard to understand how Gentiles could be saved. That was a mystery to them. But God called Paul to be a special apostle to the Gentiles, and so he went everywhere explaining this mystery, that God wanted Gentiles saved, too, and that the Gospel was good for them as well as for Jews, and that both Jews and Gentiles (the saved) would be in one body.

The body was not new. There is good evidence in Hebrews 12:23 that every saved person from Adam on to Christ's second coming will be in that "general assembly and church of the firstborn, which are written in heaven." It was the same body. The mystery was that Gentiles would be in it as well as Jews. Misunderstanding this truth, so clearly stated in the Scriptures themselves, the ultra-dispensationalists have done great harm.

We must say that the ultra-dispensationalists were first led wrong, we believe, by too much emphasis on dispensations by Plymouth Brethren and by some notes in the Scofield Bible on this matter.

VII. The "One Baptism" of Ephesians 4:5 Is Literal Immersion in Water

The ultra-dispensationalists have grossly misunderstood and misinterpreted Ephesians 4:5. That verse says, "One Lord, one faith, one baptism." But actually, that is only part of the statement. God says that, "There is one body, and one Spirit, even as ye are called in one hope of your calling; One Lord, one faith, one baptism, One God and Father of all, who is above all, and through all, and in you all" (Eph. 4:4-6). The word *one* here, actually means *the same.* God says that Christians are members of the same body, have the same Holy Spirit, have the same hope, have the same Lord, have the same faith, have the same baptism, the same God. Instead of saying that God has changed dispensations and formerly there were two baptisms and now only one, this verse really says there never has been but one, that all Christians have the same baptism. Of course the one literal, physical baptism taught in the Bible is baptism by water. To be baptized in the Spirit, or to be baptized into the body of Christ, or to be baptized with suffering—these are only figurative uses of the term. Nobody is ever literally dipped into suffering or in the Holy Spirit or literally immersed into the body of Christ; those are figurative uses of the term. The only literal and physical baptism is baptism in water, of course. And that has never changed.

If you want further help on this matter, you might see the chapter, "'Paul's Gospel' or 'Kingdom Gospel,'" in my book, *Twelve Tremendous Themes,* or you might see the discussion of the same question in my book, ***Bible Baptism,*** which shows baptism has never changed in New Testament times, and that there is no dispensational difference since the time of Christ or since the teaching of John the Baptist.

9

Spiritualists and Fortunetellers Are "An Abomination Unto the Lord"

Spiritualists and Fortunetellers Are "An Abomination Unto the Lord"

What the Bible Says About Spiritualistic Mediums and Fortunetellers and Those Who Use Them

Notice that part of the heading of this article is in quotation marks and is what God's Word says—not the words of this writer. Satan has deceived many good people who think spiritualism is simply one denomination of the Christian religion. They do not know that it is thoroughly unchristian and that the curse of God is pronounced on those who partake of its wickedness. Likewise other kinds of fortunetellers or diviners, necromancers and soothsayers are visited by Christian people who are not conscious that they are thus sinning against God and running into great danger.

In Deuteronomy 18:9-14, the Lord gave plain commands to the children of Israel in which He teaches that spiritualism and fortunetelling are an abomination to God.

"*When thou art come into the land which the Lord thy God giveth thee, thou shalt not learn to do after the abominations of those nations. There shall not be found among you any one that maketh his son or his daughter to pass through the fire, or that useth divination, or an observer of times, or an enchanter, or a witch, Or a charmer, or a consulter with familiar spirits, or a wizard, or a necromancer. For all that do these things are an abomination unto the Lord: and because of these abominations the Lord thy God doth drive them out from before thee. Thou shalt be perfect with the Lord thy God. For these nations, which thou shalt possess, hearkened unto observers of times, and unto diviners: but as for thee, the Lord thy God hath not suffered thee so to do."*—Deut. 18:9-14.

In the above passage, divination means fortunetelling. Webster's dictionary defines "divination" as follows: "The act of divining, the pretended art of foreseeing future events by supernatural or magical agencies." In the above Scripture, the terms "witch," "consulter with familiar spirits," "wizard," and "necromancer" all refer to people who pretend to be in touch with spirits, whether spirits of the human dead or spirits of devils. These words exactly describe spiritualistic mediums. The Lord commanded plainly that "there shall not be found among you any one. . . that useth divination, or an observer of times, or an enchanter, or a witch, Or a charmer, or a consulter with familiar spirits, or a wizard, or a necromancer." Verse 12 says that all that do these things are an abomination to the Lord and because of this sin the heathen nations were driven out of the land of Canaan before Israel. In other words, fortunetelling and spiritualistic seances are a part of heathenism.

Many Scriptures Condemn Spiritualism and Fortunetelling

In the Old Testament, many, many passages of God's Word condemn the wicked practices of spiritualists, fortunetellers, Hindu mystics, etc. The term "familiar spirit" refers especially, throughout the Bible, to those who claim to be on familiar terms with the unseen spirits. Read the following passages which, like Deuteronomy 18:9-14, quoted above, condemn the use of familiar spirits or spiritualistic mediums:

"*Regard not them that have familiar spirits, neither seek after wizards, to be defiled by them: I am the Lord your God.*" — Lev. 19:31.

"*And the soul that turneth after such as have familiar spirits, and after wizards, to go a whoring after them, I will even set my face against that soul, and will cut him off from among his people.*" — Lev. 20:6.

"*A man also or woman that hath a familiar spirit, or that is a wizard, shall surely be put to death: they shall stone them with stones: their blood shall be upon them.*" — Lev. 20:27.

"*And when they shall say unto you, Seek unto them that have familiar spirits, and unto wizards that peep, and that mutter: should not a people seek unto their God? for the living to the dead?*" — Isa. 8:19.

The above passages mention wizards and those having familiar spirits. A similar passage is given in Exodus 22:18 where we are told, "Thou shalt not suffer a witch to live."

The death penalty was imposed on witches, that is, those in touch, or claiming to be in touch, with spirits, just the same as for murderers. In the sight of God, fortunetelling and spiritualism are terrible sins, a part of a heathen religion, and an abomination to God.

In the New Testament, witchcraft is named with idolatry, murder, and drunkenness as terrible sins, and we are told "that they which do such things shall not inherit the kingdom of God" (Gal. 5:20,21).

Two other terms used in the New Testament referring

to fortunetelling and consulting spirits are *soothsaying* and *sorcery.*

In Acts 8:9-24, we are told of the conversion of Simon, the sorcerer, who bewitched the people of Samaria until he was soundly converted and gave up his heathen wickedness.

In Acts 13:6-12 we are told about a "certain sorcerer, a false prophet, . . . whose name was Barjesus," also called Elymas. Notice that the Scripture said he was a false prophet, that he tried to prevent others from being saved. But the hand of the Lord came on him and he was struck blind for a season and the deputy, seeing what befell him, was converted.

In every single case where the Bible mentions consulting with spirits, divining or fortunetelling, necromancers, soothsayers, wizards and witches, they are condemned in unmistakable language as being of Satan and not of God.

A Fortuneteller Converted

When Paul and Silas went on their missionary journey out of Asia Minor into Macedonia to the city of Philippi, they found there a fortunetelling girl who was possessed of an evil spirit. This evil spirit or devil helped the girl to divine or tell fortunes. But Paul, filled with the Spirit of God, commanded the evil spirit to leave her, and she was gloriously converted. Then she no longer told fortunes. Read the story in the words of Scripture from Acts 16:16-21.

"*And it came to pass, as we went to prayer, a certain damsel possessed with a spirit of divination met us, which brought her masters much gain by soothsaying: The same followed Paul and us, and cried, saying, These men are the servants of the most high God, which shew unto us the way of salvation. And this did she many days. But Paul, being grieved, turned and said to the spirit, I command thee in the name of Jesus Christ to come out of her. And he came out the same hour. And when her masters saw that the hope of their gains was gone, they caught Paul and Silas, and drew them into the marketplace unto the rulers, And brought them to the magistrates, saying, These men, being Jews, do exceedingly trouble our city, And teach customs, which are not lawful for us to receive, neither to observe, being Romans."*

This story is very important. It makes clear that if one can really tell fortunes, he does it by the power of the Devil, and that when one who does that gets right with God, he will get out of the wicked business.

The rest of the story is very interesting, too. Read it in your Bible and see how these two good preachers were put in jail, how they prayed their way out, God sending a great earthquake, and how the jailer and his family were wonderfully saved the same night.

King Saul and the Witch of Endor

Saul, the first king of Israel, rebelled against God and turned to various kinds of sin. He did not utterly destroy the Amalekites, as God had commanded; he sought to kill David, whom God had chosen to be the next king; and on the whole became a rebellious, wicked backslider. When he had become so far from God that God would not hear his prayers, he sought out a spiritualistic medium, that is, a witch, or a woman with a familiar spirit, that he might get in touch with the dead prophet Samuel and learn what would happen in the future. First Samuel 28:7-19 tells this sad story of the sin of Israel's first king:

"*Then said Saul unto his servants, Seek me a woman that hath a familiar spirit, that I may go to her, and*

***enquire** of her. And his servants said to him, Behold, there is a woman that hath a familiar spirit at En-dor. And Saul disguised himself, and put on other raiment, and he went, and two men with him, and they came to the woman by night: and he said, I pray thee, divine unto me by the familiar spirit, and bring me him up, whom I shall name unto thee. And the woman said unto him, Behold, thou knowest what Saul hath done, how he hath cut off those that have familiar spirits, and the wizards, out of the land: wherefore then layest thou a snare for my life, to cause me to die? And Saul sware to her by the Lord, saying, As the Lord liveth, there shall no punishment happen to thee for this thing. Then said the woman, Whom shall I bring up unto thee? And he said, Bring me up Samuel. And when the woman saw Samuel, she cried with a loud voice: and the woman spake to Saul, saying, Why hast thou deceived me? for thou art Saul. And the king said unto her, Be not afraid: for what sawest thou? And the woman said unto Saul, I saw gods ascending out of the earth. And he said unto her, What form is he of? And she said, An old man cometh up; and he is covered with a mantle. And Saul perceived that it was Samuel, and he stooped with his face to the ground, and bowed himself. And Samuel said to Saul, Why hast thou disquieted me, to bring me up? And Saul answered, I am sore distressed; for the Philistines make war against me, and God is departed from me, and answereth me no more, neither by prophets, nor by dreams: therefore I have called thee, that thou mayest make known unto me what I shall do. Then said Samuel, Wherefore then dost thou ask of me, seeing the Lord is departed from thee, and is become thine enemy? And the Lord hath done to him, as he spake by me: for the Lord hath rent the kingdom out of thine hand, and given it to thy neighbour, even to David: Because thou obeyedst not the voice of the Lord, nor* *executedst his fierce wrath upon Amalek, therefore hath the Lord done this thing unto thee this day. Moreover the Lord will also deliver Israel with thee into the hand of the Philistines: and to morrow shalt thou and thy sons be with me: the Lord also shall deliver the host of Israel into the hand of the Philistines.*"

So there can be no doubt about the meaning of the terms "divine" or "divination," "witch," "wizard," and "familiar spirit." Notice that they are used in this story about this woman who went into a spiritualistic seance to commune with the spirits of the dead.

The Bible does not tell us whether this woman usually had power to bring up spirits as she wished or not. We are simply given this example, and God may have done it without the witch to rebuke Saul. Saul learned nothing to his own good. He learned that God had departed from him and would not help him, that Israel would be defeated the next day in battle and that he and his sons would be slain and be with Samuel in the land of the dead.

In his early reign, Saul had obeyed the command of God to put out of Israel wizards and those that had familiar spirits. Now that he had departed from God, he sinned in patronizing this fortunetelling spiritualistic medium. In this case, God permitted him to learn the truth, but he learned nothing that did him any good, nothing to make him happy, nothing to help him meet his problems.

For This Sin Saul Lost His Kingdom

Saul had sinned in other ways, but doubtless this sin of going to a medium was the climax of his rebellion against God, and for that he was put to death. First Chronicles 10:13,14 tells us that Saul was put to death because of his transgression "and also for asking counsel of one that had a familiar spirit, to enquire of it." Read those verses and see that God is not pleased for a Christian to do as Saul did, and inquire of fortunetellers, Hindu mystics, spiritualistic mediums, astrologers, etc.

"*So Saul died for his transgression which he committed against the Lord, even against the word of the Lord, which he kept not, and also for asking counsel of one that had a familiar spirit, to enquire of it: And enquired not of the Lord: therefore he slew him, and turned the kingdom unto David the son of Jesse.*" — I Chron. 10:13,14.

Can Mediums and Fortunetellers Reveal Secrets and Foretell the Future?

Is there anything real and genuine about the work of fortunetellers and spiritualistic mediums? That is the question often asked. I answer that doubtless the average medium, the average fortuneteller, Hindu philosopher, and astrologer who offers to tell you your future, to give advice in matters of business, love, or health, is a humbug, pure and simple. Such are a bunch of charlatans, hypocrites, and racketeers who make their living off the ignorance and superstition of suckers. If you sent your dollar to get a horoscope or life reading, or if you inquired of any of this tribe of crooks, you simply helped to feed a tribe of heartless deceivers who prey on the troubles and superstitions of the ignorant.

However, the Bible clearly teaches that some people do have familiar spirits, that is, that some people are occasionally in touch with spirits of another world. But the Bible is most emphatic that such people are under the influence of devils and that only evil can come from consulting them. Simon, the sorcerer in Acts, chapter 8, was a wicked, ungodly man as long as he carried on his sorcery. Elymas, the sorcerer or fortuneteller mentioned in Acts, chapter 13, was an enemy of God, and would have prevented others from being saved. The poor slave girl, the soothsayer or medium who made money for her masters by her soothsaying, was possessed of an evil spirit, and when Paul drove the evil spirit out in the name of the Lord, she no more told fortunes, and her masters saw that the hope of their gains was gone. Any communication with spirits which spiritualistic mediums and fortunetellers have, they have under the control of the Devil. In such cases, those who use mediums are putting themselves at the mercy of the Evil One, and we may expect them to be deceived and harmed, not to be blessed or helped.

Spiritualistic mediums pretend to be able to get help for others in the matter of health, and yet I know of one who has hardly been able to leave her house for years on account of arthritis. They collect money from the gullible to foretell the turn of fortune, and yet if they could successfully do that, they themselves would have grown rich long ago. Perhaps the Devil knows more about the future than we do. If so, it is possible that he would sometimes reveal it to those who get in touch with devils through mediums or familiar spirits. But you can readily see that Satan would only reveal the things that it would please him to reveal. The Devil himself is a liar and the father of liars, and everytime he tells a half truth he tells a whole lie. The spiritual life of any Christian who attends spiritualistic readings and seances is certain to suffer. He puts himself under the influence of demons, or at the very best, under the influence of fakes and crooks. He grieves the Holy Spirit of God by disobeying the plain command of the Bible. I beg you, Christian brother or sister, have nothing to do with these evil works of darkness.

All the table walking, rapping, and secret messages of the spiritualists have been duplicated again and again by such scientific magicians as Houdini, now dead. Again and again he offered rewards of thousands of dollars to any spiritualistic medium who could secure any phenomena that he could not duplicate. He never lost a dollar. Their claims are false, their business is wicked, and all such, the Scriptures say, "are an abomination unto the Lord."

Can Christians Learn About the Future?

Thank God, Christians do not need to go to crooks and devil worshipers to learn about the future or to get advice on matters of business, love, or health. The Word of God is a rich mine of information. It tells people how they should live. The Bible has the answer to every day's problems. Consult the Word of God.

The Holy Spirit of God dwells in the body of every Christian. He is sent to us to be a Comforter, to guide us into all truth, to manifest Christ and the Father unto us. Submit yourselves to the Holy Spirit of God. Be filled with Him. Walk in the Spirit. Do not quench the Spirit.

If you need wisdom, ask of God, for James 1:5 says:

"*If any of you lack wisdom, let him ask of God, that giveth to all men liberally, and upbraideth not; and it shall be given him.*"

God will give true wisdom, soul-satisfying, reliable help in every extremity. Call upon Him today. The Spirit-filled, Bible-reading Christian will never need to sin against God by consulting familiar spirits.

"*And thine ears shall hear a word behind thee, saying, This is the way, walk ye in it, when ye turn to the right hand, and when ye turn to the left.*"—Isa. 30:21.

"*Then spake Jesus again unto them, saying, I am the light of the world: he that followeth me shall not walk in darkness, but shall have the light of life.*"—Jno. 8:12.

10

Anglo-Saxon People Are Not Israel

Anglo-Saxon People Are Not Israel

The British-Israel Theory Is Contrary to Scripture and Scientific and Historical Facts Because (1) the Jews of Today Represent the Whole Twelve Tribes of Israel, (2) the Jews Who Came Back From Captivity Represented the Entire Nation Israel, (3) Science and History Prove That England and America Could Not Possibly Be Israel, (4) the British-Israel Theory Utterly Contradicts Divine Prophecies

For a good many years I have carefully investigated all the claims of those who teach the so-called "British-Israel" theory that the United States and Great Britain are the two tribes of Ephraim and Manasseh.

Mr. Rand and other teachers of the British-Israel movement are certainly wrong in their interpretation of Scripture and are clearly contradicted by history and science. It will not take long to show you that, I think.

I. The Jews of Today Represent the Whole Twelve Tribes of Israel

I mean there are no lost tribes. Some people of all the tribes are lost, of course. But the remnant that

God counts, the only remnant that has stayed pure **in blood**, are Jews as we know them today. The Anglo-Saxons are not Israel, and no other people on the face of the earth are Israel, either in fact or in God's sight. Notice the following proofs that the Jews of today are the whole nation, Israel, representing all the twelve tribes.

1. During the time of the divided kingdom, when Judah, with Benjamin and the Levites, were counted one kingdom, and Israel, the ten tribes in the North, were counted another kingdom, Israelites from many tribes kept going to Judah more and more and settling there. For example, in the days of King Asa, II Chronicles 15:9 says, "And he gathered all Judah and Benjamin, and the strangers with them out of Ephraim and Manasseh, and out of Simeon: for they fell to him out of Israel in abundance, when they saw that the Lord his God was with him."

In the great revival under Hezekiah at Jerusalem, the sacrifices at the altar were made for all the tribes of Israel. Second Chronicles 29:24 says, "And the priest killed them, and they made reconciliation with their blood upon the altar, to make an atonement for all Israel: for the king commanded that the burnt-offering and the sin-offering should be made for all Israel." The Scripture given here indicates that by special planning the sacrifices in the nation Judah were made to represent the whole nation Israel.

Again, in the days of Hezekiah, after many people of the northern kingdom had been carried into captivity, we see that all Israel was represented at Jerusalem in the passover: Second Chronicles 30:5,6 says,

"So they established a decree to make proclamation throughout all Israel, from Beersheba even to Dan, that they should come to keep the passover unto the Lord God of Israel at Jerusalem: for they had not done it of a long time in such sort as it was written.

So the posts went with the letters from the king and his princes throughout all Israel and Judah, and according to the commandment of the king, saying, Ye children of Israel, turn again unto the Lord God of Abraham, Isaac, and Israel, and he will return to the remnant of you, that are escaped out of the hands of the king of Assyria."

Then verse 11 says, "Nevertheless divers of Asher and Manasseh and of Zebulun humbled themselves, and came to Jerusalem."

In the same chapter, II Chronicles 30:25 tells us:

"*And all the congregation of Judah, with the priests and the Levites, and all the congregation that came out of Israel, and the strangers that came out of the land of Israel, and that dwelt in Judah, rejoiced.*"

From the above it is clear that from all the other tribes of Israel many gathered to Jerusalem and were with Judah when Judah was carried into captivity.

In II Chronicles 35:3 the Scripture says:

"*And said unto the Levites that taught all Israel, which were holy unto the Lord, Put the holy ark in the house which Solomon the son of David king of Israel did build; it shall not be a burden upon your shoulders: serve now the Lord your God, and his people Israel.*"

In the same chapter, verses 17 and 18 say:

"*And the children of Israel that were present kept the passover at that time, and the feast of unleavened bread seven days. And there was no passover like to that kept in Israel from the days of Samuel the prophet; neither did all the kings of Israel keep such a passover as Josiah kept, and the priests, and the Levites, and all Judah and Israel that were present, and the inhabitants of Jerusalem.*"

There can be no doubt but that God was gathering together a remnant of all the tribes at Jerusalem, and that they represented the whole nation Israel. Thus, when Judah was carried into captivity, it was a group representing all the twelve tribes, and not only Benjamin, Judah, and the Levites.

II. The Jews Who Came Back From the Captivity Represented the Entire Nation Israel

It is easy to prove that the Jews who returned from the captivity in Babylon represented all the twelve tribes and were officially counted as Israel in God's sight. Notice the following interesting facts:

1. Cyrus, king of Persia, in his official proclamation allowing the return to Jerusalem, included all Israel. In II Chronicles 36:23, that proclamation is quoted thus: "Thus saith Cyrus king of Persia, All the kingdoms of the earth hath the Lord God of heaven given me; and he hath charged me to build him an house in Jerusalem, which is in Judah. Who is there among you of all his people? The Lord his God be with him, and let him go up." The proclamation is to "all his people"—that is literally, all of God's people in all of Israel.

The same proclamation is quoted in Ezra 1:3: "Who is there among you of all his people? his God be with him, and let him go up to Jerusalem. . . ."

Remember that Cyrus was king over the then known world, and all the twelve tribes were under his jurisdiction. In fact, those carried into captivity from the northern kingdom and those from the southern kingdom were in the same general region of Babylon, and the proclamation was as much to those of the other tribes as to the tribe of Judah.

Those who responded to the proclamation are mentioned in Ezra 1:5: "Then rose up the chief of the fathers of Judah and Benjamin, and the priests, and the Levites, WITH ALL THEM WHOSE SPIRIT GOD HAD RAISED, to go up to build the house of the Lord which is in Jerusalem." Not only those of Judah and Benjamin, the priests and Levites, but all those of other tribes "whose spirit God had raised" to go to Jerusalem, went back with the return. There is no doubt that more of the tribe of Judah went back than other tribes, but it was not the whole tribe of Judah, but just a remnant, as it was only a remnant of the other tribes which went back. Most of the whole nation Israel remained in the far country, but a remnant of all the tribes went back to Judah, and these were the Jews of the time of Christ, from whom the Jews of today are descended.

2. The remnant carried back to Judah were several times called, "all Israel."

For example, in Ezra 2:70 we are told, "So the priests, and the Levites, and some of the people, and the singers, and the porters, and the Nethinims, dwelt in their cities, and all Israel in their cities." When God says "and all Israel in their cities," it is evident that God regards this remnant which has gone back from the captivity as all Israel.

Again, a second expedition of Israelites, under Ezra, returned from captivity to Jerusalem. That is described in Ezra 7:7 as follows: "And there went up some of the children of Israel, and of the priests, and the Levites, and the singers, and the porters, and the Nethinims, unto Jerusalem, in the seventh year of Artaxerxes the king." The Bible, carefully dictated by the Holy Spirit of God, here plainly says that those who went back represented, not Judah, but the nation Israel.

Concerning Ezra's request that he be allowed to go and take an expedition to Jerusalem, Artaxerxes, then the emperor, made a decree similar to that made before by Cyrus. He said, as recorded in Ezra 7:13, "I make a decree, that all they of the people of Israel, and of his priests and Levites, in my realm, which are minded of their own freewill to go up to Jerusalem, go with thee."

It is certainly clear that Artaxerxes and Ezra, like King Cyrus, all intended that the group which went back to Jerusalem should represent the whole nation Israel: "all they of the people of Israel," in the words of the king's decree. It is equally certain that those of all Israel really returned.

In Ezra 7:28, in the last half of the verse, Ezra says, "And I was strengthened as the hand of the Lord my God was upon me, and I gathered together out of Israel chief men to go up with me." He gathered men, not just out of Judah, but out of all Israel.

3. Twelve priests were selected to represent the twelve tribes in carrying the treasure back to Jerusalem.

In Ezra 8:24 and 25, this interesting story is given:

"*Then I separated twelve of the chief of the priests, Sherebiah, Hashabiah, and ten of their brethren with them, And weighed unto them the silver, and the gold, and the vessels, even the offering of the house of our God, which the king, and his counsellors, and his lords, and all Israel there present, had offered.*"

The priests were of the tribe of Levi, of course, but twelve were selected, because they were to represent all of the twelve tribes and to carry the treasure presented by "all Israel there present."

4. When they got to Jerusalem they offered sacrifices representing all Israel. In Ezra 8:35 we are told,

"*Also the children of those that had been carried away, which were come out of the captivity, offered burnt-offerings unto the God of Israel, twelve bullocks for all Israel, ninety and six rams, seventy and seven lambs, twelve he goats for a sin-offering: all this was a burnt-offering unto the Lord.*"

Notice the "twelve bullocks for all Israel." It is clear that this immigration back to Judah is an official immigration of all Israel, and that this is the official Israel in God's sight.

5. Repeatedly through the book of Nehemiah the remnant returned to Jerusalem is called "Israel" and "all Israel."

Nehemiah 2:10 says, "When Sanballat the Horonite, and Tobiah the servant, the Ammonite, heard of it, it grieved them exceedingly that there was come a man to seek the welfare of the children of Israel."

Nehemiah 7:7 says, ". . . The number, I say, of the men of the people of Israel was this." It is clear he speaks not only of Judah, but of all Israel.

Nehemiah 7:73 says, "So the priests, and the Levites, and the porters, and the singers, and some of the people, and the Nethinims, and all Israel, dwelt in their cities; AND WHEN THE SEVENTH MONTH CAME, THE CHILDREN OF ISRAEL WERE IN THEIR CITIES." Remember, this is speaking of the remnant gone back to Palestine from the captivity, and they are "the children of Israel."

Nehemiah 9:2 says, "And the seed of Israel separated themselves from all strangers, and stood and confessed their sins, and the iniquities of their fathers."

Nehemiah 11:20 says, "And the residue of Israel, of the priests, and the Levites, were in all the cities of Judah, every one in his inheritance." Notice that though they are in the cities of Judah, the remnant is "the residue of Israel." This is the group which God officially recognizes as the whole nation Israel, and it is composed of people of every tribe.

Nehemiah 12:47 says, "And all Israel in the days of Zerubbabel, and in the days of Nehemiah, gave the portions of the singers and the porters, every day his portion: and they sanctified holy things unto the Levites; and the Levites sanctified them unto the children of Aaron." Obviously, this remnant in Palestine after the captivity, is "all Israel." Some people of all the tribes remained in Babylon, but the official representatives of all the tribes, in God's counting, were now back in Palestine.

Thus the Jews of today, as the Jews in the time of Christ, represent all the twelve tribes. There is no distinction, then, between Jews and Israel. They are the same people.

Now with this much in mind from the Old Testament, if you read the Gospels and the book of Acts and the epistles in the New Testament, you will see that the Jews in Palestine in the time of Christ are repeatedly called Israel, and are recognized as the whole house of Israel in God's sight. A simple example is Acts 2:36, where Peter is preaching at Jerusalem to the leaders of Israel. He says, "Therefore let all the house of Israel know assuredly, that God hath made that same Jesus, whom ye have crucified, both Lord and Christ." This means that Jesus was officially crucified by the leaders of all Israel, combined with Herod and Pilate. It also means that Peter was preaching to the officially responsible leaders of all Israel. The Jews in the time of Christ were the whole nation Israel.

Another example is James 1:1. There the book of James is addressed to "the twelve tribes which are scattered abroad, greeting." And the content of the book of James shows clearly that it was addressed to Christians; not to heathen people. In fact it was addressed to Christian Jews, those who had been dispersed from Jerusalem by the great persecution in the time of Saul. The book of James was likely the first New Testament book written, certainly one of the first. And the Jews to whom it was written were addressed as the twelve tribes of Israel.

III. In New Testament Times the Jews Were "All Israel"

Here we give some scriptural proof that the Jews themselves are all of Israel, and that none others are counted Israelites in God's sight.

(1) At Jerusalem at Pentecost were "Jews, devout men, out of every nation" (Acts 2:5). But Peter addressed them, "Therefore let all the house of Israel know. . ." (Acts 2:36). Therefore the Jews were properly *all the house of Israel.*

(2) People in Judaea in the time of John the Baptist and Jesus were called Jews repeatedly. But they were also called "All the people of Israel." Paul says in Acts 13:24, "When John had first preached before his coming the baptism of repentance to all the people of Israel." Those who went to hear John the Baptist preach were Jews, described in Matthew 3:5,6, "Then went out to him Jerusalem, and all Judaea, and all the region round about Jordan, And were baptized of him in Jordan, confessing their sins." That clearly shows that Jews were "*all the people of Israel.*"

(3) Romans 11:26 says that after the return of Christ, "all Israel shall be saved." But now "blindness in part is happened to Israel" (Rom. 11:25). It is the Jews who are now blinded and now are a natural branch broken off. Yet they are called Israel. Israel could not now be God's name for England and America, for there are relatively more Christians in England and America, and they are the strongholds of the Gospel. Israel is blinded so Israel is the Jews.

(4) When John the Baptist began his ministry, he was shown to all Israel. Luke 1:80 says he was in the desert "till the day of his shewing unto Israel."

(5) In Acts 4:10, Peter, addressing the Jews at Jerusalem, said, "Be it known unto you all, and to all the people of Israel."

(6) Acts 5:21 speaks of the Jews at Jerusalem as "all the senate of the children of Israel."

(7) The Jewish leaders at Jerusalem were addressed by Peter as "Ye rulers of the people, and elders of Israel" (Acts 4:8). They were elders not merely of one tribe, but elders of the whole nation. The Jews, then, are Israel.

Now, that the Jews in the time of Christ represented all the twelve tribes is easily shown.

IV. The Epistle of James Is Written to "Twelve Tribes," but to Jews

It is significant that the book of James is written "to the twelve tribes which are scattered abroad." Yet it is manifest that the message is to converted Jews. James 2:2 mentions the assembly, but in the Greek it is literally *synagogue.* There was no synagogue in the Old Testament, and none among others besides the Jews. It was evidently an institution that grew up between the Old and New Testament times. The twelve tribes scattered abroad were dispersed Jews who had been saved after Christ but still assembled in synagogues, or assemblies.

Other Scriptures are available, but I believe the above are sufficient to show that all the twelve tribes are represented in the southern nation called Judah, when it was carried captive; that representatives of all the twelve tribes returned later under Ezra and Nehemiah to Jerusalem and Judaea, and that in the time of Christ, the Jews represented all the house of Israel; the rulers of Israel were the senate of Israel and elders of Israel; the letters written to the twelve tribes were written to

Jews; Christ was the King of the Jews; the twelve apostles will judge the twelve tribes of Israel on twelve thrones. There is not a leg for the foolish Anglo-Israel teaching to stand upon.

V. Science and History Prove That England and America Could Not Possibly Be Israel

1. There is absolutely no history of any migration from the ancient country of Babylon across Europe into England, as is claimed by the British-Israel teachers. For such an entire nation to migrate, keeping its blood pure, across an entire continent, would be so startling a phenomenon that it could not be. It simply did not happen. It cannot be traced by reputable historians.

2. The Anglo-Saxon people do not have any of the ethnological inheritance that would be inevitable if they were descended from the so-called "lost ten tribes" of Israel.

Consider first that the Anglo-Saxon people have no trace of the Hebrew language, and never have had. The Hebrew language is written right to left. The Anglo-Saxon is written from left to right. They are written with different alphabets. It is only accidental that some names are similar, as is true of all languages. There is no language kinship between the English and the Hebrew. This is a scientific fact.

Consider next that the Anglo-Saxon people had no tradition whatever about circumcision. When you remember how tenaciously Jews have held to circumcision in every clime and country, amidst every kind of persecution in these twenty centuries since Christ, it is inconceivable that another group of Israelites, staying together as a nation and having the same law, the same customs, the same teaching should utterly forget the matter until there was not a tradition nor a trace of it. That simply would not happen.

Consider also that the Anglo-Saxon people had no Sabbath until it was introduced by Christian missionaries. The Sabbath was given to the nation Israel as a particular sign between her and God, as you see in Exodus 31:16 and 17 and Ezekiel 20:12. But the Anglo-Saxon people did not have any Sabbath, as an evidence that they were the people Israel. They are not.

Actually, the British-Israel doctrine is a matter of sinful national pride, a trying to assume an honor that does not belong to the English and American people. We are not Israel.

And finally, it seems silly to suppose that England would be Ephraim and America Manasseh, when we are of the same blood, insofar as we are both Anglo-Saxon people. There would be just as much reason to suppose that England was Manasseh and America Ephraim, as to suppose the contrary. However, since the doctrine started in England and Ephraim was a larger tribe, more often mentioned in the Scriptures, they chose to be Ephraim and chose that America might be Manasseh!

The idea is not only unscriptural, but utterly unscientific.

VI. The British-Israel Theory Utterly Contradicts Divine Prophecies

The British-Israel theory speaks of a throne and kingdom, but it is the throne of the house of Hanover, not the throne of the house of David. It honors British kings instead of honoring the Lord Jesus.

The land which is honored in Bible prophecy as the place where Christ will return and reign, is clearly the land of Palestine. Again and again we are told that the children of Israel will return to "the mountains of Israel," and "to their own land," "the land of their fathers," etc. That could not be England.

Again the Bible teaching is that the millennial reign will be set up by Christ in person at His return. Christ Himself will overthrow the nations and set up His kingdom. In contradiction, the British-Israel people teach that England and America must rule the world, that we are "God's battle-axe." Thus the British-Israel teaching violates all true understanding of Bible prophecy. It is a doctrine of vain and prideful men who would take to themselves and to their nation honor that does not belong to them. The only way to believe it is by a perversion of Scripture and by ignoring facts of history and science.

11

Mormonism

1. Mormonism, a False, Unscriptural Cult
   by Dr. G. Archer Weniger

2. Are Mormons Right?

1. Mormonism, a False, Unscriptural Cult

By Dr. G. Archer Weniger

Chairman of the Board of San Francisco
Baptist Theological Seminary

"Latter-Day Saints" Teach Marriage in Heaven, Baptize to Save Dead People, Go Not by Bible but by "Revelations" and the Book of Mormon, Teach Salvation by Baptism and Works; Is Not Christian

The Mormons dedicate their latest temple, a 7-million-dollar structure on an 18-acre site on a mountain promontory in Oakland, California, with a breathtaking view of the metropolitan area. The windowless structure of granite and gold is the 15th temple the Mormons have built around the world but is the 13th in current use. The central spire of the temple rises 170 feet above ground. Of the 2-million-member body, more than 300,000 live in California. This number is served by temples in Los Angeles and the new one in Oakland. The Oakland Temple District has 185,000 Mormon members. Without seeing them, one can have no idea of the immense crowds attending and the colossal traffic jams on the surrounding freeways during prededication days.

Six identical dedication services were conducted on November 17-19, 1964, and attended by over 20,000, with more than 1,000 leaders from all over the nation present, including 38 top general authorities. Members of the Twelve Apostles attended as well as the First Council of 70. Prior to dedication services, the "Gentile" public was allowed to tour the temple in silence, with 347,000 taking advantage. Each one had to fill out a ticket giving name and address. This provided a vast master list for future proselyting. Only a small portion of the temple was shown to visitors. No tours are made of the washing rooms and anointing rooms in the lower areas. When once a temple is dedicated, no tourists are allowed, not even all Mormons. One must have a "temple recommend" signed by his bishop to be admitted.

The purpose of a Mormon temple is not for regular services of worship, but rather for "priesthood ordinations and endowments, baptisms for the living and, vicariously, for the dead, and marriage ceremonies for eternity." All three of these are unscriptural purposes which lie at the very heart of Mormonism. The "endowments" have to do with the preparation of the individual for his eternal journey in which he becomes a god. Vicarious baptism for the salvation of unsaved dead is a grave responsibility for each Mormon. Several "sealing" rooms in the temple provide a place for the lengthy marriage ceremony in which marriages are solemnized and "sealed" for all eternity—even plurally. An official description of the temple said: "There are ten sealing rooms in the building, two of which have a seating capacity of sixty, four with a seating of twenty-two each, and four seating sixteen each."

Salvation by form and ceremony is taught by Mormons. In an 80-page dedication document we read on page 70 that Mormons "desired salvation in the presence of God. They understood that temple ordinances were essential to that salvation, and therefore they spared no effort in building edifices in which to obtain them. But how could a temple be so essential to one's salvation?" On page 71: "Now what are the requirements made by the gospel for the salvation of living persons? They must 'live according to God' while they are in the flesh, conforming to both the laws and ordinances of salvation including, for example, such ordinances as baptism in water. Is baptism that necessary? Jesus considered it so and was baptized himself in order 'to fulfil all righteousness' (Matt. 3:15). Can mankind do less than he?"

However, the Bible says, "For by grace are ye saved through faith; and that not of yourselves: it is the gift of God: Not of works, lest any man should boast" (Eph. 2:8,9). The Son of God needed no salvation. He is the Author of salvation.

The enormous baptistry is central in the temple, beneath the "celestial room" in the exact center of the temple. The font itself is supported on the backs of twelve life-sized oxen covered with gold leaf. The oxen are typical of those used by the early Mormon pioneers in crossing the plains, and represent the twelve tribes of Israel. This pattern of the baptistry is exact in all the temples and follows the pattern given by the "Prophet" Joseph Smith.

Vicarious baptism for the unsaved dead has been developed as an elaborate doctrine of Mormonism. Like much doctrinal error, it has built a towering structure of doctrine on a disputed passage. In this case it is I Corinthians 15:29. While there are between 35 and 40 interpretations, there are but two views which are allowed by the Greek, according to Prof. Charles A. Hauser, Jr., Th. D., of the San Francisco Baptist Seminary. The generally accepted view is that the word

"for" does not mean "baptized on behalf of" or "for the benefit of" but "in place of dead ones" or "instead of." (We believe the best interpretation of that passage simply means that baptism pictures a resurrection of dead people, the resurrection of Christ, and the resurrection of all the Christians who die. So why should any one be baptized picturing the resurrection of the dead if there is no resurrection?—J.R.R.)

Nothing is so tragic as a false way of salvation, and this is exactly what Mormons teach. In the dedication manual, on page 71: "If baptism is so essential for the salvation of the living, is it less essential for the salvation of the dead? Can we reasonably suppose that some other rite would replace baptism, such as, for instance, burning candles or saying prayers?"

The Bible is plain that baptism does not save the living and nothing can save the dead. In the fourteen epistles of the New Testament, which teach the doctrinal content of Christianity, the words "faith" and "believe" are found 278 times in relation to salvation, and not once is baptism so associated.

Baptismal regeneration is a shaky doctrine, not taught in the Bible, and constructed on disputed passages at best, while the Scriptures remain clear and plain about the way of salvation. Peter's word in Acts 2:38 is used in support of this error. "Repent, and be baptised every one of you in the name of Jesus Christ for remission [better translation: "upon remission" or "referring to remission"] of sins." First Peter 3:21 is another passage used by Mormons in this connection. Dr. Felix Runquist's free translation is good: "We are saved by the resurrection of Jesus Christ, of which baptism is a figure, which figure does not put away the filth of the flesh, but is the answer of a good conscience toward God." The Bible teaches that baptism is not essential for salvation but essential for obedience in the Christian life. In the case of every baptism in the New Testament, they believed first, and then were baptized.

The "sealing" rooms are the busiest places in the temples of Mormonism. "They represent in a way what some regard as the most basic principle in the gospel of Christ," says the dedication manual. "Husbands and wives marry for eternity, not merely until death brings an end to their union. . . family life becomes a part of our heavenly existence. It is the doctrine of the Latter-Day Saints that marriage never was intended by the Lord to be some temporary arrangement for mortal life alone."

Jesus' teaching explodes this whole doctrine (Luke 20:27-38; Matt. 22:23-33; Mark 12:18-27). Yet the manual states:

> So our temples have in them sealing rooms so-called because of the sealing and binding ordinances performed in them. Within their sacred walls bride and groom kneel at the altar and are sealed or bound in the holy order of matrimony for all eternity. Parents not previously sealed may bring their children to these rooms, that the family may be bound together for eternity by the powers of the Holy Priesthood.

"What's Wrong With Mormonism" is the title of an article by Dr. Louis T. Talbot in *The Discerner* for April, 1962, in which he said, "Every sect has some distinguishing mark which sets it apart from other systems. . . Mormonism alone—of American religions—deifies sex. While this teaching and practice characterizes some Asiatic cults, Mormonism has the distinction of being the one system in the United States whose god is man, and whose worshippers may become gods."

The "Prophet" Joseph Smith taught his people: "There must, however, be a place built expressly for that purpose, and for men to be baptized for their dead. . . for every man who wishes to save his father, mother, brothers, sisters and friends, must go through all the ordinances for each one of them separately, the same as for himself" (DHC 6:318-320). Not only are they baptized for the dead, but marriages are sealed for the dead. The manual states: "So it provides the sealing ordinances of marriage for the dead also, the living officiating in behalf of their departed loved ones."

An elaborate series of geneological records is kept by the Mormons, so that each family may "prepare its own geneologies to provide the identification needed to perform the ordinances for the dead. Properly performed ordinances for properly identified persons are acceptable with God," says the dedication manual (p. 73).

They endeavor to support this foolishness with the last verse of the Old Testament (Mal. 4:6), which speaks about the coming of Elijah: "And he shall turn the heart of the fathers to the children, and the heart of the children to their fathers, lest I come and smite the earth with a curse." They contend that these words are being fulfilled right now in the intense interest and activity of Mormons in their genealogical background and records. They contend Elijah came in 1844 when this activity really got under way. Joseph Smith states that Elijah appeared personally to him on April 3, 1836, at Kirtland, Ohio, coming in fulfillment of Malachi 4:5,6 to create this geneological interest in their forefathers.

However Titus 3:9 warns, "avoid foolish questions, and geneologies, . . . for they are unprofitable and vain." First Timothy 1:4 speaks of "endless geneologies which minister questions, rather than godly edifying. . . ."

An impregnable mountain vault has been built by the Mormon church 20 miles southwest of Salt Lake City at a cost of a million and a half dollars to provide earthquake-proof and bomb-proof security for its geneological microfilms and other church records. Six openings in the sides of the mountain lead into huge cross tunnels which serve as storage areas. The walls are painted in pastel colors, equipped with fluorescent lights, with constant heat and humidity. Mormon theology teaches that these unsaved dead may have proxy baptism and proxy marriages performed on their behalf, thus enabling them to go to Heaven, be married in Heaven, where they may continue to progress and bear children.

"**The Challenging Message of Mormonism**" is a significant message from Hugh B. Brown of the First Presidency of the Mormon Church on the subject of revelation. He said,

> The Church of Jesus Christ was established and is now directed by revelation, and that fact is largely responsible for the appeal which this new Church makes, and when I say "new," I wish to emphasize that to us it is not new but a restoration of that which was. . . . The Church is not committed to any formal or inflexible creed, but its members are taught to believe in and live by the revelations of the past and present and thus prepare themselves for the revelations yet to come. . . . We think we are justified in anticipating future revelation, and we believe that it will be surpassing in importance and glorious fulness anything that has yet been revealed.

In other words, the finality of the Bible is rejected by Mormonism (Rev. 22:18,19). Actually, then, with this "free-wheeling" program of revelation, Mormonism is without any authority. It can manufacture doctrines as it goes along, much as Roman Catholicism does, on the grounds that this is what the Lord revealed.

What Mormons think about the blood... In an official Mormon publication, "What the Mormons Think of Christ" by B.R. McConkie, we find these words,

> Christians speak often of the blood of Christ and its cleansing power. Much that is believed and taught on this subject, however, is such utter nonsense and so palpably false that to believe it is to lose one's salvation. Many go so far, for instance, as to pretend and at least

> to believe that if we confess Christ with our lips and avow that we accept Him as our personal Saviour, we are thereby saved. His blood without other act than mere belief, they say, makes us clean... Salvation in the kingdom of God is available because of the atoning blood of Christ. But it is received only on condition of faith, repentance, baptism, and endurance to the end in keeping the commandments of God. --pp. 24,25,27,28.

On the Person of Christ... Dr. Walter R. Martin, in his late book, *The Maze of Mormonism*, concludes on page 113:

> Mormonism, with its apostles, priesthood, temples, secret signs, symbols, hand shakes, and mysteries, quite literally masquerades as 'the church of the restoration'; but at its heart, in its doctrine of the Messiah, is found to be contrary to every major biblical pronouncement.

Negroes barred from Mormon priesthood.... When the late Mormon President David O. McKay, 91 years, held a press conference in Oakland the day of dedication of the latest temple in Mormonism, he was quoted in the *San Francisco Chronicle* (Nov. 17, '64), "Negroes can join the church as well as anyone else, but they cannot become members of the priesthood." *The Chronicle* said further: "The priesthood ruling—based on complexities of church dogma on preexistence and life in the hereafter—will not be changed 'during your lifetime or mine,' he said at a press conference."

Sources for information on Mormonism from an evangelical point of view would include the Utah Evangel Press, Box 348, Marlow, Oklahoma 73055, which has very extensive documents, books, and tracts. The Religion Analysis Service, 902 Hennepin Avenue, Minneapolis, Minnesota 55403, has a wide array of books and tracts. The Utah Christian Tract Society, Box 725, La Mesa, California 92041, offers a varied assortment of literature. Rev. Glen Koch, 2200 South Overland, Burley, Idaho 83318, has several booklets available. Many documents can be secured from Modern Microfilm Company,

Box 884, Salt Lake City, Utah 84110. Moody Colportage Dept., 820 North La Salle, Chicago, Illinois 60610, has two excellent books, *Is Mormonism Christian?* and *What Does the Book of Mormon Teach?* An extensive series of tracts can be had from Evangelist Harry A. McGimsey, Box 188, Hemet. California 92343. Evangelist John L. Smith, Box 348, Marlow, Oklahoma 73055, has an unusual mimeographed article, "120 Questions to Ask the Mormon Missionaries."

Strange doctrines of Mormonism. . . . Evangelist Harry McGimsey in his folder, *Mormonism's Base Attack on Christianity,* states:

> The Mormon cult, which condemns all Christian churches, believes the following false doctrines: They believe that God is an exalted man; that Christ and the Devil are brothers; that Christ was married; that the Holy Spirit is a substance or fluid; that there is salvation for the dead by proxy water baptism; baptismal regeneration; that there is no burning Hell; in genealogical research; plurality of wives; use of secret temples; in the fatherhood of God and the brotherhood of man; that people raise children after they leave the earth; in revelations beside the Bible; in the pre-existence of man; that no Negro can hold the Mormon priesthood or go through the secret Mormon temples; and in many other things that are contrary to the Bible.

"Believe on the Lord Jesus Christ, and thou shalt be saved." This is the statement of the Scriptures in Acts 16:31.

> The Mormon theology is based on an unthinking acceptance, not on reasoned thought. Whenever one drives the Mormon back on some of his fantastic beliefs his only reply is: "You have to have faith." And what he means is, you have to have faith in the word of Joseph Smith, a leader whose writings reveal amazing ignorance and undisciplined imagination and whose reputation for drunkenness, adultery and gambling is an embarrassment to his own followers. It seems to a

> Baptist that in all matters of faith and morals, any reasonable person would prefer the authority of Jesus Christ, the sinless and only begotten Son of God.

The above is a conclusive statement by Dr. F. T. Fowler, a student and observer of Mormonism from close range.

As one missionary has said,

> We long to see them wholly trust in our Saviour and have their names written in the Lamb's Book of Life instead of relying on the false hope of having their names recorded on worthless records buried in the cold stone of Utah mountain.

2. Are Mormons Right?

Mormons Claim That Their "Church of Jesus Christ of Latter-Day Saints," Has Restored New Testament Christianity With Apostles, Creeds, and Prophets, but Their Remarks Indicate That They Are a False Cult

A friend of THE SWORD OF THE LORD sent the editor a pamphlet, *Which Church Is Right?* put out by Mormons of Salt Lake City, Utah, claiming that the "Church of Jesus Christ of Latter-day Saints," or the Mormon church, has reproduced Bible Christianity. Two missionaries of the Mormon church have visited this good man's home, and told him how Joseph Smith was supposed to have had a vision; an angel, Moroni, had revealed to him where some golden plates were hidden; he was given some spectacles enabling him to miraculously read these golden plates and to translate them into what is now the Book of Mormon! Joseph Smith found very convenient "revelations" that he should marry an extra wife or two, and from time to time declared that he had word direct from God which all men were bound to heed.

In reply to our friend's question, we share with our readers the editor's answer.

Dear Brother W———:

Thank you for your letter, and for the Mormon booklet which you enclosed, *Which Church Is Right?*

I am glad to answer your questions about the Mormon church and the booklet the best I can, and I trust God will use the information. The so-called "Church of Latter-day Saints" was founded by Joseph Smith, a notorious loafer and storyteller. He pretended that he had been selected to receive a revelation from God; that some golden plates were found giving the story of how some Israelites having a new supposed revelation from God came to America before Columbus. He said that an angel revealed to him these golden plates upon which the story was written in "reformed Egyptian" language. Actually, it has been proved that he got the story from the manuscript of a novel, which he largely copied.

Later, he himself led an adulterous life and then declared that he had received a revelation from God that men should have more wives than one.

The claim of the Mormon church to be a restoration of New Testament Christianity is utterly false. There are many evidences of this.

1. The Book of Mormon is itself a proof of the falsity of their claim. In Revelation 22:18, we are plainly warned that there should be no added revelation of God to the present canon of Scripture:

"*For I testify unto every man that heareth the words of the prophecy of this book, If any man shall add unto these things, God shall add unto him the plagues that are written in this book.*"

The Bible clearly and expressly teaches that the canon of Scripture closed with the book of Revelation. So any religion which has any source of teaching which is regarded as a revelation from God like the Bible or equal to the Bible, therefore brands itself as a false religion. So with Christian Science and the writings of Mrs. Mary Baker Eddy. Her writings misinterpret the Bible and make a false basis for the Christian Science religion. So it is also with British-Israelism; the Great Pyramid is counted as inspired and as a source of divine revelation. So it is with Seventh-Day Adventism, which regards the writings of Mrs. Ellen White as inspired and authoritative. So it is with the Roman Catholic church which regards the official decisions of popes and councils, and the traditions of the church as authoritative as well as the Bible. Any religion is a false religion, a false cult, which claims any basis of authority besides the Bible itself. So Mormonism brands itself as false.

2. In doctrine the Mormon church shows itself obviously unchristian. It demands baptism for salvation, and good works for salvation. It knows nothing about the new birth. It counts Adam a god, and says that other people get to be gods. Its doctrine that men, especially elders in the Mormon churches, should have as many wives as possible, goes against the express declaration of the Bible that the bishop "should be the husband of one wife" (I Tim. 3:2). The United States government compelled the Mormon church to quit the open practice of polygamy, but it is still taught as a divine revelation received by Joseph Smith and by other leaders since his time.

3. The practice of the church is unscriptural. And their conception of Christianity is utterly wrong and contrary to the Bible.

For example, prophets were not "officers of the church." The pamphlet you sent, *Which Church Is Right?* says that the Mormon church "possesses the divine priesthood of God." But there is no human priesthood now, as an official church matter. Jesus Christ is our High Priest. All Christians are kings and priests in the sense that we can pray for one another, but we need no human priest. And we need no sacrifices; Jesus Christ paid man's debt of sin once and for all.

That booklet claims that the Mormon church "is headed by prophets and apostles as was the church in the days of Peter and Paul." That simply is not true. The apostles in the New Testament were not elected by men and they were not officers in the church in the sense that the so-called apostles of the Mormon church are officers in the denomination.

The truth is that the Mormon concept of the church of Christ is utterly unscriptural; it has the Roman Catholic idea of a human denomination. But the Bible never refers to a denomination as a church. Jesus did not establish these denominations. No man is an appointed or elected apostle of God or priest of God or prophet of God. If God's Spirit comes on one he may prophesy, but the prophet is not an office of the church. And God never intended that there should be any apostles except those that God Himself sent directly in New Testament times. We need no apostles now to reveal the divine truth, now that the Scriptures have been completed.

To become a Mormon would be a great shame. It would mean to turn one's back on New Testament Christianity and thus take part in the damnation of many, many souls who might be deceived by that false religion.

In Jesus' name, yours,

John R. Rice

12

Communism and Socialism

1. Communism Versus Bible Christianity
2. Socialism Antichristian
3. How Modernism in Religion Fits the Socialist-Communist Program

1. Communism Versus Bible Christianity

"For many deceivers are entered into the world, who confess not that Jesus Christ is come in the flesh. This is a deceiver and an antichrist."— II John 7.

Communism Is an Anti-God Political System

One who denies that the God revealed in the Old Testament, the Christ prophesied in the Old Testament, has literally become manifest in the flesh, is an antichrist and a deceiver, the Scripture says.

In I John 2:22,23 the same thing is said in effect: "Who is a liar but he that denieth that Jesus is the Christ? He is antichrist, that denieth the Father and the Son. Whosoever denieth the Son, the same hath not the Father. . . ."

Other political systems may be wrong or hurtful in some detail, but communism is basically and entirely against God, morality, and righteousness; it is the enemy of all true religion and so the enemy of the Bible.

Now it is not surprising that Karl Marx himself was an atheist, and that atheism is volubly claimed by the communists, by Karl Marx, by Lenin, by Stalin, and by other leaders of communistic countries. You see, communism is necessarily against the God of the Bible, against the Christ of the Bible, against the system of morals taught in the Bible.

Let me say also that socialism is essentially Marxism.

It is a milder form because socialism does not necessarily teach that the present governments must be overthrown by force; otherwise the basic principles are the same. Karl Marx's teaching is, and the socialist and the communist teaching is, that religion is the opiate of the people. Socialism and communism are against God, against Christ, against the Bible, against conversion, against the fundamentals of the Christian faith.

I. WHAT COMMUNISM ACTUALLY TEACHES

First, I will set out to define communism.

I have here in my hand a sermon by the late Dr. V. Raymond Edman, long-time president of Wheaton College. This sermon was used in THE SWORD OF THE LORD in 1954. It is titled, "The Big Lie," and it is a sermon on communism. He gives the Scripture about "strong delusion, that they should believe a lie," and he says communism is "The Big Lie."

About Karl Marx, the founder of the doctrine of communism, Dr. Edman said:

> It must be remembered that Karl Marx was a theorist, a doctrinaire economist, with no practical experience in the ideas which he propagated. He never earned a day's wages in his life. Once he applied for employment in an office, but his handwriting was so wretched that he was immediately discharged. He lived by the largess of others. He lived aloof, isolated, even from those who supported him out of their poverty. He was insensitive to the interests of others, irritable in the extreme, inconsiderate of everyone. Even his admiring biographers had to admit that he was "morbidly thin-skinned and jealously suspicious of the least sign of antagonism to his person or his doctrine."

1. Communism Is Against Private Ownership of Property

Karl Marx was no friend of the working man, though he claimed to be.

Dr. Edman says further:

> What are the basic communist economic principles? Karl Marx states them very graphically, with frankness that is brutal, in his *Communist Manifesto,* in which he says:
>
> "*The theory of the communists may be summed up in the single sentence: Abolition of private property.*"

That quotation is from Karl Marx in *Communist Manifesto.*

Marx goes on to say:

> You are horrified at our intending to do away with private property...in one word, you reproach us with intending to do away with your property. Precisely so; that is just what we intend.

Communism sets out to do away with private property, to seize people's property, and whether they do it by law or whether they do it without law, literally to rob people of their property, to abolish private property.

I quote from Dr. Edman's sermon:

> To achieve this abolition of private property so that everything is owned corporately by the State, a communist program was proposed by Marx. He declared that "The proletariat will use its political supremacy to wrest, by degrees, all capital from the bourgeoisie, to centralize all instruments of production in the hands of the State;" and to that end the communists plan:
>
> *1. "Abolition of property in land and application of all rents of land to public purposes."*

Notice, all property in land is to be turned over to the state, little by little, to be wrested, twisted, stolen, robbed, confiscated from people and taken by the state.

> *2. "A heavy progressive or graduated income tax."*

Now note carefully. I'll refer to that again. This is a communist proposal. What is the purpose? To steal the property of people and put it into the hands of the state. And by what one method. "A heavy progressive or graduated income tax."

> 3. *"The abolition of all right of inheritance."*

You may begin to see some likeness to the New Deal program. "Abolition of all right of inheritance." If the lands cannot go to sons, if the property cannot go to daughters, it can be confiscated in inheritance taxes by the state. Abolition of private property: this is the communist method of doing it. Again,

> 4. *"Confiscation of the property of all emigrants and rebels* [by "emigrants and rebels" was meant citizens who would flee from a communist State]."

All the people who couldn't stand that, their lives being in danger, would flee, and the government would take their property. Quoting again,

> 5. *"Centralization of credit in the hands of the State, by means of a national branch with State capital and an exclusive monopoly; and furthermore the socialization of transportation."*

That means, taking over the railroads, the bus lines, the air lines; factory production--seizing all the factories, all the mills; agriculture--seizing all the farms, all the ranches, all the gardens.

Dr. Edman continues his quote from Marx:

> *". . . and concluding with what already has long since been available, 'Free education for all children in public schools.'"*

That part we have had from many, many years back in America.

Now, do you know what the program of communism is? The abolition of private property, getting a dictatorship of some working people over the people who have owned property and have been bosses and owners and managers and foremen, then little by little stealing ("wrest" is the word Marx uses) or robbing from people all private property—all their lands, all their mills, all their garages, all their stores, all the means of production, all the railroads, all the mines.

2. Communism Would Destroy Freedom of the Individual

I'll go a little further now. Along with the abolition of private property, communism plans the destruction of individual freedom.

Karl Marx again speaks:

> *"The abolition of this state of things is called by the bourgeoisie, abolition of individuality and freedom! And rightly so."*

Again quoting Karl Marx:

> *"The abolition of bourgeois individuality, bourgeois independence, and bourgeois freedom, is undoubtedly aimed at."*

That means this: Let us get a few working people and put them in charge, make them dictators; and we intend, he says, to take the freedom away from everybody who owns any property, as well as their profits. I'll not go further into it, though there is much more. But the plan is to put people in the greatest bondage possible.

Here is another word. Another quotation. Dr. Edman says:

> To that end the bases of society must be destroyed. First, the "individual... the middle-class owner of property... must, indeed, be swept out of the way."

3. Communism Would Abolish the Family as We Know It

Next comes the family. The *Communist Manifesto* becomes savage in what it says about the family. Karl

Marx, the founder of communism, the founder of socialism, says:

> *"Abolition of the family! . . . The bourgeois family will vanish as a matter of course when its complement vanishes, and both will vanish with the banishing of capital. . . . The bourgeois claptrap about the family and education, about the hallowed co-relation of parent and child, becomes all the more disgusting . . . by the action of Modern Industry."*

Then Marx goes on to say,

> *"the community of women,* [that is, making women property of everybody and passing the women around ; *it has existed almost from time immemorial."*

That is already being done, he says, but we will legalize it. Now that is communism according to the author himself, Karl Marx, as quoted from the *Communist Manifesto.*

Actually, Russia soon found that with the breakdown of the family all human values would soon disappear, so now the communist states have abandoned largely the principle of "community of women."

II. HOW THE BIBLE OPPOSES COMMUNISM IN PRINCIPLE

Now let us take the Bible and show some things wrong with communism. Without trying to touch on all, here are a few. The Bible is out and out against communism, and in a bit you will see why communism is atheistic, why communism cannot be Christian.

1. Christianity and Communism Are Diametrically Opposed

Christianity and communism not only differ, but they are diametrically opposed. Communists and socialists are not only not Christians, but they hate Christianity and deliberately fight and seek to destroy Bible Christianity. Communism, then, is openly against the Bible.

There are in some countries political parties called the Christian Socialist Party, and sometimes people call themselves Christian Socialists. But that term is a misnomer. It is no accurate use of terminology. The one who uses it may be sincere, but he certainly is naive and uninformed as to the meaning of the word "Christian."

You may remember this. Russia claims to be the Union of Soviet Socialist Republics, and so Russia is really a socialist republic. That is, communism *is* socialism. There is no real difference. One avowedly takes the way of terrorism and murder and anarchy, while the other seeks the same end by infiltration, propaganda, creeping socialism. So communism and Karl Marx's socialism are really out-and-out enemies of the Bible.

You need not be surprised when some men in America, in the churches, say they favor communism or they are soft toward communism. These men are sometimes called "pinks"; they are sometimes called "fellow travelers"—not that they are members of the Communist Party necessarily, but they go along with communism and they are in some way victims of communism because they have such kinship with the ideals of communism and socialism.

Now why is that? That is evidently because they are modernists, religious liberals. Modernists who do not believe the Bible can be friendly toward communism because they do not have Bible standards of morals and they do not take what the Bible says as a binding standard for Christians. But on the whole, the Bible is against communism. No man who is a fundamentalist can be for communism, that is, no one who takes the Bible at face value, one who believes in the historic Christian faith as all the great orthodox men of all denominations have believed—not on incidentals but on the very essentials: the inspiration of the Bible, the deity of Christ, including His virgin birth and His bodily resurrection, the atoning death of Christ to pay for man's sins. I say, no man who is a fundamental Bible believer can believe in communism because communism and socialism are diametrically opposed to the plain teaching of the Word of God.

2. Private Ownership of Property Is Taught in the Bible

Second, I would like to talk about private ownership of property as taught in the Bible. *The Bible* teaches that private ownership of private property is right. I think private ownership of property is right but this is not a matter of human opinion; this is a matter of Bible Christianity as against communism.

Let us turn to the Ten Commandments. It is a surprising thing, when you come to think of it, that two of the Ten Commandments deal directly with this matter of private ownership of property. Is it really a sin to own property? Should all property be owned by the state and so collectively owned by the people, as communism teaches and as socialism teaches? That is not what the Bible says.

For example, there is a command in Exodus 20:15, in the Ten Commandments—the eighth one which says, "Thou shalt not steal." Now stealing is taking property that belongs to someone else. Stealing is taking what is not your own. It necessarily involves private ownership.

And in the same chapter, Exodus 20, verse 17, the tenth of the commandments says, "Thou shalt not covet thy neighbour's house." Then a neighbor has a right to own a house. "Thou shalt not covet thy neighbour's house, thou shalt not covet thy neighbour's wife, nor his manservant, nor his maidservant, nor his ox, nor his ass, nor any thing that is thy neighbour's." That is a clear acknowledgment that private ownership is a fact endorsed and supported by the Lord. And the Ten Commandments are against communism because they teach it is wrong to steal; it is wrong even to covet that which belongs to another man. That is one reason why collectivism is a sin; it is contrary to certain principles that are inherent in the nature of man. It is a contradiction of the plain teaching of the Bible about what is right and wrong.

Will you notice, then, that among the Jews there was a very strict law of inheritance of property. For example, a man might get poor and so he might come to the point where he would have to sell his property, but in the year of Jubilee, after forty-nine years, all the property must go back to original owners or their heirs. You see, God was very strict about the principle that the property was to remain in private hands and preferably that it might be retained by those who originally had a right to it and to whom it was given. That means the Bible teaches private ownership of property.

The Bible is so strict about this that one was given the right even, if need be, to kill in defense of his property. If some one came to steal in the nighttime when a person could not be identified and followed and brought to judgment, then at nighttime one had a right to kill even, in defense of his property. You see, the Bible is very clear that private ownership of property is in the plan of God.

Then there was the law of restitution. If one should steal the property of his neighbor, what should he do? He must restore five oxen for an ox and four sheep for a sheep. You see, God is making clear and is building it into the conscience of the human race through the Mosaic law that private ownership of property is right and must be respected, and that not to respect private ownership of property is a sin very clearly marked in the Ten Commandments.

You say, "I don't think so much of property rights as I do of human rights." But property ownership is a human right. And God requires respect for it. Any philosophy of government that violates this plain order of God—that people may earn or buy property and own it; that people may buy it and keep it and use it, and may reap from it, and may invest in it, and earn from the investment—any philosophy that is against that, is against the Bible plan.

Why do Americans prosper? Because the American Constitution is primarily based upon certain fundamental laws that are God's laws. It was no accident that the founders of our country put on the dollar, "In God We Trust." It is no accident that when we inaugurate a man as President we have him kiss the Bible and take the oath of office with his hand on the Bible. It is no accident that we have a chaplain pray every time the House of Representatives opens, every time the Senate opens. It is no accident that we have set out to have a chaplain for every group of soldiers and on every major battleship, to pray and preach the Gospel and stand for God. Yes, our forefathers wanted a country based on God's law.

That is the reason Americans are the best paid, have more to eat, enjoy more conveniences, are more advanced, have more leisure,—more of everything than people of other nations. We have a country that started out on God's plan, and God blessed it. Now some morons would like to throw it away.

3. Capitalism Is Taught in the Bible

Let me say that another thing taught in the Bible is capitalism, that is, the right of an individual to run a business or to use capital and get results from his capital, to hire workers and pay them and get a profit from a business which is run by some investment of savings. I say, capitalism is taught as proper in the Bible.

The hiring of workers and the gaining of reward for labor is mentioned in the Bible many times. For example, see the parable of the vineyard in Matthew

20. The Lord talks about the hiring of laborers in the vineyard:

"*For the kingdom of heaven is like unto a man that is an householder, which went out early in the morning to hire labourers into his vineyard. And when he had agreed with the labourers for a penny a day, he sent them into his vineyard.*"

Later he went and hired others. He had agreements with the laborers. He paid them a certain amount per day. He himself took the prosperity and took what gain there came from this investment of capitalism and this using of the labor of other men whom he employed. But did the Lord say that was wrong? No. The Lord Jesus did not even hint that that was wrong. He took that as the plan of God and He drew some lessons from this normal, proper use of capital.

And another thing. The Bible often says, for example, that it is right for a man to save. "Go to the ant, thou sluggard; consider her ways, and be wise." The ant saves up and so we should save. The ability to make money is given as a blessing of God, and wealth and prosperity are given as the marks of true wisdom and of good work and the blessing of God throughout the Bible.

There is the parable of the pounds and the parable of the talents. In Matthew, chapter 25, Jesus told the story of a man who was going into a far country. He called his servants, delivered unto them his goods. "And unto one he gave five talents, to another two, and to another one; to every man according to his several ability. . . ." Now notice: here is a man who hires other men of different capacities and puts different amounts in their charge, and when he returns he rewards them variously, not the same, but each according to the way he worked and according to the money he earned. Now the hiring of labor and the paying of wages, depending on productivity, is a Bible plan and is here endorsed by the Lord Jesus.

The same thing comes up in the parable of the pounds in Luke, chapter 19. The Lord said a nobleman gave ten pounds to his servants and when he came back and asked for an accounting, one man had gained ten pounds, another five pounds, and another one had gained nothing. I am just saying that the whole matter of investment of money, of hiring laborers, of making a profit through normal means is taught plainly in the Bible.

Investment and Interest on Invested Capital Approved by Jesus

Let's go a little further. In the Bible there is also the clear proposition, denied by modernists, that a part of the free enterprise system is the right to have money, to save money, to get interest on money; the right to invest in a business or in a factory or in notes and stocks and bonds--to invest and to get interest on the money. In Matthew 25:24,25, Jesus gives the story of the talents:

"*Then he which had received the one talent came and said, Lord, I knew thee that thou art an hard man, reaping where thou hast not sown, and gathering where thou hast not strawed: And I was afraid, and went and hid thy talent in the earth: lo, there thou hast that is thine.*"

A talent—how much was it? In silver, close to $2,000. In gold, close to $32,000. A talent is a certain measurement of weight of money.

"Now, I left you a talent; why didn't you use it?" Jesus said:

"*His lord answered and said unto him, Thou wicked*

and slothful servant, thou knewest that I reap where I sowed not, and gather where I have not strawed: Thou oughtest therefore to have put my money to the exchangers [invested in a bank, or invested in a loan trust], *and then at my coming I should have received mine own with usury.*"

Now Jesus Christ Himself was talking, and He said that it is proper and right to invest your money and get interest on your money. Communism, then, is against the Bible. Anyone who says a man is wrong to invest his money for honest profit is speaking against a Bible principle, one which the Lord Jesus Christ Himself approved. Anyone who tries to stop a man from investing his money is against the Bible; he saved it, he worked for it, he put it by, was thrifty when a lot of other people went on relief or went out to night spots and spent their money on luxuries and riotous living.

God's Plan for Inheritance of Wealth and Property

Now, again, the Bible has a clear word about inheritance. The Scripture tells us that Abraham had flocks and herds and much riches, and he left it all to Isaac. He gave a settlement to Ishmael and sent him away. He gave a settlement to other sons after he married Keturah, and sent them away. Then the great bulk of his estate, the Scripture says, he gave to Isaac. That is an inheritance in a Bible pattern. The Bible tells us how David had accumulated great wealth and left it in the hands of King Solomon so that Solomon was one of the richest men who ever lived. Inheritance!

That isn't all. The land of Palestine was cut up according to families and it was the law and the rule that the land, the farms, the estates should be handed down from father to son to grandson to great grandson, generation after generation. And Leviticus, chapter 25, goes into a great deal of detail to show us how that if a man fall on hard days and has to sell his inheritance, within a year's time he can go and redeem it back, because God is saying it is proper and right and it is good for society that the inheritance should pass from father to son.

Now Karl Marx's idea—and the New Deal idea in America that gifts and taxes and inheritance taxes should take all that a man has earned away from him and his heirs to buy votes with from the common people who want a free ride, and will be glad to vote for a man that will give them more—is wrong. I say, that idea is not of God. It was Karl Marx's idea, which he got from the Devil. The Bible is for inheritance and passing on of property to sons.

4. Communism Versus the Bible Doctrine of Sowing and Reaping

Oh, communism is contrary to the basic rules of right and wrong.

For example, there is the Bible law of sowing and reaping. In Galatians 6:7 and 8 the Scripture says,

"*Be not deceived; God is not mocked: for whatsoever a man soweth, that shall he also reap. For he that soweth to his flesh shall of the flesh reap corruption; but he that soweth to the Spirit shall of the Spirit reap life everlasting.*"

And then the Scripture says, "Let us not be weary in well doing: for in due season we shall reap if we faint not." There is a law in the Bible that your sins will catch up with you, you will be punished; and the good things you do earn a reward and will get a reward. A man should be paid according to his work. A man who earns more should get more.

Now the Marxist idea is that we should give, every man according as he is able, and that a man should receive according to his need, without any regard to morality and righteousness. But that is not what the Lord says. In II Thessalonians, for example, by divine inspiration Paul the apostle says, "For even when we were with you, this we commanded you, that if any would not work, neither should he eat" (II Thess. 3:10). Sowing and reaping, or not sowing and reaping, laboring and receiving rewards! Those who labor more receive more rewards. So God's plan is private enterprise and capitalism and private ownership of property.

5. Temporary and Voluntary Co-operation Among Early Christians Not Communism

In the book of Acts is another passage of Scripture to which I call your attention. From reading Acts, chapter 4, some people think that in New Testament times they had a form of communism. Look at this passage and see:

"*And the multitude of them that believed were of one heart and of one soul: neither said any of them that ought of the things which he possessed was his own; but they had all things common. . . . Neither was there any among them that lacked: for as many as were possessors of lands or houses sold them, and brought the prices of the things that were sold, And laid them down at the apostles' feet: and distribution was made unto every man according as he had need.*"—Acts 4:32,34,35.

Now some say there was a kind of Christian communism. However, I want to show you that communism is basically unchristian and that communists and socialist do not want what they had in New Testament times, and that that was not in any sense communism in the meaning of the term today. There is in these Scriptures no communism like that of Karl Marx, Engels, Lenin, Stalin, and Khruschev. That in Acts 4 is not communism in the presently accepted meaning of the word. Communism is antichristian, is against the Christian religion, because it is against the Bible. It is against the Bible because it is against the Ten Commandments, against the Christian philosophy, against the moral standards of the Bible, against Jesus Christ. And so in this matter of the church at Jerusalem there was nothing even akin to communism as people see it today.

At Jerusalem, "the multitude of them that believed were of one heart and of one soul." People there loved one another. They had been converted. They were in times of great trial and persecution, but they loved one another and they helped one another. And no one said that what he had was his own. He gave, and the apostles helped distribute to those who wanted to join in with the Christians. It was wholly voluntary. No unconverted people were in the group, and it was not commanded that they should join.

In fact, we have in chapter 5 just following an account of Ananias and Sapphira. They wanted to have credit for going along with this idea of giving up all their property, so they sold a piece of property and brought a sum of money. They said, 'This is what the place sold for, and we want to give it all.' But they lied; the place had sold for more. So Peter said, 'It was your own. You didn't have to sell it. When you sold it, the money was yours. You didn't have to bring the money. The thing is, you have lied to God and lied to the people.' So Ananias was struck dead for deceit and for seeking a reputation which he did not earn. You see, he was not required to give everything. You could give it voluntarily or not at all. So this was voluntary co-operation of Christians at Jerusalem, not communism.

The truth of the matter is that people sometimes co-operate together in that way today. Sometimes two men get together and form a partnership. Into this partnership they put certain property of their own. They have a right to do that. A man and woman marry. They now own things jointly. Neither one says that what he has is his own as separated from the other. That is wholly voluntary. Two people who are of the same mind, who love each other, who want to stay together permanently, unite in the ownership of property and live in the same house. They beget the same children. That is the way a man and wife do. That is the way the church did at Jerusalem. Will you note now that only Christians did this.

Will you note also that their voluntary sharing was temporary, during an emergency at a time before the destruction of Jerusalem and during the time of persecution. There was an emergency.

Note also that it failed, as all such plans have failed through the years. I do not say it was wrong. I think it may well be it was all right for them in this emergency to give up all their property and to eat it up soon and to be without soon, for Jerusalem would be destroyed in A. D. 70. The Bible does not say their co-operation was wrong; the Bible does not say it was right. In any case it was temporary, an emergency, and it ended up that they all had to be fed by money raised outside Jerusalem. When Quakers and Mennonites and other people have founded places where everything was owned in common, they have nearly always failed, for similar reasons.

Will you note also that no other New Testament church followed any such plan. Neither Jesus nor the apostles commanded any such thing. It was a temporary measure, done wholly voluntarily. Nobody but Christians were working together; so in this case it was temporarily useful.

Communists don't want that today. Do they want the people to say, "We will get in together and as long as we agree, we will own things in common, eat at the same table, etc."? No, no. What they want is an iron rule by dictators, forcing people who do not want to, to go in and put all their money in one hand, or socialists who want to tax it away from people who earn it and spend it on others who will vote for them. I say, communists and socialists want nothing like that today.

III. COMMUNISM IS MORALLY AND PRACTICALLY A FAILURE

Will communism take the world? No. It will lead to dictatorship wherever it becomes master. But it is failing, must fail, because it is inherently bad and unwise.

1. Is Communism Basically Good?

Now is communism basically good? Stop and think of all the murder, all the barbarism, all the lying, all the teaching of children to betray their parents, all the persecution and actual slavery that are practiced on a large scale in Russia today. Do you believe that communism is basically good?

No, communism is basically evil. It is for lying and not for the truth. It is for murder and not for respecting the individual. It is for seizing property. It is for stealing instead of respecting the rights of ownership.

It is not for the virtue of women. It soon appeared not to be wise, it seemed it did not work, but it is not surprising that for a time in Russia they set out to nationalize women and to do away with normal marriage. I say that did not work, but they tried it. Communism is basically against the home in the Bible sense. It is against the church in the Bible sense. It is against parents teaching their children about God and the Bible and prayer and salvation through faith in Christ. It definitely forbids that. Not one Sunday school runs anywhere in Russia. The churches are not allowed to teach their children. You see, communism is basically evil, barbarous. It is immoral; it is for lying and not the truth.

It is also against the freedom of the individual, against the freedom to go and come, against the freedom to work at what you want to work at, to join a union or not join a union, to vote for whom you please, to speak in public and to meet in public, against public assembly; against freedom of trial by jury, freedom of the public press and freedom to vote in such matters with the independence which we as Americans know. Communism is not for that. Communism is basically evil and wicked. It is against morals. It is against human freedom. It is against God and right.

Anybody who doubts that surely knows little about communism itself.

And I say again, those who follow Karl Marx (and if they call themselves socialists that does not change the fact) are following a system which is basically immoral and is in opposition to Christianity and is the enemy of the morals and the standards and the philosophy of the Bible.

2. Communism Not as Successful as Free Enterprise; Is Against Nature

Now one last word here. Communism cannot succeed basically. Communism has not succeeded on a voluntary basis anywhere that it has gone. It has fallen apart bit by bit. One reason is the centrifugal force of individuality and individual opinions and differences. Another thing is that no man will work as hard for the benefit of others as he will work for himself and his own wife and children. No man will work as hard for the state as he will work for his own family and his own church, for his wife, his children, and a good home and for security for the future.

Communism goes against the human nature as God has made it. Socialism does away with the divine law of sowing and reaping. It isn't bad that a man can get paid more if he works more. It is good that a man can save if he earns more, to take care of his children. It is not bad that a man can be enabled to send his children to college. But communism works against that. It has not succeeded anywhere people have the right and choice. Only for a temporary rule under absolute dictatorship and enforced by arms, only by torture and imprisonment and slaughter and purges, does a communist regime ever stay in power. A comparison of East Germany with West Germany shows at once that capitalism, free enterprise, succeeds far above communism. Communist East Germany must have a wall and soldiers to keep people from leaving for free West Germany. Communist Cuba finds the same need.

It is a failure because it puts in charge of businesses people who are not businessmen. It puts a man in to run a big business because he is a good communist, not because he is a good businessman. It puts a man in to run a collective farm not because he knows how to farm but because he "plays ball" with the government. It puts people in positions because they have standards to fit the regime, not because of character, not because of experience and suitability.

You see, there is something essentially wrong when a government ignores the matter of merit and character and honest work done for honest pay and reward according to merit; to ignore these is essentially wrong. No bureaucrat is going to do things as well when he gets his job only because he is a good Democrat or a good Republican or because he voted this way or that. No man is going to run things as well for the government as he would run it if he did it for love of country, as he could if he were elected because he was a patriot and because he had been successful in business. Communism cannot work successfully in the long run. It always fails, even when it is enforced by arms, by blood purges, by imprisonment, by starvation, by beating, by slave labor camps. Communism is doomed to failure.

And fail it does whether a communist dictator still holds people while they starve, whether communistic leaders still hold down people and lead them on to sin, and come to ghastly war. But whether it apparently holds tight control or whether it gives up the ghost and quits, communism always fails to make people happy. It fails to make a success of government. It cannot compete with free enterprise in a country where people have rights and freedoms and the standards of philosophy of the Christian religion to go by. Communism is antichristian and anti-God.

Let me read again a word in II John, verse 7. Here the Scripture says, "For many deceivers are entered into the world, who confess not that Jesus Christ is come in the flesh. This is a deceiver and an antichrist." So it is.

2. Socialism Antichristian

1. **Is It Natural and Inevitable?**

2. **Could We Properly Have Socialism With a Capable, Honest, Christian National Leader?**

3. **What Is the Bible Position on Private Property, Profits, Capitalism?**

4. **Does Socialism Always Lead to Corruption, Dishonesty, Waste?**

We have a serious and thoughtful letter with questions about socialism. The writer has studied the matter in two universities and his comments and questions are worth serious study. I am grateful for his honest questions about socialism. The Bible has clear answers on these questions, I think, and I trust the answer will be helpful to all.

Since socialism and communism are both essentially built on the teachings of Karl Marx, they have much the same principles and must be dealt with somewhat alike. So, some repetition will be necessary, but it seems wise to apply the rules here to socialism, and give the

Bible teaching on the matters that apply. The application and illustration will be different.

I. SOCIALISM AND COMMUNISM ALIKE

Now what do we mean by socialism? Let me define socialism. I have here a book, *Labor and Tomorrow's World*, by the late Bishop G. Bromley Oxnam, Methodist bishop in Washington, D. C., the most important diocese of all of Methodism.

1. Socialism, Just Like Communism, Says Do Away With Private Ownership of Property and Business

On page 90 Dr. Oxnam tells us what socialism is. This is an authoritative statement. He is a socialist, and favors it, and knows what it is.

> In a little volume now more than thirty years old entitled *Socialism Summed Up,* Morris Hillquit set forth the essential position of the socialist with exceptional lucidity. He says: "The Socialists demand that the principal industries of the nation, the business of providing the necessaries of life, be conducted by the community for the benefit of its members."

And then he says:

> Stated in more concrete terms, the Socialist program requires the public or collective ownership and operation of the principal instruments and agencies for the production and distribution of wealth–the land, mines, railroads, steamboats, telegraph and telephone lines, mills, factories and modern machinery. [That takes in most of it, doesn't it? What about that, that they are not to be privately owned but to be owned by the government? That is socialism.–Ed.]
>
> This is the main program and the ultimate aim of the whole Socialist movement, and the political creed of all Socialists. It is the unfailing test of Socialist adherence,

> and admits of no limitation, extension or variation. Whoever accepts this program is a Socialist; whoever does not, is not.

What is the program? Public ownership of all the principal instruments and agencies, production, distribution of wealth, the land, the mines, railroads, all the farms, all the factories, all the shops, steamboats, telegraph and telephone lines, mills, factories, and modern machinery. No private ownership—that is socialism. You ask the difference between that and communism. No difference in the creed. The only difference is that communism, as it is in Russia, insists on the right to take over with a violent overthrow, bloodshed, and murder, while the socialists say, "No, let us get in and do it in America. We can get a Huey Long or a Roosevelt or a Hubert Humphrey to little by little fool the people to keep giving more of other people's money so we can get enough votes and can take things away and enlarge the inheritance tax, and put on confiscatory income taxes on the higher bracket; then it won't be long until we have all the rich people poor, and the poor people will be in charge, the ones who didn't earn it." You see, there is no difference in the creed. The only difference is whether you kill somebody to do it, or whether you do it without killing.

Who is the father of communism? Karl Marx. Who is the father of socialism? Karl Marx. You know what the name of Russia is? Russia is the *Union of Soviet Socialist Republics.* What is Russia? A socialist state. No difference in socialism and communism.

2. Why Communists and Socialists Turn Up Together: They Agree

In the book, *The Witness?* Whittaker Chambers tells how strange it is that New Dealers in some naive way can't recognize the communists. President Roosevelt just could not believe that Alger Hiss was a communist and betraying his country. He just could not believe that Dexter White was a communist and betraying his country. He kept promoting him and kept whacking everybody who raised his head to defend America from communism.

Now why? Because fundamentally the real reason is that there was kinship of spirit, and so they believed alike—the one a communist and the other a socialist. They say, "Take the money away from the man who earns it and give it to the fellow who does not earn it. Take over things by the government; let the government run everything; don't let anybody make very much money. And be sure to keep enough at hand to pass out to buy votes with, buy the farmers by giving them money to plow up what they planted, or pay them more than they could get on the law of supply and demand on the natural markets," etc. But always the same principle—take it over, own it by the state, use it for political purposes, buy the votes, buy the people, put over a program with it, and finally end up in a dictatorship.

Now there is no difference in the eventual end of the socialists and the communists. The communists say, "Let us kill people and get them out of the way and do it now." The socialists say, "No, let us do it a little slower and easier. Don't kill them if we can help it." I'm not lying, nor joking, nor twisting, but giving you the facts about it.

Why is there a kinship? Why is it? Here a man says, "I'm against communism." But what he means is, "I'm against Russia." But, he says, "I'd like to make America like Russia." E. Stanley Jones would say, "Oh, I'm against communism." But he would say, "I mean, of course, Russian communism. But I'd like to help get America to be a collective state like Russia." Do you see?

II. SOCIALISM COMES WITH DECAY OF MORALS AND PRINCIPLES

He asks, "Is not socialism a natural and sensible or to-be-expected development?"

ANSWER: The development of socialism is natural in the sense that man is inherently wicked. The human heart is deceitful. For this reason, human governments usually start out better and end worse. The rise and fall of empires all over the world shows this principle. As people prosper, they decay in morals and more and more try to gain some advantage over their fellows, try some way to make a living without work, some way to be supported by the government.

For example, in the Roman Empire, shortly before its fall, the government put on great exhibitions to keep the common rabble, the plebians, content. They had great exhibitions in the Colosseum at Rome, gladiatorial combats, combats with wild beasts. They even made a lake in the Colosseum and built ships and had sea battles with the death of many, to please thousands of the idle populace and keep their support. The government furnished free bread, importing wheat.

For a season the government seemed to prosper, with its armies conquering other countries and bringing in heavier taxes. But the moral quality of the people broke down. Decay in home life and business as well as corruption in government increased until the Roman Empire fell. That is something like the story of all nations. That is why socialism or other immoral and antichristian principles are likely to prosper and are "to-be-expected" developments.

Socialism was fathered by Karl Marx. An essential part of his doctrine is atheism. Karl Marx says that religion is "the opiate of the people." The doctrines of socialism are antichristian, and he knew it; they are contrary to the Bible, and he knew it. Communism, which grew out of socialism, retained the essential teachings of Karl Marx, and socialism is always headed toward communism. The only essential difference is that socialists try to have a peaceful revolution, while communists want a violent overthrow of government for the same ends.

III. BIBLE CLEARLY OPPOSES SOCIALIST DOCTRINE AND PRACTICE

One asks, "If we had a capable, honest, respectable, talented Christian national leader, instead of the pigmy and unscrupulous ones, such as we have had, I am wondering if we would not be less opposed?"

ANSWER: But you suppose an impossibility. An out-and-out Christian cannot be an out-and-out socialist. Those who do not know what socialism means may think so, or those who do not know what the Bible teaches may think so. But those who know the Bible and who know socialism, know that they are incompatible, that they are mutually exclusive. Karl Marx knew that. It is no accident that he was an atheist and insisted that atheism must go with socialism, and that the socialist state must put down religion.

There are certain great Bible principles which outlaw socialism as unchristian and immoral. Some of these principles are as follows:

1. The Right of Private Ownership of Property

This is clearly expressed in the Ten Commandments, in the commands, "Thou shalt not steal" and "Thou shalt not covet" (Exod. 20:15,17). And throughout the Mosaic law, and throughout the New Testament epistles, it is made clear that private ownership of property is a sacred right of individuals.

Socialism teaches that it is better for property to be

owned by the mass of people, not by individuals. But there is no such teaching in the Bible. The Bible directly contradicts it.

2. Private Profit a Bible Doctrine

The principle of profit for money invested is clearly taught throughout thc Bible. Socialists speak as if profit is sinful. The Bible does not. In the parable of the pounds in Luke 19:11-27 Jesus clearly taught that the man who took one pound (a certain weight of money) and invested it in business and gained ten pounds, was to be commended, "Well, thou good servant: because thou hast been faithful in a very little, have thou authority over ten cities." The man who gained five pounds was praised, but not so much. And the man who did not have any profit on the investment is called "Thou wicked servant." Those who would try to limit legitimate profits are contrary to the Bible. Those who scoff at profits as unworthy or immoral are silly and wicked.

When you hear anyone speak slightingly of making profits, as if that were wrong, you may know that he either does not know what the Bible teaches or that he is deliberately against the Bible and God's plan for men.

Again in the parable of the sower Jesus plainly shows that men should expect profit from their labor. He tells about a farmer who sowed the ground and of the results of the seed sown. "But other fell into good ground, and brought forth fruit, some an hundredfold, some sixtyfold, some thirtyfold." In other words, it is not wrong, but proper and right, if a farmer can get his seed back a hundred times over. And the least figure given is an increase of thirtyfold, that is, three thousand per cent! This illustrates that people are to invest their time and their property and use it and expect profit from it. That is the Bible doctrine which socialists deny and which communists deny.

An authority recently revealed that the government now gets two and one-half times as much in taxes from a business as the investors who put up the money and make the business possible can get. For example, a husband died leaving his widow, let us say, $6,000. We suppose she invests that in the Bethlehem Steel Company stock or in the American Telephone Company stock, as hundreds of thousands of others have done; or she might invest it in a little dry cleaning plant in her own town, or in a garage run by a son or nephew. If she got the normal profit from the business, it might run $50 a month, which is certainly not much. But after the government takes a big slice to support all its bureaucrats and keep its hundreds of thousands of voters on the payroll, she will get, not $50 a month, but $14, the government taking two and one-half times as much for taxes as the widow gets on her life savings upon which she must depend for her declining years.

This idea that the government should discourage private enterprise and should take away all but the bare minimum of profit, is a wicked idea, wholly contrary to the teachings of the Bible. It is also deadly dangerous to the economy of America, making it unprofitable to start new businesses and unprofitable to risk capital which may be taken in confiscatory taxes and may make a normal return on money impossible.

3. It Is Not Wrong to Save, to Invest, to Get Wealth

Let us see another thing here, another principle. The Bible says riches and honor properly come to people who serve God (Prov. 3:9,10).

"*Honour the Lord with thy substance, and with the firstfruits of all thine increase: So shall thy barns be filled with plenty, and thy presses shall burst out with new wine.*"

I'll show you that socialism and communism have the same root, have the same creed. I'll show you in a moment, but right now I want you to see that socialism and communism say that for a man to earn more money is wrong, that the fellow with the muscles and the fellow who wants only a 30-hour week ought to have just as much as the fellow who schemes and plans and stays awake at night and works 16 hours a day, and so on. He says that the one ought to have as much as the other. The Bible doesn't say that. The communist says that there is no difference, and that since there is no God anyhow, it is to everybody according to his needs. But the Bible says, "Honour the Lord with thy substance, and with the firstfruits of all thine increase: So shall thy barns be filled with plenty, and thy presses shall burst out with new wine." There is a divine law of sowing and reaping, a divine law of wealth, a divine law that it is an honor to earn more money, to make good in this world, to save money, and to take care of your family.

The communistic and socialistic plan is that everybody is more or less on relief—a paternal state, a welfare state, with some laboring people in charge of it, everybody dipping into the fund so you can keep them in line, so you can buy their votes, and tell them what to do, etc.

What is the Bible plan? Take care of your own people. Paul said to Timothy, 'If anyone has a mother, or an aunt, or a widow to take care of, don't bring her to the church. You requite your own parents.' Then comes that famous Scripture which is nearly always quoted out of context, "If any provide not for his own, and specially for those of his own house [the widows of his own household, his own widowed mother or aunt, or old-maid sister, or somebody else who needs support of his own family], he hath denied the faith, and is worse than an infidel."

This socialistic idea that the government has to take care of all the old people, has to take care of everybody when the work runs out, and so on, is against the Bible plan. The Bible plan is, "Honour thy father and thy mother." Don't you think there are some people who need to be taken care of? Yes, and Paul goes on to say in I Timothy, 'Let not a widow be taken into the number if she is less than sixty years old.' Any woman under sixty will try to marry again anyhow, if she gets a chance! And a woman past sixty could be persuaded! But let a widow not be taken in unless she has been married to only one husband, and if she has washed the saints' feet, has been good in taking in strangers, has been charitable. It is all right for society to support that kind of a woman, if she is past sixty and has been married only once, and lived for God, a faithful Christian woman, and if she has no child to support her. That is the ordinary way, the American way, what we call capitalism, the free enterprise way. Do you see the difference in that and socialism and communism?

So if a good man, a church man, a professed Christian man, runs for president on a New Deal or socialistic program, then we know that he does not understand the Bible; and however good his intentions, he will lead America away from God. There will be socialists who do know what socialism means—know that it is atheistic and antichristian, and that it leads away from the Bible standard of capitalistic free enterprise.

4. Reward in Proportion to Merit—God's Law of Sowing and Reaping

Connected with this there is a very clear divine law, often stated in the Scriptures, that "whatsoever a man soweth, that shall he also reap." One who works harder ought to get more income. One who works less ought to get less. The idea that every man ought to have the same income is silly, as well as antichristian. People ought to get what they earn. This is stated also in the Scripture, "For even when we were with you, this we commanded you, that if any would not work, neither should he eat. For we hear that there are some which walk among you disorderly, working not at all, but are busybodies. Now them that are such we command and exhort by our Lord Jesus Christ, that with quietness they work, and eat their own bread" (II Thess. 3:10-12). Here the Bible clearly teaches that the man who works harder should have more to eat. The man who plans and schemes and toils ought to get greater return for his toil. The manager is worth more than the laborer, worth more to the business, worth more to society, and worthy of more honor before God.

The socialistic idea that farmers should be paid more for their goods than the law of supply and demand provides is contrary to the Bible. For the law of supply and demand is itself a part of this divine law of sowing and reaping. If what a farmer raises is of benefit to society, there will be a demand for it. He has earned what it sells for. It is good for farmers to have information and help about marketing and about how much demand for certain articles there will be, and what will be the supply. But for the rest of us to have to pay taxes to subsidize farmers and pay them money that they have not earned is sinful.

For a factory to have to take on workers they do not need or to pay men more than they earn is wicked. "Featherbed" jobs on the railroad, where a man is paid a day's wages when he does not do a day's work, are contrary to the Bible. I have rented theaters for revival services and have had to pay an electrician a full day's wages every day when he did nothing but turn on the lights and sometimes did not even do that.

That is socialistic, and it is antichristian and contrary to the Bible. The Bible rule is that people are to reap according as they sow. They are to profit according as they work. Men are to be paid according to their merits.

The socialistic idea as stated by Karl Marx that each one should work as he is able and each one receive according to his needs sounds well—but it is an antiscriptural statement. What a man receives ought to be in proportion to what he is worth to society, according to the work he does.

5. Capital, Private Investment for Profit, a Bible Principle

Capitalism is a term hated by many, but actually capitalism simply expresses the doctrine taught in the Bible, that men have a right to save up money, own property, and get return from the use of the money and the use of the property. A man bought a ramshackle old car, painted "Taxi" on the sides, and hired a man to run it. He is a capitalist, though he had only $300 invested. Another man set up a hamburger joint and hired a cook to help him. He is a capitalist.

The parables of Jesus again and again tell how He endorses capitalism. He endorsed the capitalism of the nobleman who left pounds with his servants, or talents with his servants, to run his business. He endorsed the capitalism of a man who owned a vineyard and hired workers. The idea that the workers ought to own property without buying it is utterly opposed in the Bible. And John the Baptist preached, "Be content with your wages" (Luke 3:14).

The Scripture commands, "Servants, be obedient to them that are your masters according to the flesh, with fear and trembling, in singleness of your heart, as unto Christ" (Eph. 6:5). And again and again the Bible teaches that the plan of workmen and bosses is of God, that private ownership of property and of hiring of labor is of God, that the investment of capital and taking profit from it honestly is of God.

With these things in mind, you can see that no informed Christian, well-instructed in the Bible, can be a socialist; and when a man appears to be a good Christian and runs on a socialistic platform, you may know that either he does not know what it is all about, or he is friendly to the atheism and the anti-Bible attitude of socialism.

IV. AMERICAN BUSINESS BROUGHT PROSPERITY, SOCIALISM ACTUALLY HINDERED

The man who wrote me says,

> For my part, I can't help but admit that the common man has a somewhat better economic life than he has ever had . . . .
>
> Traveling about, I see better farm homes . . . .
>
> It does seem that our present government is seeking to buy the votes of factory laborers and Negroes and farmers, but we have to admit these three groups were and have been hard-pressed, to put it mildly.

Then this friend mentions sawmill workers of the past and others.

1. How Improved Machinery and Business Enterprise Increased Wealth

ANSWER: Yes, there has been an improvement in the lot of farmers and of factory workers and of Negroes, as you say. But you are very wrong in supposing that a socialistic program made that improvement. Primarily that improvement came about by improved machinery, increased production, and by business itself, not by the government.

Let me illustrate: In my boyhood, about sixty years ago, I knew men who had worked on farms all their lives. A man was an old man, bent and worn out, at fifty years of age. He had followed a walking turning-plow, a walking cultivator, had worn himself out working twelve hours a day for many, many years in the greatest toil. But even in my boyhood walking plows gave way to riding plows. Instead of a single mule plowing a six-inch furrow, when I was ten years old, we had six mules to a big triple-disc plow. Here a small boy did six times as much work with modern machinery as a mature man had been able to do before. So farm income went up during those days, long before the New Deal.

Today modern farms produce four times as much goods per man-hour of work as they did twenty years ago. The natural increase in farm income, without government subsidies, would have greatly improved farm life. I remember that at the close of World War I it was thought there was not enough land in America to grow food for the multitudes coming. Now we know that ground can be made to produce much, much more, by modern farming methods and with modern machinery. Much marginal land has now been turned back to pasture for this reason. The growth in machinery and in modern methods has brought about a great increase in income per farmer. Likewise in industry—for the average worker now there are thousands of dollars worth of machinery used. In England, the miners who mine with pick and shovel turn out only a fraction as much as miners turn out in America with modern machinery. Don't credit the New Deal for that. Modern business, so hated by socialists, is responsible for the difference.

At one time men were hired in offices to write out business letters in longhand. Then typewriters came along and greatly increased the output of offices, and of course increased the wages of workers. Now, instead of dictating to a typist, I am dictating to a machine, saving the typist's time. She will work only about half as much in getting this chapter written as she would have a few years ago, when I dictated and she wrote in her shorthand notebook.

And at the Sword of the Lord office we have two automatic typewriters that can be set to write the same letter over and over again, with one girl running both of them and doing other things besides, and saving lots of time and money. So naturally we can pay more.

In every kind of production, American businessmen and American genius and free enterprise have so greatly increased the output per man-hour that income has risen, prices have been made more reasonable (relative to income), and the good things of life have been spread among the multitudes. The New Deal had little to do with this. And what it did have to do with it was wrong.

2. To Take One Man's Rightfully Earned Property and Give It to Others, Unearned, to Get Their Votes, Is Dishonest Demagoguery

Let us say that some people, it is true, have appeared to benefit from the New Deal. Farmers have gotten some money that they didn't earn, paid to them in subsidies, made up by the rest of the taxpayers. The Muscle Shoals and Tennessee Valley Authorities have gotten electricity to common people some cheaper than other power companies could do so, perhaps. But the rest of us have paid it in taxation providing funds with less interest than we must make up. But with taxes mounting sky-high, and with dollars buying less and less, still the government could not keep out of debt. So what really happens is that these people who got government subsidies, who got things they didn't earn, from a New Deal government which was buying their votes, simply piled up debts which they and their children will have to pay, or which will topple this government over, sooner or later. No one gets something for nothing. Somebody always has to pay. And crooked politicians who buy votes by giving people what they do not earn, after taking it away from others who do earn it, are doing no favor to America.

The truth is that the increase of prosperity was not brought about by the New Deal, but was brought about by the machine age, by modern civilization, by science applied to daily life; and the government had practically nothing to do with these factors except to hamstring them by public criticism and by enormous taxation, and expensive and crippling red tape.

V. CORRUPTION, WASTE, INEFFICIENCY AND DISHONESTY NATURALLY GO WITH SOCIALISM

Our friend says, "Again I say, it seems to me that socialism is a part of destiny, but the corruption and the moral rot and dishonesty on the part of our leaders is what makes socialism seem so nasty."

ANSWER: But you are mistaken, and all sincere socialists are mistaken, in supposing that corruption and moral rot and dishonesty of the New Deal administration does not inherently go with socialism. It does. Socialism never did work successfully and it cannot work now for several reasons.

1. Enlightened Self-Interest Expressed in Profit and Wages Are Proper Motives for Work

Enlightened self-interest is a proper motive, and the strongest motive, to get people to work. Wages according to one's work, on the part of labor, and profit according to one's ingenuity and vigilance and careful administration, on the part of management—these are God-appointed motives for work.

Put two people up to work on two jobs, right across

the street from each other, and see how it works. Let one man be working under the O. P. A. (Office of Price Administration) system, and paid by the government, irrespective of his merits. Let another man be working at his own job, to make money, and you will see that private enterprise works better than socialism. It always has been that way and it always will be that way. Again and again groups of serious, idealistic people, often Christian people, have gotten together to start a communal or collective enterprise, where each would work the best he could and all would share alike. They have never succeeded for the simple reason that people do not work well where the law of supply and demand, the Bible law of sowing and reaping, does not have proper play. If people are not paid more for more work, they will not do more work.

In management it works the same way. The post office department runs at a deficit all the time. It is owned by the government, and the postmaster general's office is used as a reward for political service. So it costs Americans millions of dollars in taxes to keep up our post office system. But side by side with the postal system, the American Express Company, run by private enterprise, does the same kind of work and makes a profit. And it gives better service. If you don't believe it, try ten different post offices and ten different express offices and see which place you get the most courteous treatment, the most eager service! Bureaucracy is itself hurtful and wrong and anti-social.

If government owns business, then a man can keep his job not by doing more work but by keeping a political pull. Then the boss who has political pull can give jobs to those who pay him a little on the side. He does not have to make the business pay—the government (meaning the rest of us taxpayers) pays all the bills anyway! The more government meddles in business, the more it hires employees, that much more corruption and dishonesty is inevitable.

In England, it has been proved beyond any doubt that the steel mills owned by the government will not turn out as much steel as when they are controlled by private industry. Coal mines owned by the government and run by the government will not turn out as much coal as when the mines are run by private enterprise. And as the government succeeds in socializing medicine, hires the doctors, and runs the hospitals, then there will be more malingering by people who are not sick but who want attention, there will be more crookedness among doctors, there will be poorer service in hospitals and by physicians, because in taking away initiative and private enterprise and enlightened self-interest, and in killing the profit-motive, we "kill the goose that lays the golden egg." Socialistic government kills moral principle, kills initiative, so that necessarily waste, dishonesty, and higher expenses of government administration inevitably come.

For instance, even the poorest people who think they have been helped by government subsidies—money taken away from people that earned it by governments who wanted to use that tax money to buy votes with, would find that if we could be rid of all the bureaucracy, the red tape, the waste and extravagance of a socialistic government, and if we had only the simple, primitive government of the United States of forty-five or fifty years ago, business would have increased so much more that the commonest working man would have gained far more in actual benefits than he has by the dishonesty of a socialistic government, which has piled billions of dollars of debt upon the people, and has grabbed from others their rightful earnings, to buy votes of labor and the farmers and other favored classes who had more votes. Actually we have lost in prosperity, not gained, by the socialism in America.

2. Wasteful Meddling of the New Deal Prolonged the Depression, Now Makes Waste, Decreases Production and Prosperity

It is a silly idea, advanced by mountebanks and rabble rousers, that President Hoover brought on the depression, and that the New Deal saved America out of the depression. Actually the exact opposite is the truth. America had had great depressions before, but they never lasted more than a few weeks or months at most. But America quickly recovered because the law of supply and demand, the law of sowing and reaping, was allowed to take effect and even things up so there could be a quick comeback. But with the meddling of Roosevelt and the New Deal, wages in the union were kept abnormally high, and wherever possible prices were kept high. If men had been allowed to work for whatever they could get, there would not have been unemployment. There was still need for plenty of labor. If farmers had been allowed to sell their goods at whatever the market would bring, they could have sold all their goods. It was silly and wasteful and wicked to kill hogs when people were without food, to plow up one row out of every three in cotton, when millions did not have enough clothes, and pay subsidies to the farmers for keeping their products off the market. All this interference with God's own economic laws prolonged the depression for years, when it would have cured itself automatically in a few months had God's law been allowed to take effect.

Men may think that artificial regulation of economy is better than God's law of sowing and reaping, the law of supply and demand; but it is not. There is never any reason for scarcity, if we let God's laws work. There are always people who could buy normal amounts of food, of grain, of steel products and manufactured goods, if we let our market find its own level. There are always jobs to be done, at proper wages, relative to the need, if we allow wages to seek their proper level. Artificial pegging of standards that have no relation to God's laws is back of much of our trouble.

I am for high wages. I am for big production. I am for normal prices. But let goods sell for what they are worth. Let labor bring what it is worth. Keep the market open. Do not kill the labor market by the closed shop practice. Do not kill the market for goods by pegged, high prices. Sometimes in emergency cases, such as in wartime, there should, perhaps, be a top limit on wages and prices. But that is the unusual thing, and even so, conditions will soon adjust themselves, for the more demand there is for labor, the more labor-saving machines will be installed and more people will work, and the more demand there is for any goods the more of those goods will be supplied, to make a profit. God's economic laws, like all of God's laws, always work. Interference with these laws, or deliberately breaking these laws, always brings trouble.

It is true that Roosevelt and the New Deal administration and more recent welfare administrations did buy the votes of many people by "distributing the wealth" as these socialists called it. That means they took money from some who had earned it and gave it to others who had not earned it. No doubt there was some charity of heart, but their motives were selfish in the main; they were simply buying votes, and that philosophy fitted their craving to stay in power. But to teach that socialistic measures brought America out of the depression is silly and contrary to the facts. There would have been far more economic prosperity if men had simply followed God's laws of supply and demand, without such high taxes, without such extravagance and waste and red tape.

3. Class Hatred So Carefully Cultivated by Liberals, Civil Rights Workers, and Communists Is Wicked, Unchristian and Un-American

Another terrible result of socialism is inevitable, that is, the setting of class against class. All this talk about "dirty capitalists," all this talk of "sweat shops," of "slave labor laws" (referring mendaciously to thc Taft-Hartley Law) is wicked. All this setting up of a political party to get the votes of labor, to get the votes of the farmers, as opposed to other classes, is wicked. But that is essentially the doctrine of socialism and the method of socialism.

One has a right to suspect the patriotism and the integrity of any man who sets out especially to say he is "for labor" or "for the farmers" or "for colored people," as if these groups or any other groups should have their champions against the rest of the people. Why not just be for God and the country and for people everywhere? Why not simply be an American and be for Americans? Why should not every man who goes to Congress, and every man who seeks the Presidency, just be for the good of the whole of America? What is good for one is good for all of us. Anything that cripples one part of our nation cripples all of us eventually.

To raise racial hate or class hate and to arouse enmity against management, against big business or little business, against capital, is essentially wicked and un-American. The man who encourages oppression of big business today will tomorrow be hurting small business and labor. The man who takes away the liberties of any of us will find his own liberties involved sooner or later. If President Truman can illegally seize the steel mills (private property, legitimate and scriptural according to the philosophy of the Bible), tomorrow a President can seize your home or your car or your cow or the Sword of the Lord. Socialism necessarily means buying the votes of the group of people who have the most votes by attacking the group that has the fewer votes. And that is wrong. It necessarily means higher taxes for people of more enterprise, more education, more hard work, or more genius, in order to buy the votes of people with lesser energy or lesser skill or lesser integrity.

In other words, socialism is essentially corrupt; it goes against God's laws, against Christianity, against the Bible, against true Americanism. It goes against the things that make for good character and prosperity. The corruption and waste and extravagance and debt of the New Deal are a part of the lack of principle involved. They are inevitable with socialism.

3. How Modernism in Religion Fits the Socialist-Communist Program

Here is a book, *Labor in Tomorrow's World,* by G. Bromley Oxnam—"A distinguished interpretation of the labor movement in relation to the world-wide mission of the Christian church." You will be interested to know that this book is dedicated to Francis John McConnell, the most radical modernist of the Methodist church, now retired, and who, I believe, recently died.

Here is another book, *Preaching and the Social Crisis,* edited by G. Bromley Oxnam, and this has a great many series of lectures delivered for the Boston University School of Theology. Contents:

"Preaching and Socialism," by Kirby Page;

"Communism's Challenge to Christianity," by Jerome Davis;

"Preaching and the Industrial Order," by Harry Frederick Ward, the man who started the Methodist Social Action Committee and sworn before Congress to be a communist, a professor in Union Theological Seminary and the teacher and mentor of Bishop Oxnam himself. Dr. Oxnam used to be his secretary;

"Preaching and the Race Problem," by William Nelson DeBerry;

"The Preacher and Revolution," by G. Bromley Oxnam; and other chapters by Francis McConnell, Burris Atkins Jenkins, etc., more of the same kind.

Do you remember the method that Karl Marx said communism should use to take property away from the people and to get it in the hands of a dictatorship? Listen and I'll read you his statements. Here they are:

"1. Abolition of private property in land and application of all rents of lands to public purposes:

"2. A heavy progressive or graduated income tax."

Now why, if one man be taxed not beyond a certain low limit so a man will have a chance, beyond that—why not everybody 10% or everybody 20%? No, because the man who made more money may want to take it away from you, Marx says, so let us get 90% of his while we get 20% of somebody else's. So says Marx and some other people you've heard about.

I'll read on:

"3. The abolition of all right of inheritance."

Let's take it away in taxes instead of letting a man give it to his children.

"4. The confiscation of the property of all emigrants and rebels," those who may have left the State.

"5. Centralization of credit in the hands of the State, . . . furthermore, the socialization of transportation, factory production, agriculture."

We're pretty far gone toward that in agriculture now. I'm just reminding you of how closely alike are communism and socialism. Those are two of the triplets that are fairly to be called members of the same party!

Modernists Openly Avow Socialism

We go a little further. How are modernism, communism, and socialism alike? Now, I think I have showed you there would be no doubt that communism and socialism are alike. But now how is modernism like socialism and communism? Here are the facts. For example, this book edited by G. Bromley Oxnam on

Preaching and the Social Crisis is not about the Gospel, is not the plan of salvation, is not what the Bible teaches us, but is about preaching and the social crisis of turning everything that we can into socialism in this country. Now, why would that have to be by a Methodist preacher and why would three of the sermons in here be by Methodist bishops? On page 19 I read in this book by a modernist preacher (See if you think this is socialism or not) in this sermon by Kirby Page, edited by Bishop Oxnam:

> It is supremely tragic that at this late day evidence must still be produced that Socialism is much closer akin to Christian gospel than capitalism.

That isn't so, but that's what he says. So he's a socialist, isn't he? All right, quoting again from page 19:

> For the Christian Church to disentangle itself from the meshes of capitalism [the American free enterprise system, private ownership of property] is as crucial and urgent in our time as it was for the church of our forefathers' day to break with slavery.

Another quotation, page 32. Are modernist preachers socialist and communist? Listen carefully now:

> Surely, it is obvious that the co-operative method of Socialism is much closer akin to Jesus' way of life than is the competitive combat of capitalism.

So Kirby Page said, with Bishop Oxnam's approval. Here is another one. On page 38, Jerome Davis, a famous modernist and socialist, says in this book, edited by Bishop Oxnam:

> They demand a dictatorship of producers. They [the communist leaders] believe it is possible to own, control and use all property for the benefit of the workers through a system of state Socialism.

You see, they know socialism and communism are the same.

> Nothing must be run for the profit of the individual;

> everything must be run in the interests of the masses--the real producers. Production must be for use and not for profit. Furthermore, they demand that all property relations be humanized, that we must revolutionize factory conditions in the interests of the workers. All income must be socialized. [Nobody's income according to his work, but according to what the State decrees, you see?] The effort of everyone in society shall be planned and directed for the common good.

No one will work where he wants to; he works where he is told. Nobody to get what he agrees and bargains to work for; he will get what the state, run by dictators, tells him he can get. Now, the statement is by Jerome Davis, modernist preacher, and edited by the late Bishop G. Bromley Oxnam of Washington, D. C., once the most prominent bishop of the Methodist church and one of the presidents of the World Council of Churches.

Modernist Leaders Say They Are Leaders in Socialist-Modernist Revolution

Here is another quotation by Jerome Davis, on page 55:

> "As ministers of Jesus Christ, we must recognize again that we are leaders in a revolutionary movement. . . ."

Well, then, what is the Methodist church training preachers for? To be leaders in a revolutionary movement. What is the National Council of Churches insisting that preachers do? Be leaders in a revolutionary movement. Listen now: ". . . which is seeking nothing short of the complete overthrow of special privilege [that is, a man keeping what he earns], economic selfishness [I'll earn it and I'll get paid for it], and racial discrimination." This involves not only a revolution of human heart but a revolution of the social order.

Change the American way of life to the Russian way of life: socialism, communism.

How Modernists and Communists Are Alike in Being Against the Bible

Now, why is it that G. Bromley Oxnam, for example, admitted before an investigating committee of Congress, that he had joined nine different communist-front organizations? Note, he did not say he was a communist, and nobody accused him of being a communist, but if he were a communist, he wouldn't tell it. I don't know; I don't say he was. But he admitted that he had joined nine different organizations which, it turned out, had been organized by communists and for communist purposes in America. Now, why is it that modernists run with that crowd? And those that are not red are pink. I want to show you why they are alike.

Listen carefully. First of all, they start alike against the Bible. The communists hate the Bible. The communists say that all religion is the opiate of the people. They start alike in that they do not believe the Bible. The modernists don't believe the Bible. They say, "We will not have that authority." The communists say, "We will not have that Bible as authority." The socialists say, "We will not have the Bible as authority." Does anybody know why, as soon as we got a pro-socialist New Deal government in the country, we repealed the Eighteenth Amendment? The Bible standards do not fit with socialism and communism.

They are alike in that they all reject the Bible. Listen to me! Don't put a modernist in with Christians. Put him with infidels. The man who does not believe that the Bible is true, who does not believe that Jesus was born of a virgin, who believes that the Bible is a book of myths and legends as well as some good things, and who does not believe in the atoning blood—that man is not a Christian but is an infidel! He is an unbeliever! You rate a modernist not with Christians but with communists and with infidels, with Tom Paine, with

Bob Ingersoll, with Voltaire. On all the principal essentials they agree exactly. Yes. Now do you see why they are alike?

Modernists, Like Communism, Have a Philosophy Based on Evolution, Not Supernatural Creation

Second, they are alike on evolution. Modernists believe that the world came not by direct creation of God but by evolution, that man came by slowly evolving from lower forms of life. They trace man from apes on back to one-celled animals, etc. They believe that man came by evolution. But that is a part of the particular doctrine of Karl Marx. And to whom did Karl Marx dedicate his book, *Communist Manifesto*? To Charles Darwin! Yes. He says that the human race is evolving upward and that therefore, little by little, society is growing into a better state and eventually we will not have any private property, and everybody will own everything together. And he says that evolution is absolutely certain to bring communism over the whole world. So Stalin taught, so all communists believe. So you believe when you believe in evolution instead of direct creation by God, when you believe not that God's Bible is authoritative but that just whatever will work out to fit your scheme is all right.

Modernists, Like Communists and Socialists, Exalt Man as Good

Do you see the difference? Now, third, modernists, evolutionists, socialists, all believe alike on the creation of man. The Bible says that man was created in God's image but fell, that man is a fallen creature, that the heart is desperately wicked, that a man must be born again or go to Hell, that man is an enemy of God, estranged from God from the womb. But modernism says, "No." They say, "Man [Christian Science puts it this way, too] is the unfallen son of God." The modernist declares that there is good in every man. He says God is the Father of all and that all are brothers. He says men do not need to be born again—they are already born of God. I have a book by Harry Emerson Fosdick, *The Hope of the World*, in which he says in a sermon on "The Peril of Worshiping Jesus," "Do you believe that Jesus is divine? Yes," he said, "I do, like my mother was divine." Is he blaspheming?

Now, communists, socialists, modernists, *all* agree that man is essentially good, and it is just the system that is wrong. If man had a chance he would come out all right. Do you see why modernists turn naturally to socialism? Do you know why the modernist or liberal will be working toward a collective state and for uniting all the churches and uniting world government, and for everybody getting together to own the property collectively instead of by private enterprise? Because he does not believe what the Bible says about man, but he believes man is essentially good, like the socialists and the communists believe! The modernists and the socialists and communists all come out alike on that matter. Do you see why they run together? They do not always know why, but it turns out that way because they are alike. They have the same doctrinal background.

The Deceitful Morality of Communism and Modernism Alike

Fourth, the modernists and the communists are alike in a certain wicked immorality. The Bible declares that with feigned words these modernists will make merchandise of you; ". . . with deceitful words," the Scripture says. They are false prophets come to you in sheep's clothing. They are wolves in sheep's clothing. What do I mean? They are pretending to be sheep, but they are wolves. They are pretending to be preachers of the Gospel, but they are infidels. They will come as angels of light, Paul said, but they are enemies of your souls, they are wicked spirits. Do you see what the Bible teaches?

A communist says, "I don't agree with the Bible, so I am not bound by the Ten Commandments." He says, "There is no God, so there is no morality, and there's nobody holding me to account. If I can get by with it, I'll get by with it." There is no right and wrong to a communist except, "What will advance communism and what will not?" If lying will win, if murder will win, if stealing will win, if rape will win, that is all right. The communists have no morality. A man is a fool to trust Russia, because Russian leaders are all communists, which means they will tell as big a lie as they want to; they've no conscience on it. They say if it prospers Russia, and if it prospers communism, then it is right to lie.

What about a modernist? What do you think about a modernist who comes in and is ordained as a Baptist preacher and says that he agrees with the New Hampshire Confession of Faith. "What do you believe? Were you converted? What do you believe about the inspiration of the Bible? What do you believe about Hell? What do you believe about the blood atonement? How do you believe people are saved?" Are preachers asked those questions still? Now what about a Baptist preacher who says he believes the Bible, says he believes the virgin birth, believes Jesus rose from the dead, says he believes man is a sinner and must be born again, but takes those vows tongue in cheek, then little by little sets out to break down faith and to deny the Bible that he promised God and men he would support?

A Methodist preacher wrote me, and I answered his letter just today. He said, "I wish you would have that SWORD OF THE LORD stopped. I don't want it coming to my place." And he said some mean things. I wrote him that I would stop the paper that someone sent him because they loved him. But I asked him, "Why don't you be honest about it and say, 'The truth is, I am against the historic Christian position; I do not believe the Bible; I despise the Christ presented in THE SWORD OF THE LORD' ? Why don't you say that, instead of running me down and accusing me of being a troublemaker?" I went on to say, "You were ordained, and every Methodist preacher who is ordained once took solemn vows that he believes the Articles of Religion of the Methodist church which are unchanged down through the years. And you vowed publicly to teach them and defend them. Now, then, suppose you took them tongue in cheek. Never mind; you will meet God and give an account. Yes, we will stop THE SWORD OF THE LORD but what can an honest man do when he finds he is not a Christian and is against historic Christianity and against the Christ of the Bible and he is pretending to be a Gospel minister?"

I am saying there is a fundamental kinship of immorality and deceit and wickedness with a man who is a modernist, just like the man who is a communist. Isn't it terrible that men should creep in and try to steal secrets and betray the United States government? Yes. Well, what is the difference for a man to teach in Louisville Seminary, supported by honest Baptist money, and there break down the faith of young men in the inspiration of the Bible, knowing he is paid by the sacrificial gifts of Baptists who believe it all? That is as fundamentally wicked as murder. Yes, sir!

Do you see that communists and modernists are of the same stripe? They are wicked, rebellious sinners, against God and against Christ, against the Bible and against Bible morality and Bible doctrine and Bible truth. They are triplets—communism, socialism, modernism.

For the Christian It Must Be Christ and the Whole Bible or Nothing

Now a final word. We need to say, "It is the Bible and Christ, or nothing." Somebody may say, "It is the Baptist denomination or nothing." But you are wrong, brother, sister. One will soon go into modernism unless he believes in Christ and the Bible, come Hell or high water—Christ and the Bible wherever He leads, whatever it teaches!

Somebody wrote about me, "Brother John Rice used to be such a sound Baptist but now he is for so-and-so." Sound Baptist? Maybe so, maybe not. But I've always been for Christ and the Bible, the blood atonement, the virgin birth, the bodily resurrection, Heaven and Hell. If God said it, it is so. I dare you to find any time I have ever wavered on that.

You say, "But my friends!" Friendship isn't first. It is Christ and the Bible first. You say, "It is the program." Not the program first! Christ and the Bible. "But I'll lose friends!" Well, lose them.

America is doomed unless we say, "I will stand for Christ and the Bible, friendship or no friendship; Democratic Party or no party; whether the people lead or don't lead; whether it pays or doesn't pay; whether I get cheaper electricity or not, I will stand for Christ and the Bible." We had better get back to the American way of life, private ownership of property, paying honest debts, receiving what we deserve, paying what we owe. That is the American way.

And in Christianity it is back to Jesus Christ, the blood, the infallible Bible, and "I will follow it if I lose every friend in the world, and have to break with everybody." I would rather shake the hand and call "brother" any Catholic priest who loves Jesus Christ and believes the Bible than to shake hands with a Baptist who does not believe the Bible!

There is just one safe place and that is in saying, "By God's grace I am going to stick right here with the Word."

Closing Prayer

O God, do put some iron in the backbones of preachers. O God, put some holy conviction in the hearts of Christians. Help people to say, "I will not, God helping me—not with a dime of money, not even with an encouring word—I will not back up infidelity and modernism, the enemies of Jesus Christ." Help us to say, "O God, if Jesus says, 'Die for, Me,' I'll die; if He says, 'Lose friends,' I'll lose them, but I'll stay true to Christ and the Bible." Help us in Jesus' name, Amen.

(For further reading, see *Masters of Deceit* by FBI head, J. Edgar Hoover, published by Pocket Books, Inc., 630 Fifth Avenue, New York, New York 10020.)

13

Modernism--Religious Liberalism

Modernism—Religious Liberalism

There are infidels who claim to be Christians. They fit exactly the dictionary definition of infidels, denying the essentials of the Christian faith. They have exactly the position of Bob Ingersoll, Tom Paine, and Voltaire, but they are in the church and willfully deceive God's people because they want the prestige, the income, the influence of the Christian religion.

I. HOW OFTEN THE WORD OF GOD WARNS OF THESE!

Jesus said in Matthew 7:15, "Beware of false prophets, which come to you in sheep's clothing, but inwardly they are ravening wolves."

That warning in more detail is given in II Peter 2:1-3, as follows:

"*But there were false prophets also among the people, even as there shall be false teachers among you, who privily shall bring in damnable heresies, even denying the Lord that bought them and bring upon themselves swift destruction. And many shall follow their pernicious ways; by reason of whom the way of truth shall be evil spoken of. And through covetousness shall they with feigned words make merchandise of you: whose judgment now of a long time lingereth not, and their damnation slumbereth not.*"

How wicked these false prophets are to be, is pictured

here: 1. They come in privily, that is, secretly, pretending to be true prophets of God. 2. Their heresies shall be damnable—"even denying the Lord that bought them." Though they use the name of Jesus, they teach that He is not really God, not an atoning, virgin-born Saviour. 3. So many shall follow these false prophets that principal truths of the Bible "shall be evil spoken of." Whole denominations shall be led away to discard faith in the virgin birth of Christ, His bodily resurrection, the absolute necessity of being born again, the infallible inspiration of the Bible. 4. Covetousness, this Scripture says, will lead these modern liberals to use "feigned words," lying, deceiving, "making merchandise of you." 5. Their awful "damnation" will come speedily because they are unconverted, this Scripture teaches, and they will go to eternal torment with other unbelievers.

Oh, the awful infection of unbelief among professed Christians, especially among those who seek leadership in the ministry, that the Bible warns against, again and again! The Apostle Paul was inspired to say of some who opposed him and his Gospel preaching:

"*For such are false apostles, deceitful workers, transforming themselves into the apostles of Christ. And no marvel; for Satan himself is transformed into an angel of light. Therefore it is no great thing if his ministers also be transformed as the minister of righteousness; whose end shall be according to their works.*"—II Cor. 11:13-15.

And Jude, in verses 3 and 4, tells us, "Beloved, when I gave all diligence to write unto you of the common salvation, it was needful for me to write unto you, and exhort you that ye should earnestly contend for the faith which was once delivered unto the saints. For there are certain men crept in unawares, who were before of old ordained to this condemnation, ungodly men, turning the grace of our God into lasciviousness, and denying the only Lord God, and our Lord Jesus Christ." Such liberals are "ungodly men," unconverted, denying the actual deity of the Lord Jesus. So it is necessary to "earnestly contend for the faith." God grant we may contend for the faith earnestly, as we are here commanded.

Such warnings are given also in I Timothy 4:1-3, in II Timothy 4:3,4, in Galatians 1:6-9, in II Peter 3:3-5, and in II John, verses 7-11. One who does not obey the warning of Jesus to "beware of false prophets, which come to you in sheep's clothing," sins, and is in great danger of supporting infidelity and even of being led into wreck of his faith.

II. WHAT ARE THE ABSOLUTE ESSENTIALS OF THE CHRISTIAN FAITH?

The New Testament often speaks of that body of essential doctrine without which one cannot be a Christian. It is called sometimes "the faith." We are to earnestly contend for "*the faith*" (Jude 3). Church members at Corinth were exhorted, "Examine yourselves, whether ye be in *the faith*" (II Cor. 13:5). Paul, about to die a martyr's death, could rejoice, "I have kept *the faith*" (II Tim. 4:7).

This is called "the faith of the gospel" in Philippians 1:27. And that helps to define it. Paul states the saving Gospel he preached in these words:

"*. . . how that Christ died for our sins according to the Scriptures; And that he was buried, and that he rose again the third day according to the scriptures.*"—I Cor. 15:3,4.

Here then are the essentials of the Gospel by which one can be saved, the "faith of the gospel."

1. *The sinful, lost state of man.* Christ "died for our sins."

2. *The atoning, substitutionary death of Christ.* He died "for our sins."

3. *Christ is Deity.* He is God so He arose from the dead, the one sign of His deity He insisted upon in Matthew 12:39,40. His resurrection, then, authenticates His virgin birth, His sinless life, His pre-existent deity.

4. *These truths are as recorded in the Scriptures,* as we are twice told here. So the inspiration of the Bible, as God's Word, is part of the faith of the Gospel.

One may be wrong on lesser matters of doctrine and be saved. Jesus said that certain matters are "weightier matters of the law" (Matt. 23:23). One may be mistaught about baptism, about some Christian duties, about the Lord's Supper, about the pattern for a New Testament church and still be a born-again Christian. One may be saved by faith in Christ as Saviour and not realize that this salvation is guaranteed to be eternal. But one who does not believe what the Bible says about Christ's death for our sins and His absolute deity, is not saved. Christians believe the Bible whether they understand it or not. Christians believe Jesus is all He claims to be in the Bible—the virgin-born, unique Son of God, who died for our sins.

III. ONE WHO DENIES THESE ESSENTIALS IS NOT SAVED, NOT A CHRISTIAN

In Matthew 7:15 Jesus warned of false prophets, who are not sheep but wolves. In verses 21 to 23 of the same passage, Jesus said:

"*Not every one that saith unto me, Lord, Lord, shall enter into the kingdom of heaven; but he that doeth the will of my Father which is in heaven. Many will say to me in that day, Lord, Lord, have we not prophesied in thy name? and in thy name have cast out devils? and in thy name done many wonderful works? And then will I profess unto them, I never knew you: depart from me, ye that work iniquity.*"

So these false teachers who claim they have "prophesied in thy name...cast out devils...and in thy name done many wonderful works," will be told by the Saviour, "I never knew you: depart from me, ye that work iniquity." Those who do not come to Christ as God, as an atoning Saviour, do not do "the will of my Father which is in heaven" about salvation, but reject the Bible and the virgin-born Christ of the Bible, they "work iniquity." These false prophets cannot go to Heaven.

That is clearly stated for us, also, in II John, verses 7 to 11, as follows:

"*For many deceivers are entered into the world, who confess not that Jesus Christ is come in the flesh. This is a deceiver and an antichrist. Look to yourselves, that we lose not those things which we have wrought, but that we receive a full reward. Whosoever transgresseth, and abideth not in the doctrine of Christ, hath not God. He that abideth in the doctrine of Christ, he hath both the Father and the Son. If there come any unto you, and bring not this doctrine, receive him not into your house, neither bid him God speed: For he that biddeth him God speed is partaker of his evil deeds.*"

One who rejects the Bible doctrine of Christ, of His deity and atoning death for our sins "hath not God," is not saved. One who abides or rests in this Bible truth about Christ "hath both the Father and the Son."

IV. HOW WILL YOU KNOW A MODERNIST, A RELIGIOUS LIBERAL?

Religious liberals come "with feigned words," the

Scripture says; they "come in privily" or secretly. They deliberately deceive and "make merchandise" of common Christians. They are wolves but they wear sheep's clothing.

1. Deceiving Liberals and Compromising Denominational Leaders Make It Hard

Many actual Christians are so deceived by the liberals, the unbelievers, that they quote and defend the modernists, support them in Christian schools—so some born-again Christians compromise until it is hard to tell the scabby, dirty sheep from the wolf in sheep's clothing.

The term "modernist" became a reproach a few years back, so now a few people claim to be modernists. The president of a blatantly liberal seminary wrote me a letter protesting that I had called the seminary a modernist school, where, he said, "not a single teacher here calls himself a modernist." I wrote back and told him if he and the teachers would write me that they now believed in the virgin birth of Christ, His substitutionary, atoning death and His bodily resurrection and in the infallible inspiration of the Bible, I would openly announce that they were not modernists. There was no reply.

Dr. Nels F. S. Ferre, who says it is wrong to worship Jesus, to follow the Bible, says Jesus may have been the illegitimate son of a blond German soldier and harlot Mary—is advertized as "an evangelical," has been welcomed at Southern Baptist Seminary and other "Christian" institutions, as have Dr. George Buttrick, most outspoken opponent of the virgin birth, the blood atonement and inspiration of the Bible. So is Dr. Elton Trueblood and many others who are actually unbelievers.

It is the folly and tragedy of the churches today that denominational leaders prefer united support for their denominational programs to any clear division between Bible-believing Christians and the unconverted infidels who have "privily," with "feigned words" stolen into positions of influence. The false prophets, "ravening wolves," as Jesus said, have on sheep's clothing and, according to II John, verse 7, "many deceivers are entered into the world," and as the Lord Jesus said in Matthew 24:24, "if...possible, they shall deceive the very elect."

2. It Is Possible to Know These False Prophets

Jesus said of these "false prophets," in Matthew 7:15, 16, "Ye shall know them by their fruits." Their fruit is their teaching. If one teaches or writes against the virgin birth of Christ or His bodily resurrection or the blood atonement, then he does not believe in the deity of Christ and is a false prophet, an unconverted infidel. If he denies the inspiration of the Bible, the need for men to be born again, then he is against the faith, is not a Christian. If one transgresses on this matter and does not abide in the Bible doctrine about Christ, he "hath not God," says II John, verse 9; he is not saved, must not be counted a Christian nor given support or Christian recognition, says the Scripture.

So Christian people are plainly commanded to "beware of false prophets," even if they do come in sheep's clothing. To support or approve a modernist, an unbeliever in the Bible, is to be "partaker of his evil deeds," says II John, verse 11.

IV. SOME MARKS OF RELIGIOUS LIBERALISM, UNBELIEF

Those who are false prophets do not openly say so. They use "feigned words," so we may not expect them to openly say the Bible is false, that Christ was a bastard, an imposter, that the Christian religion is a false religion. Their approach is more subtle than that.

1. The Liberal Approach to the Bible

These religious unbelievers claim to use historical criticism to learn more about the Bible. So they accept the "conjecture" of lewd Dr. Astruc, carried further by infidels Graff and Wellhausen, that Genesis was not really written by Moses. But they say that some lying "redactor" collected writings of different unknown sources they may call "E" or "J" or "P" or something else, and that the editor patched together the Pentateuch centuries after Moses lived, and then declared it was by Moses.

They say, of course, the Bible is, in some sense, for religious purposes, the Word of God, or at least contains the Word of God but that the first chapters of Genesis were simply taken from Babylonian myths or legends and carried down by oral tradition; so they believe God did not create the world by direct miraculous act, and did not create man in His own image, as the Word of God declares, but that all things, including man and the Christian religion, are simply the products of evolution, by natural causes.

They say that the Bible *contains* the Word of God, and the naive and trusting may believe they mean the Bible is the inspired Word of God. But they simply mean there are good things in the Bible and so, in a general sense, are from God, but each one they teach must pass judgment for himself and find any parts of the Bible he can believe or thinks may be helpful.

2. Pretending to Have Christ, They Deny His Deity and Sinlessness

Liberals, of course, do not attack Christ directly, do not say they hate the Christ of the Bible, as they really do. They make for themselves another Christ who would condemn no one, a gentle, unlearned child of

His age who probably believed the Old Testament, or did not want to disillusion His followers by calling attention to its mistakes!

They do not say openly that the Gospels are human documents with many contradictions and errors as they really believe. They simply invent a "Q" manuscript, in theory, though no one ever saw such a manuscript and there is not even a mention of it in the Bible or any ancient documents, and say the synoptic Gospels were copied, more or less, from that and from each other! So, of course, they feel free to select parts they think are in error. Thus the recorded words and actions of our Saviour are made doubtful or considered inaccurate.

Liberals usually do not at first openly deny the resurrection of Christ. They may begin by denying the story of Jonah because Jesus said Jonah's three days in the belly of the sea monster was a sign of His three days in the grave, and His resurrection. Or one may say, like Buttrick or Ferre, that the Gospel accounts are "contradictory," so doubt is cast on Christ's resurrection and so on His deity.

Liberals use Christian terminology, but make it mean less than the Scripture means. They speak of "the gospel," but insist that it is primarily social. They do not mean the Gospel of the Bible, the Gospel that Christ died for our sins and all should believe on Him for everlasting life and salvation. Note, they say "gospel," but mean civil rights, labor unions, poverty programs, government housing, and socialism in general.

They often repeat the Scripture that "God was in Christ, reconciling the world unto himself" (II Cor. 5:19). But they do not mean literally that Christ is God and so our Saviour literally by His substitutionary death: they mean God used the man Jesus to be an example we should follow.

The folly of religious liberalism is that it sets man to judge the Scriptures instead of being judged by the infallibly inspired Bible themselves. They are of this world's wisdom, not of divine wisdom.

The neo-orthodox theologian first deceives in his name (neo-orthodoxy is not orthodoxy). It claims what it knows it is not. Then it says the Bible is the Word of God only as it speaks to you and as God reaches you through it, but that it is not, objectively, always, the revealed will of God.

V. WHAT SHOULD CHRISTIANS DO ABOUT MODERNISM, RELIGIOUS LIBERALISM?

God's Word has clear instructions about what Christians should do about these who claim to be Christians but deny the essentials of the Christian faith, and are, in fact, infidels. No one has to argue or try to weigh reasons why support of modernists, fellowship with modernists, might do more good than exposing them, leaving them.

Here is what God's Word says do:

1. "*Beware of false prophets,* which come to you in sheep's clothing," Jesus said (Matt. 7:15). Call it "witch hunting"? Well, it is still what Jesus commanded. Be on the lookout for infidels in your church or denomination.

2. "*Examine yourselves, whether ye be in the faith*" (II Cor. 13:5). Have you been misled by such infidel Sunday school literature or teachers in college or seminary?

3. "*Earnestly contend for the faith*" (Jude 3). One is a poor Christian who is not insulted when Christ's deity is questioned or when the infallible authority of the Bible is questioned. Contend earnestly, we are commanded. Defend the Bible and Christ.

4. *Do not put yourself and your children under the influence of such false teachers,* for "Blessed is the man that walketh not in the counsel of the ungodly, nor

standeth in the way of sinners, nor sitteth in the seat of the scornful" (Ps. 1:1). To use such Sunday school or other literature, to read such books, to sit under such teachers as question the plenary, verbal inspiration of the Bible, or the virgin birth or bodily resurrection of Christ, is to 'walk in the counsel of the ungodly'; often it is to 'sit in the seat of the scornful.' It is wrong.

5. *Do not let any man teach a class you are in, nor stand in a pulpit* for which you are partly responsible who is a religious liberal denying or questioning the essentials of "the faith." Second John 9-11 says:

"*Whosoever transgresseth, and abideth not in the doctrine of Christ, hath not God. He that abideth in the doctrine of Christ, he hath both the Father and the Son. If there come any unto you, and bring not this doctrine, receive him not into your house, neither bid him God speed: For he that biddeth him God speed is partaker of his evil deeds.*"

One who does not stay with the Bible doctrine about Jesus Christ "hath not God," is unconverted. You are not to receive him as a Christian, not to receive him into your house as a Christian, not to give a dime to support him, not even to bid him Godspeed! To give money to a denominational program that includes colleges or seminaries with any liberal teachers is a sin, strictly forbidden.

6. *You are not to be in the unequal yoke of membership* in a local church or denomination whose official stand is wrong on the essentials of the faith, such as the new Presbyterian Confession of Faith or the new curriculum prepared for the United Church of Canada. To have your name and presence thus putting your tacit approval on infidelity, thus encouraging others to support it, is to be responsible before God for ruin and eternal damnation of some. Thus you are 'partaker of their evil deeds' who deny Christ and the Bible.

So it is with the preacher who stays in a ministerial association which has Catholic priests or rabbis or modernists in it, thus indicating that he regards them as Christian brothers, when they are actually unsaved. One may have fellowship with born-again Christians who differ on lesser matters, but one who denies some essential of the Christian faith is not a Christian, should not be thus endorsed as a Christian. So what to do?

"*Be ye not unequally yoked together with unbelievers: for what fellowship hath righteousness with unrighteousness? and what communion hath light with darkness? And what concord hath Christ with Belial? or what part hath he that believeth with an infidel? And what agreement hath the temple of God with idols? for ye are the temple of the living God; as God hath said, I will dwell in them, and walk in them; and I will be their God, and they shall be my people. Wherefore come out from among them, and be ye separate, saith the Lord, and touch not the unclean thing; and I will receive you, And will be a Father unto you, and ye shall be my sons and daughters, saith the Lord Almighty.*"—II Cor. 6:14-18.

If you are a member of the big Methodist church, since most of your bishops are unconverted, unbelievers, your colleges and seminaries liberal, your denominational literature openly liberal, then leave them all! Your local church cannot decide its program, select clean literature, call a sound preacher; so leave it! That is hard, but God commands it.

So with you Presbyterians with your new openly liberal statement of faith, to stay in the denomination means you compromise your convictions, disobey the Bible, and very likely lead to the eternal ruin of your children by destroying their faith.

Baptists, if your local church program is such that you cannot be in full fellowship without supporting, through your Cooperative Program, seminaries and colleges, and denominational literature that is liberal, then come out! No one has a right to talk for Christ in testimony meeting and then talk against Christ and the Bible with his money. "Put your money where your mouth is!" Live like you talk!

Must one leave friends of a lifetime for Christ? Yes, very often. Must one give up a Sunday school class in a modernistic church when he teaches them the Bible? Yes, or really you are teaching them to stay where it is wrong to stay, to attend liberal colleges it is wrong to attend, to study literature that is against Christ, to follow preachers who are false prophets and who will break down their faith. Yes, the Bible says, "Come out from among them."

Do you love Christ and His Word more than your denomination, more than your false leaders?

Further Reading

1. *Is Jesus God?* by John R. Rice; the six chapters: "Is Jesus God?" "Letter to a Modernist," "The Virgin-Born Saviour," "Old Testament Prophecies Miraculously Fulfilled in Christ," "The Resurrection of Christ," and "What Is Wrong With a Modernist?" Obtain from Sword of the Lord Publishers.

2. *Death in the Pot*, by J. Elwin Wright; paper-bound; Fellowship Press, 9 Park Street, Boston, Mass. 02122.

3. *The Ecclesiastical Octopus,* by Ernest Gordon; Fellowship Press, 9 Park Street, Boston, Mass. 02122.

4. *Christianity and Liberalism,* by J. Gresham Machen; Wm. B. Eerdmans Publishing Co., 225 Jefferson Avenue, Grand Rapids, Mich. 49502.

5. *These Issues We Must Face,* by Dr. W. A. Criswell (the chapter on modernism); Zondervan Publishing House, Grand Rapids, Mich. 49506.

6. *Ecumenical Folly, Modernism of National Council of Churches as Shown by San Francisco General Assembly,* by G. Archer Weniger; pamphlet of 32 pages, Sword of the Lord Publishers, Murfreesboro, TN 37133.